From Left to Right

From Left to Right

Maternalism and Women's Political Activism in Postwar Canada

BRIAN T. THORN

UBC Press • Vancouver • Toronto

25 24 23 22 21 20 19 18 17 16   5 4 3 2 1

Printed in Canada on FSC-certified ancient-forest-free paper (100% post-consumer recycled) that is processed chlorine- and acid-free.

Library and Archives Canada Cataloguing in Publication

Thorn, Brian T. (Brian Thomas), author
From left to right : maternalism and women's political activism in postwar Canada / Brian T. Thorn.

Includes bibliographical references and index.
Issued in print and electronic formats.
ISBN 978-0-7748-3208-3 (hbk). – ISBN 978-0-7748-3210-6 (pdf). –
ISBN 978-0-7748-3211-3 (epub). – ISBN 978-0-7748-3212-0 (mobi)

1. Women – Political activity – Canada – History – 20th century. 2. Women political activists – Canada – History – 20th century. 3. Feminism – Canada – History – 20th century. 4. Political parties – Canada – History – 20th century. 5. Right and left (Political science) – Canada – History – 20th century. I. Title.

HQ1453.T56 2016   305.4097109'045   C2016-901209-3
C2016-901210-7

Canadä

UBC Press gratefully acknowledges the financial support for our publishing program of the Government of Canada (through the Canada Book Fund), the Canada Council for the Arts, and the British Columbia Arts Council.

This book has been published with the help of a grant from the Canadian Federation for the Humanities and Social Sciences, through the Awards to Scholarly Publications Program, using funds provided by the Social Sciences and Humanities Research Council of Canada.

Printed and bound in Canada by Friesens
Set in Garamond by Apex CoVantage, LLC
Copy editor: Joanne Richardson

UBC Press
The University of British Columbia
2029 West Mall
Vancouver, BC V6T 1Z2
www.ubcpress.ca

This book is dedicated to
Allan and Patricia
Jack and Jane
Bryan and Joan
Michelle, Austin, and Dylan
... and to the women and men of the right and left who have resisted capitalism, imperialism, and war over the many decades

Contents

Acknowledgments

This book has taken me a long time to complete, and I want to thank the many people who have contributed to its publication. Bryan Palmer and Joan Sangster, Margaret Hobbs, Pauline Rankin, John Wadland, Jim Struthers, and Alvin Finkel provided advice and support for an aspiring academic during the period when this study was originally conceived. Although we have gone our separate ways, Trent colleagues Molly Blyth, Donica Belisle, Mark Dickinson, Maggie Quirt, and Henk and Amy Warnar-Brown are not far from my thoughts as I move on in academic life. Many years ago, the late Michael Fellman suggested a study on right-wing women; I hope that he would be pleased with this book. My MA thesis supervisor Mark Leier's example is never far from my thoughts.

I appreciate UBC Press's unwavering support of this book, especially when it appeared that it might never be published. Darcy Cullen has been a model editor, pushing *From Left to Right* towards publication. Lesley Erickson was a fine and attentive production editor, and Joanne Richardson's editing suggestions improved the prose substantially. I am greatly indebted to UBC Press. My colleague and friend Mark Crane prepared the index. The three anonymous reviewers secured by the press all provided judicious and helpful criticism, and I thank them. Of the many archivists who assisted with my research, I am especially grateful to George Brandak and Linda Turner of the University of British Columbia, Special Collections Division, and Francis Fournier and Enid Britt of the Simon Fraser University Archives. I thank the editors of *Peace and*

Change and *Histoire sociale/Social History* for allowing portions of Chapters 3 and 6 to be reprinted in the book.

My years teaching at Simon Fraser University, Douglas College, Queen's University, Trent University, and Nipissing University have been exceptionally rewarding. I thank all of the students from whom I have learned over the years, especially the students in my History 4615 (Canadian-American Relations) seminar in 2012–13 at Nipissing. I thank various department chairs at Queen's, Trent, and Nipissing Universities for their support, notably David Parker, Richard Greenfield, Dimitry Anastakis, Robin Gendron, Katrina Srigley, Laurie Kruk, James Murton, and Gyllian Phillips. Chris Dummitt has been a good friend and colleague over the years, as have Tyler King, Peter McMahon, Samir Goel, and Andy Corbett.

My years at Nipissing University – in both the History and English Departments – have been among the most rewarding of my life. Many people at NipU have played a key role in shaping *From Left to Right,* whether they know it or not. I think especially of Mark Crane, Hillary Earl, Gordon Morrell, Darren Ferry, Rhiannon Don, Lindsey McMaster, Robin Gendron, Gillian McCann, Herminio Texeira, and Nestar Russell and Susan Cahill, among many others. Mark Crane's and Gillian McCann's kindness in giving me places to live in North Bay has gone beyond anything that I might expect. I also thank the Nipissing University Faculty Association for standing up for the rights of part-time faculty members in a time of austerity. Sandra and Richard Martin, Michael Kary, Jeff Smardon, and the other members of the (now defunct, sadly) CampoVerde social club of Vancouver provided support as well. I am obviously solely responsible for any errors and omissions in the text.

This book is dedicated to four groups of individuals who have been a key part of my life for many years. Although my views have drifted somewhat from what they might deem acceptable, I am deeply grateful to Bryan Palmer and Joan Sangster for all they have done for me over the years. It was Bryan who first inspired me to become a historian, and I have not forgotten his example. Joan, too, has taught me much about historical materialism, feminism, masculinity, and historiography. If there are any two individuals to whom this book is addressed, it is certainly Bryan and Joan.

The same situation prevails with regard to Jane Power and Jack O'Dell of Vancouver. From the moment I met Jane and Jack, they treated me almost like a member of their own family. I can only hope to follow their example in politics, activism, and life. It goes without saying that I appreciate the help and support of my parents, Allan and Patricia Thorn of Peterborough, Ontario, as well as my sister, Andrea Thorn, and her husband, Brent Greenham. My in-laws Ed Martin of Nanaimo, British Columbia, and Grace Martin of Surrey, British Columbia, also offered support. Suffice it to say that they stand for all of the positive elements that women of the left and right endorsed. In keeping with the traditionalist values of many conservative women, I have not forgotten my roots in rural Ontario! But this is not all.

My greatest debt is to my partner, Michelle Martin, and to our children, Austin and Dylan. They have put up with me for more years than I care to remember. Michelle has gone through moving, job changes, and tension, and, through it all, she has stood firm. I dedicate *From Left to Right* to all of these people, in hopes that the future might be better than the world that has preceded it. Above all, this book is for Michelle and the children, who have made my burdens much lighter. I hope that they realize why this book is, finally, dedicated to them.

From Left to Right

Introduction

Postwar Canada was a society on the verge of great change. At the end of the Second World War, many suggested that a new nation – built on peace, prosperity, and unity – would come to pass. New and different visions of what Canada could look like under ideal conditions emerged. Since "Central Canada" – a euphemism for the business and political interests of the Toronto–Ottawa–Montreal axis – still largely ruled Canada,[1] voices of dissent and discord came from the periphery. In Alberta and British Columbia, the two western-most regions, new visions came from both the left and the right of the political spectrum. These ostensibly different political viewpoints had some aspects in common. As part of a speech to an Alberta Social Credit Party convention, prominent provincial member of the Legislative Assembly Cornelia Wood argued that the objective for Social Credit, and for other movements of protest, was "to usher in the New World Order."[2]

Wood's notion of inaugurating the "New World Order" was an integral part of the ideologies that left- and right-wing western Canadian women held during the period from 1945 to 1960. I chose these dates because they represent a distinct historical period, one that bridged the gap between the era of the Second World War and its aftermath and the very different era of the 1960s, which heralded the onset of the New Left and second-wave feminism. Women in the Communist Party of Canada (CPC), the Co-operative Commonwealth Federation (CCF), and the Social Credit Party (SCP or Socreds) all espoused some version of the New World Order. These parties asserted that they had the power to usher in a new vision of life for Canada. All argued that the immediate post-Second World War period represented a time of danger as well as promise. During the late 1940s and 1950s, the world faced the possibility of moral and military disaster because of the onset of the Cold War – that is, the battle for world supremacy waged between the capitalist, Western bloc nations (led by the United States) and the Communist, Eastern bloc nations (led by the Soviet Union). The Cold War lasted from 1945 to 1991, with the latter year seeing the dissolution of the Soviet Union. At various junctures, notably the Korean War from 1950 to 1953, the world seemed perilously close to a "hot" war breaking out between the two hostile power blocs.[3] The period from 1945 to 1961 was also a time of promise, when it seemed that new, positive visions of the world might come to pass. With the defeat of fascism during the Second World War, and the economic prosperity that followed, individuals and groups of all political stripes (including the three parties discussed here) argued that a time of peace, development, and equality – in short, a new world order – had begun.

From Left to Right examines the different perspectives that left- and right-wing women's groups brought to bear on the idea of the New World Order. Each of these political parties had a somewhat different conception of what it would look like; however, all three visions reflected a maternalist perspective. Political women's views often cohered with those of the men in their parties and with others who held similar ideological viewpoints. Yet previous scholars and political activists have made too much of the perceived differences between ostensibly "left-" and "right-" wing political perspectives. In fact, gendered ideologies often led to a shared perspective among women from seemingly different political backgrounds. This being the case, I present three main arguments. First, I argue that a common maternalist ethic sometimes united left- and right-wing women in the *tactics* and *discourses* that they used, even if the ultimate political goals for which they fought were very different. Maternalism, for example, was a key part of women's political activism of both the right and the left during the postwar period. Second, I argue that the use of a maternalist ideology led to an *increase* in women's social and political activism in these three parties. When these women ceased to use maternalist arguments in their writing and activism, women's power declined in the CP, the CCF, and the SCP. Finally, women of the right and the left used maternalism to break down barriers between the "public" and the "private" – the "domestic sphere" of the home and family and the outside world of work and politics. Women of all political stripes saw the home and family as being a positive and empowering rather than a negative and constricting aspect of life. Indeed, they wanted to unite the two spheres of home/family and work/politics in ways that would enhance both. Still, the ultimate goals for which these women fought were very different. Within their respective movements, political women used a common maternalist ethic to battle fiercely for different viewpoints. All critiqued modernity and capitalism, although in very different ways. As we shall see, where left-wing women of the CPC and the CCF fought for an increased welfare state, Socred women battled for a return to pre-capitalist and pre-industrial values.

I join with other authors in suggesting that there was considerable political activism among different groups of women during the 1940s and 1950s.[4] Indeed, the CP, CCF, and SCP could scarcely have survived without women's efforts. Yet previous scholars, whose focus, to be fair, lay elsewhere, have failed to notice that gender and ideas about motherhood functioned to unify women from different political parties.[5]

Feminist historians conclude that women's activism did not disappear during the period from 1920 to 1960, the period between the two feminist "waves." In particular, the 1950s, sometimes portrayed in popular culture as a time of conservatism and retreat for women, was a period of challenge and change in gender roles.[6] Recent historians of the women's movement eschew the use of the wave metaphor.[7] It is more helpful to think of feminist politics from the nineteenth century to the present time as a continuing process of activism rather than as a series of starts and stops. A number of scholars argue that, during the 1940s and 1950s, a vibrant "left feminism" developed in labour and left-wing movements in North America. Many groups and individuals who were part of this labour feminism continued their battles into the 1960s and 1970s.[8] I concur with these arguments and suggest that a vibrant tradition of protest and activism also existed among right-wing women in Canada and the United Sates during the 1940s and 1950s, as well as in later decades, even if the stated goal of right-wing women's activity was to return to a more conservative period. I define "feminism" as a movement that fights for the equality of *all* groups of women. Moreover, I see feminism as an ideology that, if properly applied, must acknowledge the existence of a patriarchal system and a belief that this system disadvantages all groups of women, even if some groups – working-class and ethnic minority women in particular – face harsher consequences because of their class, racial, and/or ethnic status.[9] By this definition, the women I discuss were not feminists, even if their actions helped to pave the way for the rise of second-wave feminism.

I see *From Left to Right* as part of a growing literature, primarily in the area of American historiography, that discusses right-wing women as active agents of history and discusses the complexity of their views and activism.[10] It also provides one of the only looks at right-wing women in the Canadian context, particularly in the postwar period.[11] While they *rhetorically* opposed the expansion of women's roles, right-wing women's activity outside the home during the 1940s and 1950s *implicitly* suggested that women deserved a larger role than that of being mothers and wives. All of these women – of the left and of the right – used the conservative-sounding language of maternalism, which emphasizes motherhood and family, as part of a strategy to reconceptualize the home and family as a place of radicalism (or at least, in the case of SCP women, of activism) and not of retreat. All fought to reshape public society in the image of the home, thereby breaking down barriers between the public and private spheres.

Postwar political women used a maternalist viewpoint to argue for an increased female role, and their maternalism had specific elements. First, maternalist thinkers from the 1940s and 1950s suggested that there existed a uniquely female value system, based on care and nurturance. Second, they suggested that women, as mothers, shared a collective responsibility to protect the world's children and families in the face of various threats, most notably economic scarcity, the prospect of nuclear war, and capitalist modernity. All three groups of women were, to some degree, critical of aspects of postwar modernity:[12] increased urbanization, the increasing numbers of women working outside the home, and the perceived decline of Christianity and rural values. Finally, right- and left-wing women asserted that their work, experience, and socialization as mothers made them uniquely able to lead certain kinds of reform and political campaigns.[13]

Women of the right and left perceived gender in a specific manner. Women in the CPC, CCF, and SCP had very particular ideas surrounding what roles were appropriate for women and what roles were appropriate for men. Many women *were* mothers and wives during the 1940s and 1950s. With this in mind, political women of the right and of the left used maternalism in two ways. First, they used maternalism strategically (see Prentice's idea of "strategic essentialism") – that is, they took a narrow definition of a woman's role and applied it to a specific context in order to draw more women into political movements and to extract concessions from the dominant system.[14] Political women used maternalist arguments to draw other women – many of whom were otherwise uninterested in political ideologies – into their respective movements. Second, and more significantly, many CPC, CCF, and SCP women perceived the home and family differently from second-wave feminists.

Political women from the 1940s and 1950s did not see the home and family as a site of retreat or female submission. Indeed, women of the right and of the left supported maternalist politics in the belief that it affirmed family life in the face of modernity and capitalism. These women did not necessarily see either conservative or leftist economic policies as superior one to the other; rather, many, perhaps most, joined political movements as part of an effort to maintain family lives – materially and spiritually – by transforming an unjust society into a new order. Women in all three political parties endorsed the gendered division of labour – the idea that men should work to support families by making money in the public sphere while women should safeguard the domestic sphere – but right- and left-wing women did not see the latter sphere as inferior to the former.[15] In fact, they attempted to use the home as a site of activism and as part of an effort to increase women's power in the public sphere.[16]

As historian Temma Kaplan argues, women's activism – of the left and of the right – is connected to a "female consciousness" – that is, the notion that women organize to defend the family and to fight against anything that they feel will interfere with their ability to preserve life and family as they know it.[17] Therefore, political women sought to break down barriers between the workplace and the home, the public and the private spheres. Similarly, some prominent women in these parties introduced policy initiatives that pushed women's equality forward; this was particularly the case for SCP women since their party held power in Alberta and British Columbia during substantial portions of this period. This, in turn, helped to lay the groundwork for the huge increase in women's activism during the 1960s and 1970s.

Ironically, where these women, especially those of the right, attempted to valorize the home and family, the result was that, in the 1960s and 1970s, more and more women became involved in activities outside the home. The idea of "family" was a key part of women's politics. Many of these women wanted to reinforce their particular conception of the family in opposition to the deprivations of the public world of capitalism. Family was also important in a more literal sense: political women of both the right and the left often came from families with long histories in conservative or leftist politics. These political women wanted to use the idea of family – particularly the maternalist idea that women's maternal and familial roles justified their political activism outside the home – as well as their actual, existing families as resources for attempting to change the Canada of the 1940s and 1950s into a new world order. Therefore, women of both the left and the right used maternalism as a discourse (i.e., they valorized motherhood and child-rearing in their speeches and public pronouncements and made this language a key part of their announcements and platforms) and as a mechanism to attract new recruits and volunteers. The left used maternalism to argue for stronger state support for families in the form of better housing and education for children, while the right argued that capitalist modernity was destroying the traditional nuclear family. Both right- and left-wing women believed that the provincial government should attempt to return women to the home so that they could help to reconstitute the mythical patriarchal family.

My focus is the CPC and the CCF (the "left" parties) in British Columbia and the Social Credit Party (the "right" party) in Alberta. For many years, region was a key issue in Canadian history, one of Canada's "limited identities." Particularly over the last fifteen years, however, Canadian studies scholars have downplayed region as a causal explanation. Western historian Gerald Friesen convincingly argues that it is no longer useful to think of "the West" as being a coherent, monolithic region unto itself. He argues that the West does not exist as a unified whole and that it is better to think of it as being four separate provinces with different economies and identities.[18]

Friesen's argument is borne out in this book. While the CPC and CCF branches in British Columbia were larger and, in some ways, more successful than were their counterparts in other provinces, their similarities with other provincial branches outnumber their differences. Broadly speaking, CPC and CCF supporters across Canada shared the same views on most issues: the role of women in the party, war and violence, class, and youth delinquency, to give only a few examples. The same situation prevailed with the Socred Credit Party of Alberta and the Social Credit Party of British Columbia: from the 1950s onward the two provincial parties shared a similar perspective. Socred governments in both provinces introduced many of the same economic policies. Indeed, on certain issues, many Socred women held views that were similar to those of women in the CPC and the CCF.

Yet the political context in the two provinces differed, and this had implications for SCP women's ideological focus. Alberta was effectively a one-party province from 1935 to 1971, with the Socreds dominating political and economic life. In British Columbia, however, a two-party system emerged, with the CCF/NDP and SCP vying for power. BC Socreds had to moderate their policies in order to appease voters who did not subscribe to "rightist" views. W.A.C. Bennett's nationalization of BC Hydro in 1961, a key campaign plank for the NDP, represents an example of this strategy of "moderation." British Columbia's tradition of relatively powerful labour and left movements provided a base of support for the CPC and the CCF/NDP that did not exist in Alberta.[19]

Women's views, rather than being the product of their experience of an entire region, were the product of their experience of their hometowns and adopted communities in Alberta and British Columbia. In other words, their ideologies emanated from their communities of origin and those in which they lived, worked, and engaged in political activism. "Place" consists of three basic elements: (1) the setting in which social relations exist, (2) the geographical area in which social and economic relations occur, and (3) the "sense of place" that creates the political and social atmosphere of a particular community.[20] These elements are closely connected to the different political economies that are "embedded" in different locales.[21] For example, women and men who lived in resource-based communities such as Nelson, Trail, or the Cowichan-Ladysmith section of British Columbia (areas where mining, logging, or fishing were prominent) tended to be supporters of the CPC and the CCF. In contrast, rural and farming towns such as Lethbridge and Medicine Hat in Alberta or the Okanagan and Fraser Valley areas of British Columbia – all rural areas with traditions of religious conservatism – developed a different political economy. The provincial branches of the SCP received strong support from local residents of these areas.

Even within particular areas of these provinces, there were political and economic differences. In northern British Columbia, for instance, some ridings voted CCF and had strong traditions of communist labour militancy, while other working-class areas responded to W.A.C. Bennett's populist appeal. This was also true in Alberta. Working-class areas of Edmonton, and, in some instances, Calgary would vote CCF or Liberal, but in most areas of rural and suburban Alberta, the SCP had little to no competition for votes from the 1940s until the late 1960s. In short, looking at the specific places or communities in which these women lived and worked helps to explain their views.[22] This is not to say that views have not changed over time in these different areas, but it does suggest that place and location matter a great deal when it comes to explaining the particular political choices that these women made.[23]

While the bulk of this book focuses on the 1945–60 period,[24] it is necessary to say a few words about the earlier origins of these three political parties. Founded in 1921, in Guelph, Ontario, the Communist Party of Canada, heavily influenced by its ties to the Soviet Union, argued that only a socialist revolution, propagated by the working class, could solve the problems of capitalist society. Many Canadian leftists had been members of organizations like the Socialist Party of Canada and the Independent Labour Party. The Russian Revolution of 1917 convinced many of these radicals to form communist parties, following the model established by the Communist Party of the Soviet Union. Members of communist parties all over the world asserted that following the Soviet model was the only way to create a socialist society.

During the 1920s, Canadian communists adapted to the viewpoint of the Communist International (Comintern) in Moscow, the governing body of all national communist parties until 1943.[25] However, after 1935, with the onset of the Popular Front,[26] the CPC largely moved away from working towards revolution and instead concentrated on implementing piecemeal reforms. Even during the 1920s, the CP, although it asserted that only a revolution would truly change society, focused on achieving such government reforms as legal protection for unions and a national system of unemployment insurance. Most of the illegal activities in which the CPC engaged, even during the 1920s, were non-violent (e.g., the CPC often helped evicted tenants and assisted in organizing strikes). This fairly moderate approach continued into the 1930s and into subsequent decades. In keeping with this desire to appear "mainstream," many CPC members expressed an increasingly conservative view of women and gender. CPC men and women embraced the nuclear, heterosexual family, decrying capitalism because it failed to provide the means to support this ideal.

The 1950s and the rise of Cold War anti-communism saw the defeat of communism as a major political force in Canada and worldwide. In 1956, Soviet tanks crushed a potential revolution in Hungary; many communists in Canada and around the world quit their parties and became disillusioned about the prospect of radical change. After this point, the Communist Party of Canada played no meaningful role in the country's political life at the federal and provincial levels or even, for the most part, in activist circles.[27]

For its part, as an ostensible social democratic party, the CCF argued that capitalist nations could gradually be changed into welfare statist societies.[28] As previously seen, the CP, in practice, was little different: it endorsed a stronger welfare state and eschewed non-legal, non-electoral strategies. The CCF emerged from a variety of different, sometimes contradictory, political groups and positions. Scholars and partisans describe the CCF's ideology as consisting of farmer, labour, and urban socialist elements. In the 1920s and 1930s, the poverty that many western farmers faced pushed them towards the CCF's position, which emphasized farming cooperatives, rural electrification, and increased state funding for rural areas.[29]

The labour movement, and its political supporters in Parliament, also represented a major part of the CCF's base. Activists in the Independent Labour Party, which had provincial branches across Canada, were early members of the CCF. Independent Labour Party members fought to effect a socialist society using legal electoral means. This "legalist" approach to social change remained constant throughout the history of the CCF-NDP. Labour activists collaborated with radical farm organizations in western Canada. When the CCF was established, initially at the Calgary Conference of 1932 and then, more permanently, at the Regina Conference of 1933, a number of prominent members of the United Farmers of Alberta and the United Farmers of Canada, Saskatchewan Section, joined the new party.[30]

Many provincial wings of the Independent Labour Party joined the CCF at that time. Indeed, the early BC CCF was effectively a fusion of several smaller labour and socialist parties into one non-communist, left-wing group. The failure of the BC branch of the Canadian Labour Party resulted in the more or less permanent exclusion of communists from mainstream labour and left movements in British Columbia.[31] Urban intellectuals from the universities, as well as religiously minded reformers, also joined the CCF. These members became increasingly important during the party's ideological changes over the years.[32]

With the onset of the Cold War in Europe, the CCF committed to the Western military alliance and to Cold War anti-communism. In 1949, the CCF voted to support the founding of the North Atlantic Treaty Organization (NATO). NATO was intended to be an instrument of anti-communism: it united Western nations under American hegemony against the perceived threat of Soviet expansionism.[33] More radical CCF members challenged this view; they criticized Western, especially American, imperialism and supported anti-war causes. These radicals formed the Socialist Fellowship in 1951 to oppose the CCF hierarchy; however, the conservative faction won out. The year 1956 saw the publication of the Winnipeg Declaration, signalling an even more mainstream direction for the party. In 1961, with its electoral future in doubt, the CCF implemented a formal tie with organized labour and became the openly moderate New Party, later called the New Democratic Party (NDP).[34]

CCF supporters lauded "welfare state" nations such as Great Britain (under the Labour Party) and Sweden as examples that Canada should follow. Many of the best known CCF women, notably Mildred Fahrni and Laura Jamieson,[35] had backgrounds in social work. In keeping with this, many social democratic women – and men for that matter – held technocratic viewpoints, a perspective that emphasizes the role of the efficient welfare state and the growth of bureaucracy as a means of reforming society.[36] They combined this perspective with anti-communism. Particularly after 1951, with the expulsion and marginalization of the left, the party endorsed a reformist ideology with regard to capitalism.[37] The CCF also expressed support for the nuclear family, albeit in a somewhat different manner than did the CP. CCF women and men suggested that, while it was acceptable for women to work under capitalism, a social democratic society would allow women to stay at home by providing a combination of higher wages for men, social insurance programs, and a more equitable taxation system.[38]

Like the CCF, the Social Credit Party emerged out of conditions that resulted from the Great Depression. Alberta in the 1930s was a poor province, dependent on agriculture, with the vast majority of its population living in rural areas. Unemployment and drought led to the failure of many farms and to thousands of people being on relief. In these circumstances, the people of Alberta were ready to listen to someone who would offer a solution to their economic problems. Such a person was William "Bible Bill" Aberhart, a Calgary high school principal and Presbyterian minister. According to his biographers, the suicide of one of his impoverished students convinced Aberhart that the root causes of the Depression needed to be addressed.[39]

Aberhart became a follower of the monetary theories of Scottish engineer Major Clifford Hugh (C.H.) Douglas. Douglas was responsible for the "A plus B theorem," the convoluted basis for Social Credit economic theory. Douglas argued that "the people," a vaguely defined term often meaning farmers and small business owners, did not have enough purchasing power. This, Douglas surmised, was the cause of economic problems in capitalist society, notably the Depression. If governments provided annual dividends to the people, then there would be more money going into the economy, which would solve the problems of the Depression. In his 1935 election campaign, which resulted in the Socreds coming to power in a landslide victory, Aberhart promised that, if elected, each month the SCP would provide all adult Albertans with a cheque for twenty-five dollars.[40]

During the years of Aberhart's leadership, many SCP supporters possessed left-leaning views. As Alvin Finkel notes, the Aberhart government introduced Canada's first male minimum wage laws, compulsory membership in the Alberta Teachers Association, and legislation restricting various trades to licensed individuals. The proposed twenty-five-dollar dividend, Aberhart's "funny money," was never implemented. In 1937, Canada's Supreme Court declared that the proposed legislation to create the Social Credit dividend lay outside the boundaries of provincial responsibility. The failure to implement the dividend, coupled with the subsequent failure of other SCP legislation, signalled a turn to the right for Aberhart, whose parliamentary caucus had always contained right-wing as well as left-wing members.

With Aberhart's death in 1943, and Ernest Manning's takeover as premier of Alberta, SCP ideology and practice changed even more dramatically. Manning, Aberhart's chief lieutenant and a close friend, was a conservative Christian. Manning's brand of capitalistic, pro-business Christianity differed from Aberhart's vision of the church as a supporter of farmers and workers. During his years as premier, from 1943 to 1969, Manning had no compunction about repudiating the earlier gains made by the labour movement and other progressives.[41]

The SCP in British Columbia turned to conservatism at an earlier stage than did its counterpart in Alberta. Its origins lay in the machinations of the party's first leader, the Kelowna hardware merchant William Andrew Cecil (W.A.C.) Bennett. After his defeat in a 1950 provincial Conservative Party leadership convention, Bennett began to express support for the ideals of Social Credit as practised in Alberta. He presented himself as a populist outsider, hostile to traditional, Victoria-based politicians who were out of touch with the concerns of farmers, workers, and small business owners. In March 1951, Bennett announced his intention to sit as an independent in the BC Legislature, although his true political leanings lay with the SCP.

The BC Social Credit League, an offshoot of a similar organization in Alberta, enthusiastically supported Bennett as an independent MLA. Although the league had existed since 1932, it was not until the early 1950s that its membership began to grow. Disgruntled Liberals and Conservatives joined the new party, which elected former Albertan Ernest Hansell, a fundamentalist Christian minister, as its leader. After the SCP won the 1952 provincial election in British Columbia, a vote of all sitting Socred MLAs elected W.A.C. Bennett as the leader of the party and, consequently, as the premier of the province. In June 1953, Bennett forced another election; the Socreds won a clear victory and Bennett remained the premier of British Columbia until 1972.[42]

SCP women favoured a return to what they termed "traditional" Christian values. They also emphasized the importance of the nuclear family. SCP women rejected the values of secularism, liberalism, the welfare state, and socialism. Much of the SCP view of life was, on the surface, "reactionary."[43] Socreds endorsed turning the clock back to an earlier, undefined period of history when the problems of modernity did not exist. They opposed unions and other organizations that limited what they saw as "individual freedom."

SCP ideology was contradictory. Many supporters liked to promote their views as being "scientific" and based on "rational" thought. SCP leaders endorsed capitalist economic development in the form of corporate mergers, road- and dam building, and the development of new forms of resources (most notably oil in Alberta). These are all aspects of a modern political economy, with its reliance on state-centred economic projects. As we see in later chapters, the SCP was divided between (1) "traditionalist" conservatives, who emphasized anti-modernism, individual rights, and evangelical Christianity and (2) economic, or "modernist," conservatives, who emphasized development, big business, and the growth of the provincial state.[44]

Analyzing women's activism in the Co-operative Commonwealth Federation, the Social Credit Party, and the Communist Party of Canada in the provinces of British Columbia and Alberta allows me to compare and contrast the experiences of left- and right-wing women in different political settings. The BC sections of the CPC and the CCF were among the most active, disciplined, and largest of their kind in Canada: only Ontario and Saskatchewan possessed CPC or CCF branches that were equivalent in size and influence.[45] Similarly, the SCP became a lasting presence only in British Columbia and Alberta. Alberta's left-wing parties fell into disarray owing to the SCP's ability to mobilize public opinion in conservative directions. After 1945, much of mainstream Albertan society opposed left-wing parties and leftist viewpoints.

For these reasons, I do not discuss the Alberta wings of the CPC and the CCF. Left parties played far smaller roles in Alberta politics than they did in BC politics. As Alvin Finkel, a historian of the SCP, notes, the 1950s saw the provincial Liberal Party emerge as the primary challenger to Social Credit in Alberta: in the 1955 provincial election, the Liberals won fifteen seats in the Legislature. During the course of the three provincial elections fought in Alberta from 1952 to 1959, the CCF lost the two seats that it had previously held, while, by 1959, its share of the popular vote had fallen to 8 percent. The CPC's slide was even more dramatic: during the 1950s, the CPC received, on average, 0.5 percent of the popular vote in elections, and its membership and influence decreased markedly. In the same vein, after 1947, Alberta's oil wealth allowed Socred governments to massively fund infrastructure and welfare state programs, thereby undercutting the appeal of the province's left.[46] While voting patterns are not the *only* barometer of political consciousness, the fact that the number of votes for left-wing parties dropped so dramatically during a relatively short time span suggests that leftist options lost favour with many Albertans during the 1950s.[47] I found virtually no mention of women or gender in archival sources dealing with the Alberta CPC and CCF during the 1945–60 period.[48] The same holds true for archival sources dealing with the BC SCP.

A number of factors led to the formation of these three parties, religion being one. Where CPC members were anti-religious and CCF members were often social gospel Protestants or non-religious, many Socreds in both Alberta and British Columbia espoused support for evangelical Christianity, or "evangelicalism." Evangelicals adhere to a belief system that has four main pillars. First, they argue that active proselytizing is necessary to recruit new members to their faith. Second, they believe that the Bible should be taken literally: they see it is the word of God speaking directly to the faithful. Third, they emphasize a Christ-centred faith, arguing that Jesus Christ died on the cross in order to save humanity from its sins. This distinguishes evangelicals from more liberal Protestants and Roman Catholics, who often downplay the focus on humanity's innately evil nature. Finally, many evangelicals, particularly in the United States, classify themselves as "Born Again." These people state that they have a personal relationship with Jesus Christ and that this relationship is responsible for saving them from a sinful life. Evangelicalism is also associated with a kind of charismatic and physical religious experience.[49]

Support for evangelical versions of Protestantism was a key aspect of SCP ideology in both Alberta and British Columbia. Robert Burkinshaw writes that, during the period from 1952 to 1956, 22.5 percent of BC SCP members belonged to evangelical groups – notably, Baptists, Methodists, Presbyterian, Pentecostals, and Nazarenes. Another 72 percent were involved in mainline Protestant sects, as compared with 65 percent of BC CCF members. Burkinshaw further suggests that 71.5 percent of fundamentalist church ministers supported the SC, while none supported the CCF. Not surprisingly, more liberal churches, especially those affiliated with the social gospel, were inclined to support social democracy: only 7.6 percent of United Church ministers supported the SCP, while 61.5

percent stated that they voted CCF.[50] Mennonites in British Columbia's interior were also strong supporters of the SCP, particularly in the 1952 election that first brought the party to power.[51]

Fundamentalist Christians associated the CCF with theological liberalism, the social gospel, and socialism and communism. Burkinshaw contends that the evangelical proportion of the population in British Columbia stood at only 7 percent in 1952; however, in close elections, this group played a significant role in turning the province over to SCP governments.[52] Many of the leaders and public faces in the Socred movement, especially during the party's early formative years, were followers of these conservative Christian sects. This strong evangelical influence was a uniquely western Canadian phenomenon. Although SCP women did not commonly express this viewpoint, part of the SCP's ideological appeal lay in its stated support for western Canadian values in opposition to the perceived power of Ottawa and of the banks and financial interests in Toronto, Ottawa, and Montreal.[53] SCP support for evangelical Protestantism, and the relative strength of evangelicalism in the western provinces, became part of the West's opposition to the perceived secularization of central Canadian society in urban Ontario and Quebec. SCP leaders asserted that their Christian values were part of the libertarian, western Canadian, pro-capitalist heritage. However inaccurately, they portrayed themselves as the defenders of this heritage against the secular, liberal powers in Ottawa and Quebec.[54] These factors cast doubt on the notion that all of Canadian society was becoming increasingly secular during the post-Second World War years.[55] Clearly, there were pockets of support for conservative theology in parts of the country. Political parties and branches of Christianity developed in the West in opposition to their more mainline Liberal and Conservative, and Protestant and Roman Catholic, counterpart in the east.

My study of political women engages two theoretical approaches: (1) elitist/populist and (2) socialist feminist. "Populism" implies support for workers rights, decentralism in government, anti-war and anti-imperialist views, popular democracy, and, in the case of Socred populists, for individualism and evangelical Christianity. Socred populists fought to uphold the traditional, nuclear, heterosexual family against any perceived threat, including from big business and big government, from liberals and leftists, and from those who supported war and imperialism. Alvin Finkel argues that there is a difference between left- and right-wing variants of populism. Left populism sees large-scale capitalist organization of the economy as the major social problem and seeks to solve it by calling for socialists/communists to take over the state. Conversely, right-wing populism only superficially critiques the economic system and sees small, conspiratorial groups (like bankers, Jews, and bureaucratic governments) as the problem. According to this perspective, if a small group of people could be removed from power, then the capitalist system would function effectively.[56]

In contrast, "elitism" refers to support for party leaders and bureaucratic tendencies, centralization of power (within political parties and within government itself), pro-war viewpoints, and, in the case of the SCP, for big business and monopoly capitalism (particularly in the oil, lumber, and mining industries). Finkel is correct in defining left- and right-wing populism in this manner. Populist women in the SCP saw big business and big government as uniting to destroy small business, traditional family values, Christianity, and rural areas. SCP women argued that the solution to societal problems would be found in a return to traditional, Christian values – lost in the transition to an industrial, consumerist economy – and in the small-scale ownership of land and materials. SCP women, like some American populist conservatives from the late 1960s and subsequent decades, condemned the "free market" and big business for destroying traditional morality through modern forms of media and their introduction of a more "permissive" society.[57] I contend that "traditionalist" SCP members like Cornelia Wood and Lydia Arsens – with their suspicion of, if not hostility towards, capitalist modernity and their support for anti-war politics – had some ideas in common with "left populist" CCF members such as Evelyn Smith. This is true, even though the SCP's ultimate goal was very different from that of the CCF.[58]

A large number of women in these parties were populists rather than elitists. In fact, attitudes towards women's roles in politics broke down around elitist/populist lines, with many women supporting populist viewpoints and increased roles for women in public life. In contrast, elitists in these parties, including many men in leadership positions, often opposed an increased role for women. This populist versus elitist framework does not apply to CPC women. CPC women like Becky Buhay, Annie Buller, and Mona Morgan embraced introducing more democracy, fairness, and workers' rights into society: indeed, CPC women fought alongside men, at the grassroots level, to organize unions, fight against war, and help the poor. While the CPC ostensibly followed the dictates of the Soviet Union on many issues, in practice, Moscow and the Comintern did not direct, or even support, CPC activities at the grassroots level.[59] Nonetheless, on the whole, the populist versus elitist framework is useful for understanding political women's activism in the CCF and the SCP.

With regard to my second theoretical approach – socialist feminism – one can say that certain general assumptions are central. For example, historical materialism – a vision of history that focuses on how economic structures influence human behaviour – is seen as a useful tool for understanding the world, even if other feminist theories, from radical feminism to poststructuralist feminism, contend this.[60] Socialist feminism argues that working-class men, while also exploited under capitalism, have more freedom than do women to work and live in the competitive world. Socialist feminist scholars seek to understand how class has defined women's experiences and how gender has defined women's and men's lives.

Socialist feminist scholarship emphasizes that women's experiences differ economically from men's. Capitalism has exploited working-class women brutally, using them as cheap labour and structuring their work so that it constitutes an onerous double day consisting of paid work outside the home and unpaid domestic work and child-rearing inside the home. In the elusive "last instance," historical materialism – in effect, class – and gender are seen as the overarching forces that shaped women's experiences in the western Canada of the 1940s and 1950s.

I chose the case studies presented in the following chapters because of their prominence in the discourse of left- and right-wing women and because they reveal much about the politics of these women's groups. In Chapter 1, I present a series of biographies of left-wing women. Through these biographies, I offer a study of left-wing women's views on collectivism, a key idea in communist and social democratic ideology. In Chapter 2, again using a series of biographies, I provide a discussion of SCP women and their individualistic views. I chose the women in the first two chapters because of their prominence in their respective movements and because of the extent to which their experiences are representative of women in the CPC, the CCF, and the SCP. These two chapters are mirror images of each other: they argue that there are some differences in the class, ethnic, religious, and rural/urban positions of the women under discussion and that these differences account for their choice of political party. Yet these women held common views on many issues (e.g., their belief in the importance of family connections united all three groups of women). In these two chapters, I outline the book's cast of characters, many of whom reappear in later sections, where their views serve to illuminate different aspects of their respective political ideologies.

In the remaining chapters I offer case studies that demonstrate the views of these women and their parties. In Chapter 3, I deal with CPC and CCF women in the peace and anti-war movements. Here, and throughout the book, I continue a critical dialogue with the idea of maternalism. In Chapter 4, I discuss SCP women and their perspectives on issues surrounding peace and nuclear disarmament. I show that many right- and left-wing women shared an anti-war perspective. It becomes clear that anti-war activism was less of a concern for leftist men than it was for leftist women, while SCP men largely endorsed war, particularly the Cold War against communism. For their part, conservative women supported a maternalist ideology, which they used to argue against sending their husbands and sons to fight and die in wars started by men.

In Chapter 5, I discuss women-only organizations in all three parties, most notably the women's auxiliaries of left-wing trade unions and the Social Credit Women's Auxiliary. Here I suggest that, in all three parties, women-only groups led to a stronger voice for women. In Chapter 6, I offer a discussion of the discourse of juvenile delinquency and its uses. Women in all three parties used the idea of juvenile delinquency to buttress their ideological views. Left-wing women saw delinquency as a moral problem but one with material roots: delinquency indicated that young people needed the benefits of a stronger welfare state – notably, improved housing, public recreation, and social programs – to give them hope. Conversely, Socred women saw delinquency as being solely an ethical issue with religious overtones: society had moved away from the traditional concerns of family and Christianity, and this, in turn, had led to increased youth crime. Only a return to the time-honoured values of church and the nuclear family could stem the tide of leftism and modernity. Still, all three groups of women saw delinquency as evidence that post-Second World War Canadian society was heading down the wrong moral path.

Although I focus on the geographical and political margins of Canada, *From Left to Right* reveals much about how the mainstream "centre" operates in terms of politics, place, and gender. This contributes to new directions and new views of Canadian women's history.[61] In studying Canadian women of the right and the left, we must seek to examine the complexity of their lives and to break down traditional political and societal categories, most notably the division between left- and right-wing political ideologies. I show that left and right had some things in common in post-Second World War Canada. The three groups of women under discussion all asserted that reinventing human society – and the character of human beings – was possible. Maternalism is the common thread that united their different visions of the New World Order. Ironically, all three groups possessed what many might see as essentialist views of women and motherhood. Despite the fact that very few of the women discussed here endorsed an explicitly feminist viewpoint – a perspective that endorses equality for *all* groups of women – the increase in women's political activism during the 1940s and 1950s laid the basis for the second-wave feminism of the following decades.

1

Women No Longer Need Fear Want or Illness

Women on the Left

The years directly after the Second World War were a time of optimism for communists, social democrats,[1] and conservatives in Canada and elsewhere. Women of all political stripes were especially hopeful. During the war, women had come out of the home to work in war-related industries; many commentators suggested that women's work and actions had helped the Allied nations win the war. After the defeat of the fascist powers, women hoped that the events of the war would foreshadow stronger legal rights and social advancement. This was particularly the case for left-wing women, who argued, optimistically, that the postwar years would lead to better health care and educational programs, including nursery schools for children and a national health insurance plan. Encapsulating this perspective, Co-operative Commonwealth Federation member Laura Jamieson wrote that women would "no longer fear want or illness" for themselves or for their children and families.[2]

Communist Party of Canada and CCF women endorsed a "collectivist" vision of society – that is, they advocated for societal solutions to the problems engendered by capitalism. CPC and CCF women stated that people, especially workers, the poor, and other oppressed groups, should work together to advance solutions to the problems of inequality and class struggle. Both groups of women also suggested that taking control of state and governmental structures was necessary to effect change in society. This was leftist women's vision of the New World Order. A sense of "place" was also key in shaping left-wing women's political choices. The political economies of the particular towns and areas from which left-wing women came strongly predisposed them towards supporting leftist and collectivist solutions to societal problems. Left-wing women came from families with strong traditions of leftist activism; this was true for women from both the CPC and the CCF. Many leftist women came from families with strong traditions in radical politics and the labour movement. Both left- and right-wing women reified the ideal of the nuclear, heterosexual family, using their biological families as well as their vision of the male-breadwinner, male-dominated family as a spur towards political activism. These women did not see their roles of raising and maintaining families as being inferior to men's roles of working outside the home.

CP and CCF women expressed similar views regarding the prospect of women's advancement. Most leftist women asserted that, in a more equal society, women would not have to work for pay outside the home; socialist men would make enough money to "keep" a family on one wage. Thus, leftist women held similar values to those of left-wing men. Other women endorsed a vision according to which they would play a larger role in shaping Canadian society. They would step out of the home and into public life, albeit in such a way that would not threaten the male-breadwinner model. Leftist women, like their counterparts on the right, "gendered" men primarily as fathers, sons, husbands, brothers, political leaders, protectors, and, especially, as breadwinners who worked outside the home to make money to support their families. In short, political women portrayed male roles as related to the family and the private sphere: that is, men earned money *in order to support* women and children in the private sphere. Women's view of men was a limiting one and was very much a product of its time; indeed, we might say that women of both the left and the right saw men as being workers and *producers* rather than as people of leisure and consumption. The 1960s and subsequent decades ushered in very different views of the role of men and masculinity.[3]

In order to understand the vision of the New World Order that these women wanted to inaugurate, it is first necessary to look at the system that they wanted to replace. CPC and CCF women favoured reform of the dominant capitalist economic system. Capitalism argued for individualism, the free flow of market forces, and (rhetorically) anti-statism (even though, in practice, most conservatives used the state to ensure the power of large corporations and monopolies, thereby hindering any true free market).[4] The capitalist system emphasized the family and the individual as the building blocks of society. While still, in practice, upholding the family, left-wing women argued that class forces shaped society in fundamental ways. They further argued that collective action on the part of left-wing organizations was necessary to bring about societal and economic change, including more state support for working men, which would, in turn, keep women out of the paid work force.[5]

These views are reflected in the collective biographies of left-wing women. In this chapter, I present a series of biographies of CPC and CCF women: most of these women were well known in their respective organizations, while others were rank-and-file party members. I chose these women because of their prominence in their parties and because they left behind sufficient information to provide detailed biographies. Some of these women appear later on, where their views highlight the ideologies of the left- and right-wing parties to which they belonged. My, at times, thin treatment of some of these women is related to limitations in the source material. The biographies I offer in Chapters 1 and 2 do not provide detailed accounts of the lives of these women (other scholars have seen to this);[6] rather, they offer a basic portrait not only of the typical left- or right-wing woman activist but also of the leading women in the CP, the CCF, and the SCP. The biographies set the stage for the case studies that demonstrate the actions and gendered ideologies of the right and the left in post-Second World War western Canada.[7]

Left-wing women came from diverse backgrounds. All are drawn from British Columbia, which is not surprising given the relative strength of left-wing movements in the Pacific province.[8] Some left-wing women had urban origins; others, especially in the CCF, were from rural areas. Leading women in these parties, like Grace MacInnis and Dorothy Steeves, had a great deal of formal education, while more proletarian members, like Effie Jones and Gladys Hilland of the CPC, forged their ideology in the union struggles of the 1930s and 1940s. The women's lives also span different periods. CCF women often had their political origins in the suffrage movement. In contrast, CPC women often dated their introduction to radical politics from the 1930s. Given the conservative orientation of some first-wave feminists, this helps to explain the moderate ideological direction taken by many CCF women. These biographies tell us much about left-wing women's social backgrounds, about what brought them into communist or social democratic politics, and about their views and ideologies.

In order to clarify left-wing women's views on such issues as peace, juvenile delinquency, and feminism it is important to first define their personal perspectives. The biographies show that left-wing women came from specific backgrounds and possessed a particular ideology.[9] Communist women were largely from working-class, often immigrant, backgrounds and were largely non-religious. CPC women had usually emigrated from the British Isles or Continental Europe. They often lived in urban environments or in resource-based communities like Nanaimo, Nelson, or Trail, where trade unionism flourished. Most CPC women were married and had children (like many, perhaps most, women during the 1940s and 1950s). CPC and CCF women sometimes dealt with issues of particular importance to women, most notably abortion, childcare, and birth control. They usually considered these issues from a class, as well as from a maternalist, perspective: poor or working-class women had far fewer financial resources than did middle- or upper-class women. This foreshadows the views expressed by second-wave socialist feminists during the 1960s and 1970s.[10]

Relatively little archival material exists concerning the nature of left-wing women's grassroots and bureaucratic organizations. Nonetheless, it is fair to say that left- and right-wing women's groups were organized in similar ways, even if their political perspectives differed. Left-wing women's groups, most notably the CCF Women's Council and the women's auxiliaries to left-wing trade unions, had an official status within their parent parties. All appointed delegates to provincial conventions and to the parties' annual meetings. These groups, like their right-wing counterparts, possessed presidents, two vice-presidents, and secretary-treasurers who ran the unions and auxiliaries. The CCF Women's Council was an official organ of the party and was required to turn over part of its fundraising contribution to the CCF provincial and federal executives. Union auxiliaries were established on a slightly different basis. The CPC and its unions required that at least five women join an auxiliary in order for it to be considered official. Some union locals, especially in rural and isolated areas of British Columbia, lacked auxiliaries since not enough women were interested to justify starting them up. It is difficult to judge the exact number of participants in women's councils and auxiliaries, but it was probably, at most, around fifteen hundred women. There were significantly more women who were members and supporters of the CPC and CCF parties but who were not official members of the women's councils or auxiliaries. At one time, between 1945 and 1961, several thousand women were members of the councils and auxiliaries. The overall female – and male – membership of the CCF was larger than that of the CPC (which is not surprising, given the more mainstream appeal of the CCF), but the exact number of women members is impossible to estimate. Women in the CPC and the CCF constituted about 30 percent of their parties' memberships. So women represented a minority of party members, albeit a highly significant one.[11]

My information on left- and right-wing women comes from a variety of sources, including newspapers, archival collections, personal papers, transcriptions of oral interviews, and contemporary published works by prominent members of the three parties under discussion. These sources have their limitations. In particular, the published works and the party newspapers largely reflect the "party line"; there is little debate over issues such as capitalism, Christianity, modernity, morality, unions, war and peace, women's issues, or delinquency. All of the printed sources are, effectively, propaganda tools. Even the interviews, conducted many years after the period in question, largely attempt to place the interviewees and their partisan ideologies in a positive light. Nonetheless, the fact that the sources, most notably the published works and newspapers, often focus on women and familial concerns suggests that women's activism was an important force.

CPC women in western Canada saw the world from a standpoint that – they argued – would produce a new world order of equality and socialism. One such woman was Mary (Mollie) Crowe of Nelson, British Columbia. In November 1957, Crowe having recently died at the age of fifty-four, the CPC published an obituary for her in its newspaper, the *Pacific Tribune*. Calling her a "pioneer supporter" of the labour movement, the CPC offered a commentary on Crowe's life.[12] She came from a family of Welsh miners who had immigrated to Canada when she was only two years old.[13] Initially settling in Alberta's Crowsnest Pass region, which was known for the volatility of its miners' strikes, the family soon moved to Nanaimo, where mining was also a key industry.[14] Crowe's father took part in the 1912–13 miners' strike in British Columbia, which resulted in Premier Richard McBride's bringing in the 72nd Highlanders to smash the embryonic union.[15] The province's coal operators blacklisted Crowe's father from the mines on account of his union involvement. The family later relocated to Nelson. Eventually, along with her husband Jack, Mollie Crowe joined the CPC, under the auspices of the International Union of Mine, Mill, and Smelter Workers (Mine-Mill).[16] Prominent CPC official Tom McEwen officiated at Crowe's funeral, which was held in Nelson.[17] Crowe represented the CPC's image of the "ideal" rank-and-file party supporter in many ways: she was from a working-class background, strongly supported unions, and had a sense of class consciousness. She and her husband became active supporters of the class struggle as organizers for, and members of, the CPC. Left-wing women often explained their introduction to radical politics by portraying it as a response to the suffering of poor and working-class people. This was the social "hook" through which they explained their ideology. The theme of family emerges as an explanation for Crowe's decision to join the CPC (she and her husband were both party members) as does the theme of place: coming from a mining family, Mollie Crowe, like so many other Scottish and Welsh migrants, came to Nanaimo and then to Nelson, both communities that replicated the radical, leftist mining culture of the old country.[18]

Betty (née Dunbar) Griffin was a more prominent CPC supporter than was Mollie Crowe. Born in Vancouver in 1923, Griffin explained her radicalism as resulting from the context of the Great Depression. Indeed, the Depression was an important factor in the radicalization of many left-wing women. Owing to the suffering faced by poor and working people, and the indifference of government and local officials, many on the left argued that statist solutions – actions taken by government on the people's behalf – were necessary to deal with society's problems. Like many other women of her generation, Griffin worked in industry – at Boeing – during the Second World War. She had attended the University of British Columbia for a year when, in 1942, she went into war work. This provided her with her first taste of factory work as well as her union membership. She worked with Local 756 of the International Association of Machinists to sign up new members for the union. These experiences – seeing the poverty engendered by the Great Depression and helping to organize workers during the Second World War – brought Griffin into the orbit of left-wing ideology. During the war, she met her husband, CPC member Harold (Hal) Griffin. She joined the CPC shortly thereafter. As a new CPC member, Betty Dunbar attended Hal's classes on Marxist and socialist theory. After their marriage, Griffin remained at home for some years to raise the couple's children; because of her pregnancy, the school board fired her from her teaching position in Burnaby.[19]

During the late 1940s and into the 1950s, Griffin wrote for the Woman's Page of the CPC newspaper. She presented opinions on a diverse array of topics, some of which were of particular importance to women: consumption, juvenile delinquency, peace and anti-war issues, and the problems associated with raising children in working-class households. She remained a CPC supporter after the Hungarian Revolution of 1956 and was heavily involved in her local of the British Columbia Teachers' Federation. In more recent times, Griffin lived in West Vancouver after her husband's death in 1998 and was involved in anti-war and anti-nuclear campaigns.[20] Unlike some former activists, most of the women mentioned here maintained their left-wing views throughout their lives, even after many former supporters, disillusioned by the revelations concerning the authoritarian nature of the Soviet Union, left the party. In recent interviews, Griffin's recollections of her life reflect her politics, and her sense of radical identity, which she clearly never lost.

Mona Morgan's life history is indicative of those of many other left-wing women. Her parents, Dora and Paul Bjarnason, were of Icelandic origin. They were both born in the United States and, after coming to Canada, lived in Wynyard, Saskatchewan, for many years. The family came to Vancouver in 1934 and remained there. Paul and Dora had seven children, Emil, Val, and Mona being the ones best known to left-wing historians because of their association with the CPC. Soon after coming to Vancouver, Mona Bjarnason married Nigel Morgan, a strong CPC supporter who eventually became the leader of the International Woodworkers of America (IWA), a CPC stronghold until the 1948 purge that removed leftists from the union's leadership and membership. In the 1946 province-wide strike of British Columbia's woodworkers, Morgan hosted a radio broadcast, "Five Minutes with Mona," which presented working-class issues from a woman's point of view. She helped to organize and lead the "Trek to Victoria" in 1946 to support male strikers in the logging industry. As a member of the Housewives Consumers Association, Mona Morgan was also involved with the fight to lower food prices in order to attain a better standard of living for working families. On one occasion, she ran, unsuccessfully, for city council in Vancouver.[21]

CPC women and men often became involved with radical politics through family connections. Nigel Morgan's mother, Kathleen Morgan, a resident and "pioneer settler" of Galiano Island, had been involved with the suffragette movement in England. She was an ally of Emmeline Pankhurst and was among those who had padlocked themselves to the gates of Buckingham Palace to protest against women's being denied the vote. At age sixty-four, Kathleen Morgan became a member of the Kensington Club of the CPC and worked "with tireless energy" in the cause of peace and the party.[22] The Bjarnason/Morgan family was one of a number of significant "Communist families" in the Vancouver area. The Greenwell and the Gidora-Dewhurst families also numbered among the important CPC supporters in the city. Donald "Dusty" Greenwell was a community organizer in Vancouver, heavily involved in establishing community centres and local parks; his wife Betty was also an active CPC member.

Alf Dewhurst was a leading member of the IWA; however, the anti-communist purge of unions in British Columbia and throughout Canada forced Dewhurst, like Nigel Morgan, to leave the union in 1948.[23] He would later undertake visits to communist nations like China, the Soviet Union, and (later) Vietnam. Dewhurst's wife, Viola, helped to organize laundry workers on Vancouver Island and on British Columbia's mainland. Their children and grandchildren continue to be involved with the CPC and other progressive organizations in the Vancouver area.[24]

The phenomenon of the "Communist family" suggests how family ties and personal relations intersected with, and reinforced, political loyalties. This was also the case with women involved in the CCF and the SCP, and with the mainstream Liberal and Conservative parties. Political women used their family connections to assist them in forging careers in public life. Even today, many politically active people of various ideological stripes come from families who have been involved in public life for several generations.

The examples of Betty Griffin and Mona Morgan are particularly instructive in that both women had a working-class background and met their husbands through the CPC. Unlike some earlier CPC women, such as Jeanne Corbin, CPC women from the postwar period were not single women who devoted themselves to the cause of class struggle.[25] These women married and had children and families. CPC women – at least the small group of BC activists with which I am concerned – were a relatively homogeneous group: most knew each other through social and political contacts. These Vancouver-based activists all came to the party in similar ways, usually because of parental influence or in reaction to the suffering caused by the Great Depression. CCF women also shared many similarities, and a community of like-minded CCF women did develop in Vancouver; however, theirs was not as homogenous a group as was that comprised of CPC women. From this we can see that left-wing women in British Columbia forged a distinctive, "alternative subculture" of CPC activism.

We might consider Griffin and Morgan, as well as Mollie Crowe, as being part of the populist wing of the left. All supported grassroots activism, workers rights, community-based solutions to social problems, increased democracy, and anti-war activities. Although there were elitist elements in the CPC (given the party's ultimate subservience to the dictates of the Soviet Union), this was not the whole story. CPC women activists fought for grassroots change to western Canadian society in many areas – particularly those related to consumption and high prices, anti-war activism, and workers rights – and they cared deeply about the concerns of the common people.[26] In spite of the elitist framework of their party's hierarchy – party leaders in the Soviet Union and Canada referred to their policy as "democratic centralism" but, in practice, the party's male hierarchy made most of the important decisions – CPC women were all left-wing populists.

Elspeth Gardner, another important CPC woman, also came from a working-class background. Like Mona Morgan, her family history included many people who fought for progressive causes. Her mother, Elsie Munro, was a renowned cook who had worked in many upper-class houses in Scotland before immigrating to Canada. Elsie married Peter Munro, a CPC member and a trade unionist with the Street Railwayman's Union in Vancouver. Before he agreed to marry her, Peter Munro insisted that Elsie become a socialist. During the 1930s, Elsie Munro was involved with women's organizations like the Housewives' League and the Mothers' Council.[27] Elspeth Gardner was a strong public speaker who often gave public addresses on left-wing and progressive causes. She "married late" in life and became a labour lawyer: she was called to the bar in 1942 and articled under the CPC's lawyer, John Stanton. During the 1950s she defended Gordon Martin, a lawyer who had been disbarred because of his left-wing affiliations. Elspeth Gardner worked in anti-war and pro-peace campaigns as well as in labour and civil rights struggles. She remained a CPC supporter after 1956.[28]

Effie Jones was another immigrant woman from the British Isles who became involved with the CPC. She was born in Somersetshire, England, but was brought up in Wales until she was six. Her father, the principal of a boys' school, had died, so Jones went to live with her mother, also a principal, in England. Before his death, her father had insisted on her move to England, fearing that she would not get a good education in the economically depressed area of Wales in which she lived. At various intervals, Effie Jones returned to Wales to live with her great-grandparents who were "like a mother and father" to her. Jones encountered class struggle at a young age, when she saw a group of unemployed miners walking through central Wales. During the early 1900s, while in her teens, Jones went to visit her uncle, a trade unionist who organized railway workers in Swansea and who had a strong influence on her thinking. She later remarked, on her experiences in Swansea: "From then on I knew where my place was in society."[29]

Effie Jones's political awakening was similar to that of other left-wing women. She explained her ideological standpoint as having resulted from a particular social hook, in this case her identification with struggling miners. A sense of place, or location, was also key to Jones's political background. She had lived in a mining area of Wales; as part of this milieu, she had lived beside working-class, pro-union people and had strongly identified with them. This led her to support left-wing activism and state-centred social reform. While, in practice, the CPC, the CCF, and the SCP often shared similar views on a number of issues, women of the left and of the right did come from different geographical backgrounds. This led them to make different kinds of political identifications. The case of mining-based areas is instructive. Many mining families, who were originally from iron-producing areas of northern England, Scotland, and Wales, came to places like Nelson, Trail, Nanaimo, Newcastle, and the Crowsnest Pass, where they started up labour and socialist parties.[30] In this way, a sense of place played a key role in the formative process of left-wing women's political ideologies. While resource-based areas where logging or mining was strong (such as those in British Columbia) often produced leftist and pro-union groups, small towns and rural areas with political economies based on farming (such as those in Alberta) often produced a more conservative political culture.[31]

After having taught in Britain for nine years, Effie Jones, aged thirty, came to Canada on Christmas Day 1919 and was married that same day. Jones's husband worked for BC Electric and later for BC Telephone (for thirty-three years) and was a member of the Telephone Pioneers of America. He was also a socialist and supported Effie in her political career.[32] Effie Jones began her journey in politics as a member of the CCF. She was also involved in the Housewives' League (HWL) from its inception.[33] The Liberal Party women who had founded the HWL were "not very active although they did meet socially."[34] The CCF's ostensibly more moderate ideology did not satisfy Jones, and she soon moved on to the CPC. As a party member, Effie Jones took up many causes. She assisted her Vancouver neighbours against evictions, and, along with many CPC comrades in the HWL, she supported the post-office sit-down strikers in 1938, providing them with sandwiches and later arranging for their defence in court.

In 1947, Effie Jones ran for mayor in Vancouver against a conservative candidate, Charles "High Fare" Jones. Effie called herself "Low Fare" Jones because she opposed the BC Electric's monopoly and its constant rate increases. Effie Jones ended up losing in a close race, in part, she said, because the opposition brought in drunks and nuns to vote against her. She also remarked, tellingly: "I lost the election in the business district, where I had no support." She would later run, on several occasions, for city council. Although she always polled respectable numbers, she never won an election. During the 1950s, she was a leading figure in peace marches and the Housewives Consumers Association. She was also president of the Civic Reform Association, a successful, communist-inspired attempt to influence local government in Vancouver. The association dealt with such issues as police corruption, high electrical rates, and public ownership of utilities. Jones continued to be a CPC supporter until her death in 1985.[35]

Although Effie Jones was not elected to City Council, other progressives were. CPC members, often criticized as "ultra-leftist" radicals, were willing to work within traditional structures in order to effect change. This lends credence to the view that, particularly from the Popular Front period onward, the CPC had largely abandoned the idea that only a socialist revolution could bring change to Canadian society. Instead, Canadian communists, not unlike CCFers, had decided to work within the dominant system to bring about practical reforms that would be of benefit to working people. Clearly, CPC women's views had changed from the left-sectarian of the "Third Period."[36] The Popular Front position continued from 1935 into the post-Second World War period. In fact, this support of a more moderate direction for the CPC lasted until the late 1950s, when anti-communism led to the demise of the CPC as a political force in North America.

Union women, particularly in communist-led organizations like the IWA, were also important to the CPC. Gladys (née Shunaman) Hilland was an important member of the IWA and the CPC. She was born in Dunkirk, Saskatchewan – roughly forty-eight kilometres south of Moose Jaw. As a young girl, she laboured both on her family's farm and as a domestic servant. Hilland finished Grade 11 in 1932 and worked at an orphanage in Moose Jaw. She attended meetings of the Farmers' Unity League between 1929 and 1935, her first experience with the CPC. Later, the On-to-Ottawa-Trek had a strong influence on her, particularly when, in 1935, she watched trains carrying single unemployed men come through Moose Jaw.[37] Hilland's rural background was common to many women. Migration from rural areas to large urban centres had been a feature of North American history for many years, and this accelerated during the Depression, with the decline of farms. Rural origins were even more common among CCF and SCP women than among CPC women.

Hoping to find work in British Columbia, Gladys Hilland migrated there in 1940 and found employment in a hotel in Hope and then as a domestic in Vancouver. During the latter years of the Second World War she worked for Sitka Spruce (later BC Forest Products), which processed spruce for airplanes and washboards for the army. During this period, Hilland became an IWA member and, in 1942, secretary-treasurer of IWA Local 217, a position that was usually filled by a man. As secretary-treasurer, she helped to organize women workers. She later remarked that she had to be careful where she went in Vancouver since it was common for company thugs to assault union supporters.[38] This fear of violence was typical among left-wing women; even CCF members had to be careful about revealing their affiliation in the party's early days. Hilland, and others like her, would go to a plant's lunchroom and speak to the workers on a variety of issues. She also organized special "women's day meetings" in order to appeal to female workers.[39]

As an IWA member and union official, Hilland was involved with the 1946 province-wide strike of lumber workers. She noted that the union got "fantastic support for the strike." The Native Brotherhood, the Bakers' Union, Mine-Mill, and the Fishermen's Union numbered among the various groups that supported the IWA's efforts. After the 1948 split in the Woodworkers' Union, Hilland, as a communist, was blacklisted and never returned to the IWA or to the union movement. Instead, she raised a family and later established and ran her own boarding house. In her later years in Maple Ridge, British Columbia, Hilland operated a private hospital for senior citizens. She was also involved in the peace movement.[40]

These biographies of CPC women have implications for how historians see the international connections among national communist parties. CPC women could claim membership in numerous organizations, notably parent-teacher associations, the Housewives Consumers Association, peace organizations, and local government. This suggests that, while Moscow had the "final say" in what the CPC hierarchy did, communist women, like their male comrades, often worked at local levels in order to achieve reform in the "here and now" in ways that Moscow could not control.[41] Far from not "living in the real world," as historian Aileen Kraditor puts it, communists were often very present-minded and concerned with everyday issues of interest to working people.[42] Indeed, as we have noted, neither Moscow nor the Comintern supported the grassroots achievements of CPC women or men.

These biographies suggest a different way of interpreting the history of CPC women from the 1920s to the 1950s. The views of CPC women from the postwar period differed in significant ways from those of CPC women during the prewar years. In many ways, the Women's Labour Leagues (WLLs) of the 1920s and early 1930s represented a high point for women's activism in the CPC. The WLLs fought for many radical causes, notably the right of women to choose to have abortions and the legalization of birth control. During the Third Period, the WLLs were placed under the control of the CPC-led Workers' Unity League. This, along with the death of party organizer Florence Custance in 1929, led to the demise of the WLLs and the curtailing of women's activism in the CPC. During the period of the Popular Front, CPC women's activity in the party increased somewhat, although in ways that did not hearken back to the days of the WLLs. CPC women forged temporary alliances among women of different political stripes, especially with CCF women, and this led to the promise of a "popular front" of women's activism.[43] However, during the Cold War period, anti-communism became an unremitting ideology that led to the demonization of CPC supporters, including women, in all sectors of society. Owing to the negative associations of communism in this era, the CPC was anxious to convey to Canadians of all political opinions that it was a mainstream organization with conventional views on all issues, including the roles of women. Among CPC men, this meant downgrading women's activism in the party. Like men in the CCF and in the SCP, those in the CPC's hierarchy were largely hostile to women's activity. During all of these periods, CPC women used maternalist language and views to convey their ideological perspective concerning the value of motherhood as a spur towards political activism. This was even more the case during the post-1945 period since CPC women were, no less than CPC men, concerned with conveying a mainstream image.

The biographies of CCF women also suggest new interpretations of female experiences in political parties. Like their communist counterparts, social democratic women argued that they had a duty to participate in effecting change at the local, national, and international levels. Mildred Osterhout Fahrni was a particularly significant social democratic woman. She was born in Rapid City, Manitoba, on 2 January 1900, to a Dutch father and English mother. The Osterhout family came to Vancouver soon after her birth. Fahrni's father, a minister in the Methodist Church, emphasized to his young daughter the importance of education. The family moved frequently since A.B. Osterhout was continually looking for a congregation that would provide his family with stability. Mildred Osterhout obtained her BA and MA degrees at the University of British Columbia, where she studied philosophy and English. At UBC, she came under the influence of a Dr. Boggs, the head of the Department of Economics. Boggs led Fahrni to socialist study groups, where she became convinced that the capitalist system needed to be changed. At these study groups, Fahrni read the works of radical thinkers like Harold Laski, Sidney and Beatrice Webb, and Karl Marx. She was also a member of the pacifist group the Fellowship of Reconciliation, which was established during the First World War. Fahrni represented the social gospel wing of the CCF, with its emphasis on using religion to improve life for humanity.[44] This differentiates her from other CCF supporters, notably the technocrats of the League for Social Reconstruction, who favoured rational and scientific, rather than religious or spiritual, solutions to social problems.[45]

Mildred Osterhout joined another pacifist group, the Student Christian Movement, during the same period.[46] As a young girl she had attended trade union and Industrial Workers of the World meetings in Vancouver's East Side. In her spare time, she was involved with the Young Women's Christian Association. In 1930–31, Fahrni attended Bryn Mawr College in Pennsylvania, where she was a student in the Department of Social Economics and Social Research and where she received a certificate that qualified her to be a social worker. While at Bryn Mawr, she continued her work with single unemployed women in working-class areas of Philadelphia. She then spent six months teaching at the London School of Economics, where she lectured in economics, sociology, psychology, and mental hygiene.[47]

Given her background in social work and left-wing causes, it is not surprising that Fahrni was involved with the CCF from its inception. She attended the first CCF conference in Regina, travelling there from Vancouver with Frank MacKenzie and Dorothy Steeves. She remarked in 1982 that the founding of the new party filled her with "great enthusiasm." Later, in the 1930s, Osterhout travelled through Europe and to India, where she encountered Mahatma Gandhi. She had first met him in London at Kingsley Hall in 1931 during her stay at the London School of Economics. Back in Vancouver, Osterhout assisted in establishing the West End Community Centre and was its director for four years during the 1930s. She married Walter Fahrni in August 1941. Unlike many others in her party and in the CPC, she opposed the Canadian government's relocation of the Japanese Canadians during the Second World War and taught at an internment camp in New Denver, British Columbia, during the war.[48]

Fahrni ran for public office on a number of occasions but was never elected, perhaps because she was unwilling to compromise her anti-racist, pacifist sentiments. She joined numerous women's and socialist organizations in Vancouver, notably the CCF Women's Council and the Vancouver Women's School for Citizenship, an organization established to teach women about voting and politics. Fahrni played a "small role," as did her comrade Laura Jamieson, in the Vancouver Council of Women.[49] She was also a key member of the Women's International League for Peace and Freedom. As a pacifist, she argued that taking a human life under any conditions was morally wrong. Fahrni supported peaceful resolutions to such conflicts as the Arab-Israeli wars, she opposed colonialism and nuclear weapons, and supported the United Nations. Fahrni remained a critical supporter of the CCF/NDP until her death in Vancouver in 1992. However, she had become largely disillusioned with the CCF after 1945, particularly with its compromises, its support for the Second World War and the Cold War, and its willingness to support the Canadian establishment. Mildred Fahrni's encounter with Gandhi had a profound impact on her, as did her encounters with other non-violent crusaders such as J.S. Woodsworth and, later, Martin Luther King.[50] Fahrni marched in favour of black civil rights in Alabama in 1956, opposed the Vietnam War during the 1960s, and protested against nuclear weapons during the 1980s.[51] Fahrni's socialist politics seems to have been inspired by the example of "great" individuals like Woodsworth and King as well as by her father's social gospel background; unlike other left-wing women, her ideology did not originate in a reaction to specific economic or social conditions. Given her uncompromising support for the anti-war movement and her opposition to colonialism, we might see Fahrni as a representative of the populist wing of the CCF/NDP. Unlike other women discussed here, Fahrni was never removed from her party for being too radical.

Other CCF women's lives followed different paths. Laura Jamieson was born Laura Emma Marshall in Park Head, Bruce County, Ontario, near Owen Sound, in 1882. She was educated at Owen Sound Collegiate and later at the University of Toronto, where she was an arts major, graduating in 1908. She worked, initially, as a school teacher and then briefly as a secretary for the YWCA in Stratford, Ontario. Since teaching jobs were not plentiful in Ontario at the time, Marshall moved to British Columbia to find employment. She first taught part-time in 1901 and then acquired her Normal School certificate, which allowed her to become a teacher anywhere in Canada. She was accepted at the Country School Board, fifty miles from Vancouver, where she taught summer school to save money for university.[52] After finishing at the University of Toronto, Marshall moved to Vancouver in 1911, where she remained for the rest of her life. Soon after moving to British Columbia, she married lawyer J. Stuart Jamieson, whom she had met previously while teaching summer school. The couple had two children who survived to adulthood, Laura Jean and Stuart Jr., and one who died in infancy. Stuart Jamieson Jr.

would later write a number of important texts on Canadian labour law from a leftist, political-economic perspective. Here, again, we see that politics are often associated with family ties.[53]

Jamieson, like Mildred Fahrni, supported the peace movement, particularly the Women's International League for Peace and Freedom, from its early stages in Canada. Like most other CPC and CCF members, she endorsed reform through "progressive, legal" means. She became a member of the Vancouver Council of Women and supported suffrage rights.[54] Jamieson is the oldest woman discussed here, and she is the only one who was able to trace her political activism back to the suffrage era – the era of first-wave feminism in Canada. Jamieson had a more openly moderate, and legalistic, perspective than did many other left-wing women, largely because of her involvement with the battle for the vote. Many left-wing women viewed the fight for suffrage, not without cause, as a battle for the rights of middle- and upper-class women.[55] Jamieson, however, was different. She used a maternalist analysis to critique war and capitalism; however, she endorsed Western colonialism in the Middle East, Africa, and Asia. Like social gospel activists from the "Progressive Era" (an era of widespread social reform stretching from the 1890s to the 1920s), Jamieson argued that whites needed to "uplift" those in the "Third World" and transform them into white Christians.[56] CCF women's political origins were more varied than were those of CPC or SCP women, a reflection of the fact that many different, sometimes opposing, groups of people came together to form the CCF in 1932–33.

Laura Jamieson's life course soon led her into electoral politics. Following the death of her husband in 1926, she was offered his job as a juvenile court judge in Burnaby. She worked as a judge from 1927 until 1938, when she decided to run on the CCF ticket for the BC Legislature. She won election in the Vancouver Centre riding in 1939 and represented that constituency until her defeat in 1945. She would later be elected to represent the same riding in 1952 and was a member of Vancouver City Council from 1948 to 1950. During the Second World War, in addition to writing a pamphlet on Canadian social and economic conditions, she organized and operated a cooperative residence for working-class and poor girls. The residence was intended to provide accommodation for girls, like Jamieson herself, who came to Vancouver from rural areas of British Columbia and Canada to look for jobs.[57] Later in life, Jamieson sat on the Board of Directors for the New Vista Society, an organization established to secure housing for senior citizens. She died in Vancouver in 1964.[58] Like other CCF members, she had many different interests in life, all of which involved serving some sector of the public. CCF members like Jamieson had an optimistic view of humanity, believing that it was possible for human beings to change and, ultimately, to adapt to a welfare statist society. Jamieson was a tireless worker for the CCF. She supported deserted wives and was responsible for introducing legislation that brought in equal pay for equal work, a step forward for women's rights in British Columbia (although the law was not well enforced). This may be seen as an example of how women from earlier eras paved the way for the rise of second-wave feminism. Owing to her support for statist and bureaucratic solutions to society's problems, as well as to her rather uncritical support for colonialism, Jamieson may be seen as being part of the elitist wing of the CCF.

Contemporaries often contrasted Dorothy (Gretchen) Steeves's temperament with Jamieson's. Born Dorothy Gretchen Biersteker in Amsterdam, Holland, on 26 May 1891 to a Dutch father and an English mother, Steeves was educated in Holland and studied at the University of Leiden, where she earned the degree of doctor of laws. During the First World War she was legal adviser to the Dutch government's Rationing Bureau. In 1917, she met her husband, Rufus Palmer Steeves, a Canadian military officer who was one of a contingent of British Commonwealth prisoners of war on parole in Holland. Gretchen Biersteker and Rufus Steeves were married in The Hague and then went to Canada in January 1919. Rufus was a teacher and a "proud seventh-generation Canadian."[59] The CCF's Daisy Webster later remarked that Rufus Steeves was a "liberal" who "kept quietly out of politics" and supported his wife's political endeavours.[60] Rufus Steeves ran the CCF federal campaign in the Vancouver-Burrard riding in the 1939 election but never voted in a Canadian election. Harold Winch argues that Rufus was "very pro-British" and had wanted to enlist when the Second World War broke out; however, Gretchen forbade this. Their only child, Hugh Douglas Steeves, an RCAF pilot, was killed in 1943.[61] This was a key event in Gretchen Steeves's life. Her pacifist views became stronger, as did her intolerance of war and of those in the CCF who had supported Canada's entry into the Second World War.

Gretchen Steeves supported the women's suffrage movement in Holland and gained much experience lecturing and writing.[62] The suffrage movement introduced her to labour and socialist politics. Steeves's life serves as an example of how more women were becoming involved in electoral and party politics with the advent of suffrage rights. This is not to say that women's political work began with suffrage. This is clearly not the case, especially when we consider the numerous examples of many nineteenth-century women who supported religious and reform organizations.[63] Still, women's suffrage increased the number of women who were interested in, and willing to engage in, political activism. Suffrage work set the stage for these women's later political activity in various groups. Laura Jamieson, in Canada, and Dorothy Steeves, in Holland, both participated in campaigns for women's suffrage, which later led them to support other kinds of reformist politics as members of the CCF.

The Depression deepened Gretchen Steeves's commitment to social democratic ideals. Like CPC women, social democrats often explained their politics through a particular social hook: in this case, it was a response to the conditions spawned by the Depression. Steeves attended the first CCF convention in Regina in 1933. Later that year, she ran, unsuccessfully, for the CCF in the BC riding of Point Grey. In 1934, she was elected to the BC Legislature in a North Vancouver by-election and was twice re-elected; she was finally defeated in 1945. Steeves supported organizations like the BC Civil Liberties Association, the Fellowship of Reconciliation, the Canadian Committee for Nuclear Disarmament, the Women's International League of Peace and Freedom, the Society for the Abolition of Capital Punishment, the Kitsilano Consumers Credit Union, and the Society for the Prevention of Cruelty to Animals.[64] According to Harold Winch, Steeves was the "mother of the credit union movement in British Columbia" as well as of the cooperative movement.[65] Her role in establishing these services suggests that political women had an influence on Canadian society that belied their relatively small numbers. It also offers support for the argument that the 1950s were not simply years of repression for women: clearly, some politicized women fought outside the home for social and economic change.

As the CCF's foreign affairs expert, Steeves, for many years, wrote a column in the *CCF News* on international issues. She was bitterly disappointed when the CCF voted to support Canada's entry into the Second World War. Many CCF members suggested that her anger at her son's death during the war intensified her hatred of war. She became progressively more anti-war, helping to establish the Socialist Fellowship in 1951. She deplored the Canadian government's internment of Japanese Canadians, although she did not speak out against it as strongly as did Mildred Fahrni. Nonetheless, Harold Winch remarks that, during the war, Steeves and her close friend Colin Cameron "let loose" in the BC Legislature over the horrors of war and, because of this, "came within a hairline of being charged with treason."[66]

CCF comrades described Steeves as a "sparkling woman" with a "biting wit." She was highly educated during a period when many people had little formal education.[67] Daisy Webster noted that Steeves had little use for feminism: she preferred the company found in mixed socialist groups.[68] Other colleagues suggested that she did not care for women much, although those who liked her said she was "kind" and "thoughtful." Apparently "women were jealous of her" but "men were not."[69] Her antagonism towards the Second World War alienated many of her North Vancouver constituents, and she was not re-elected after 1945. Hilda Kristiansen remarks that Steeves went blind shortly before her death and that this "tore her apart" because she could not stand being dependent on others.[70] Jessie Mendels argues that it was a tragedy for both Steeves and the party that she did not get elected as a federal MP since she would have "shone in Ottawa."[71] Husband Rufus Steeves retired from school teaching in 1958 and died suddenly in 1960; Gretchen died in 1974.[72] Although she supported state-centred solutions to problems of poverty and wealth, Steeves's anti-imperialism and support for the Socialist Fellowship places in her in the populist category of CCF women.

In contrast, Grace MacInnis was part of the CCF's leadership and was born into social democratic politics. Born in Winnipeg in 1905, Grace Winona Woodsworth was the daughter of J.S. and Lucy Woodsworth, who helped to found the CCF. J.S. Woodsworth was the pastor at Winnipeg's Grace Church at the time of his daughter's birth. The family left Winnipeg in 1917 after J.S. wrote a letter to the right-wing *Winnipeg Free Press* protesting Prime Minister Robert Borden's introduction of conscription. Grace Church fired J.S. Woodsworth as a result of this letter, and the family headed for Victoria. A church at Gibson's Landing, British Columbia, subsequently dismissed J.S. for refusing to support the First World War from the pulpit.

Grace Woodsworth attended the University of British Columbia for one year and eventually graduated from the University of Manitoba with her bachelor's degree. She later went to the Sorbonne in Paris, where welfare state theorist Harold Laski heavily influenced her. Following this, Woodsworth taught grade school and worked as a secretary for her father in Ottawa. During her first year in Ottawa, she met her husband, Angus MacInnis, a working-class social democrat, originally from Prince Edward Island, who was a stalwart of the Independent Labour Party and the Socialist Party of Canada. They married in 1932. According to Grace, this was when her "real political life" began.[73]

In the early years of her marriage, Grace remained at home since Angus had a good salary and the male-breadwinner ideology dictated that women whose husbands had paid work should run the domestic sphere.[74] During the 1930s, Grace met fellow CCF members Laura Jamieson and Dorothy Steeves through organizations like the Women's International League for Peace and Freedom. Unlike Steeves, Grace MacInnis supported the CCF's decision to vote for Canadian participation in the Second World War and (later) Canada's entry into NATO. She stated that, because of her father's pacifist convictions, this was the "hardest decision [she] ever had to make." MacInnis opposed the formation of the Socialist Fellowship, arguing that it encouraged "anarchy" and did not foster free speech.[75]

Grace MacInnis, later a supporter of abortion rights, did not support feminism. Both Steeves and MacInnis argued that women's subordinate position in society resulted from capitalist social relations and not from patriarchy. As the federal MP for Vancouver-Kingsway from 1965 to 1974, MacInnis fought for lower food prices, rent controls, improved housing for working people, better schools, and larger pensions. She also advocated for a more equitable division of labour among men and women, suggesting that creating a better balance between work and child-rearing was key to improving Canadian society. MacInnis preferred the company of mixed groups of male and female social democrats to feminist or women-only organizations. In this way, she was typical of many left-wing women whose political views were formed during the 1940s and 1950s and who eschewed the gender-based analysis of society that came to be associated with second-wave feminism. In her support for statist bureaucracy, top-down solutions to problems, and Cold War anti-communism and NATO, MacInnis was a member of the elitist faction of the CCF. Political scientist Walter Young says that MacInnis was a member of the party's predominantly male leadership group.[76] Daisy Webster remarks that "middle-of-the-road" CCF supporters preferred MacInnis's politics to those of Gretchen Steeves. Nonetheless, MacInnis became an icon for CCF/NDP veterans. She died in 1991.[77] When the CCF helped to expel communists from the trade union movement during the late 1940s, an act that MacInnis supported, it became the dominant force on the mainstream left in Canada. Populist CCF members like Steeves made common cause with Colin Cameron in the Socialist Fellowship, while more mainstream party members (like MacInnis) tried to push the CCF onto a more centrist path.[78]

Unlike Steeves or MacInnis, Evelyn Grey Smith (Eve or "Evie" to her close family) is the subject of relatively little scholarly or popular writing. Smith held more consistent socialist views then did either Steeves or MacInnis. Therefore, it is perhaps not surprising that she never held public office. Eve Smith was born in 1904 on Samuel Island, between British Columbia's mainland and Vancouver Island. Her father, Ralph Grey, a descendent of former governor general of Canada Earl Grey, was a farmer. Like some rural men, he was sympathetic to women's liberation (suffrage struggles often grew out of rural contexts). Eve Smith attributed her father's support for suffrage to the fact that he had "batched" for a number of years before he married and so was used to making bread, doing his own laundry, and mending his own socks. Both of her parents were from wealthy English families who had become impoverished over time. The family's previous wealth indicates the diversity of CCF women's backgrounds. Some social democratic women, like Laura Jamieson, were from relatively poor, rural backgrounds, while others, like Mildred Fahrni and Eve Smith, came from middle-class or wealthy families.

Eve Grey's father was a member of the Socialist Party of Canada; he was also patriotic and had worked in the shipyards during the First World War. He later followed his daughter into the CCF. For Eve Grey, as for so many other political women, family connections played a role in her introduction to politics.[79] We are talking about a group of educated women, both rural and urban, from a particular stratum of the working class. All of these women – of the right and of the left – came from families whose parents encouraged their education and activities outside the home. This occurred in the context of the post-suffrage era, when many women were playing increased public roles. The western Canadian context also had an effect. Given the rural and relatively isolated status of many western cities and towns during this period, the onus was on women to be independent-minded and to work in the public sphere. Eve, along with her sister Constance (or "Contie"), attended St. Margaret's School in Victoria; however, Eve left school at sixteen to work because the family needed money. She initially found employment looking after the baby of a local woman who was expecting another child. By this time, the Smith family had moved to Esquimalt. During the war, at an infants' hospital, Eve Grey took a six-month course on how to looking after babies.[80]

When the First World War ended, Eve became engaged to Ronald MacEwen, a logger from Scotland who came to Canada to study logging techniques under the tutelage of Eve Grey's uncle. For reasons that are unclear, the two never married. Smith contracted tuberculosis after having just finished her nursing training in Vancouver at the age of twenty-three. She spent three months in Honolulu, Hawaii, and then, back in

British Columbia, lived in a sanatorium at Tranquille, near Kamloops, from 1928 to 1932. At Tranquille, Eve first encountered social democratic politics. CCF members, Ernest Winch among them, visited the sanatorium and left literature for patients to read. Eve joined a CCF club in Kamloops in 1933.[81] Smith, like Mildred Fahrni, explained her politics by referring not only to the influence of strong individuals like Winch but also to her family background.

Eve Smith remained in Kamloops until 1937, when she moved permanently to Vancouver. There she met her future husband, Don Smith, then the editor of the CCF newspaper. In 1939, at a CCF convention in Edmonton, Eve and Don met J.S. Woodsworth and other prominent CCF members. Like other political women of her generation, Eve did not identify with an explicitly feminist ideology, later recalling: "My whole attitude was that you liberate everybody, not just women." In an interview during the 1980s, Eve admitted that an unequal sexual division of labour had existed within the CCF. She recalled: "It was the women who got the sandwiches and usually served the coffee and washed the dishes." Often, in retrospect, left-wing women note that male leftists did not treat them equally, in this perhaps reflecting the liberal feminism of the 1990s and the twenty-first century. There were clearly divisions among left-wing women on the issue of whether or not to support female liberation. Those women, notably Laura Jamieson, who participated in suffrage struggles, endorsed more female involvement in society and attempted to put forward legal measures that would facilitate this end. Others, like Smith and Dorothy Steeves, did not view women's liberation as an end in itself; rather, these women believed that female liberation would come with the introduction of a democratic socialist society. Most of these women, regardless of their ideological orientation, used a maternalist ethic to explain their politics.

In spite of a lack of enthusiasm for a feminist ethic, Eve Smith was very much on the left of the CCF, and we can place her as a member of the populist wing of the party. She strongly opposed the CCF's vote in support of Canada's participation in the Second World War, and she alleged that right-wing CCF members were tarnishing J.S. Woodsworth's legacy and the ideas contained in the Regina Manifesto.[82] Like Dorothy Steeves, Smith was a member of the Socialist Fellowship. Members of this group were, Smith noted, "opposed to working-class people going out and killing other working-class people for the sake of saving General Motors and Gulf Oil."[83]

Owing to this contrary view, members of the CCF hierarchy expelled Eve Smith. At a 1950 CCF convention in Vancouver, Smith was in charge of a table that displayed left-wing literature. David Lewis, later to lead the federal NDP, objected to a pamphlet on the table published by the Socialist Party of Great Britain and entitled *Is the Labour Party Socialist?*. Lewis was a friend of British Labour Party leader Hugh Gaitskell, and he wished to move the CCF to a more openly moderate – some might say conservative – position in a manner similar to that reflected in Gaitskell's vision for the Labour Party.[84] Lewis demanded that Smith remove the pamphlet. When she refused, he enlisted the support of Donald MacDonald and Tommy Douglas, who forced Smith to remove the offending document. Lewis asserted that the pamphlet was overly critical of the British Labour Party, which, at the time, was considered a CCF ally. BC CCF members Ernest and Harold Winch, along with radicals like Rod Young, Colin Cameron, and Dorothy Steeves, supported Smith. They argued that there should be no censorship of thought or speech in the party. Smith later remarked that "the CCF executive [had] hauled [her] over the coals." The party set up an investigation committee, headed by MLA Arthur Turner, to discuss Smith's case.[85]

Shortly after this, Colin Cameron, Dorothy Steeves, and others established the short-lived Socialist Fellowship. The fellowship soon rejoined the party, although several of its members left the CCF. Smith was one of those who left, joining the Socialist Party of Canada soon after the investigation committee voted to censure her. Later in life, Smith supported causes related to animal welfare and the environment, hardly a common practice for the time, even among those with leftist views. Thus, Smith's ideas, although originating with the "Old Left," borrowed from ideas that came out in 1960s- and 1970s-era "New Left" activism.[86] Eve Smith supported the Society for the Prevention of Cruelty to Animals and was a founding member of the BC branch of the Voice of Women, often considered the first second-wave feminist organization in Canada.[87] Like the communists and many Socred women, Smith opposed the fluoridation of Vancouver's water supply in 1958–59, viewing it as an example of unwarranted state intervention in the lives of individuals.[88]

Social democratic women were united by a number of common characteristics. Some, like Dorothy Steeves, were immigrants, though most were born in Canada. The most prominent women were middle class and highly educated, while others, like Laura Jamieson, came from working-class or rural backgrounds. Mildred Fahrni's father, like J.S. Woodsworth, was a minister and a strong proponent of the social gospel. Those women who had received formal education were the most likely to be found among the party's leadership. Even in a supposedly egalitarian organization, those from more privileged economic and social backgrounds stood out. This was also the case, to varying degrees, in the CPC and the SCP. Tensions existed between the urban, educated sections of all political parties and the rural, sometimes more proletarian, rank and file. Educated CCF women asserted that they had an obligation – it was a kind of noblesse oblige and was typical of the condescending attitude that some Progressive Era reformers had towards working people and the poor – to use their skills to help improve public life for workers, women, and other marginalized groups. Many CCF women, notably Mildred Fahrni and Laura Jamieson, had backgrounds in social work or social service causes. A belief in Progressive Era values like evolutionary change, reform, and human improvement distinguished CCF and CPC women from their SCP counterparts. Left-wing women possessed an optimistic view of human nature: they believed that, given the proper social and economic situation, human beings could change for the better.

Social democratic women explained their ideology, and their introduction to politics, in a variety of ways. Like CPC women, they often emphasized a collective response to human suffering (as occurred in the Depression) or the need for women's suffrage as their entry point to the party. The influence of family or a particular individual pushed some CCF women into public life. Social democratic women's lives and views are located between those of CPC and SCP women, which is perhaps fitting. CCF women's entrance into politics resulted not only from responses to collective forms of oppression (like that of CPC women) but also from individual influences (like that of SPC women).

This biographical information also tells us something about the changes in CCF women's ideology during the years from the party's founding until the end of the 1950s. CCF women's views in the postwar period differed from those of their counterparts before the war. The social gospel tradition in the party, which was very strong before the Second World War, declined in the war's aftermath, perhaps as a result of the secularization of Canadian society.[89] The women discussed here, Mildred Fahrni excepted, did not subscribe to the social gospel viewpoint, and even Fahrni became much more critical of the CCF during and after the Second World War. Many early CCF women, Rose Henderson and Lucy Woodsworth among them, came into politics and activism, at least in part, because of the influence of maternal feminism and early suffrage campaigns. Although "maternalism" remained a crucial idea for many left-wing women, the influence of maternal feminism, with its link to suffrage campaigns, became progressively less important to CCF women.

By the late 1940s and 1950s, women had been voting in elections for more than twenty years and, in some instances, had been in public life since the 1870s and 1880s. For this reason, earlier feminist traditions in the CCF, connected to the suffrage movement and the social gospel, began to die out, albeit slowly.

During the postwar period, many CCF members were anxious to appear "respectable" and "mainstream" in order to stave off the charge that the party was soft on communism. We might think of these more moderate social democrats as "advanced welfare liberals," given that their views were often not far removed from the "welfare statist" wing of the federal Liberal Party. Women's activism within the party suffered as a result of the increasingly conservative atmosphere within the CCF. Although there were many women who used motherhood, and ideas surrounding women's alleged innate capacity for nurturance, as a spur to political activism, the party hierarchy took increasingly regressive stances on issues like women's paid work outside the home and the legalization of abortion and birth control. The CPC, too, often took conservative stances on issues specifically related to women and gender, and the onset of the Cold War only exacerbated this trend.[90]

What does this biographical and intellectual information regarding radical women say to us about gender in North American history? In many ways, these women held to a similar ideology: they all had a tradition of public service and they all believed in a vision of a new, more egalitarian, world order. Left-wing women subscribed to a statist ideology. They argued that people had a responsibility to care for one another. The state, as the representative of the people, had to be expanded in order to help its citizens. While left-wing women came from different family and ethnic backgrounds, they all employed a maternalist ideology. This emphasis on motherhood was particularly important during the late 1940s and 1950s. Many people in positions of power advanced an ideology of "hetero-normativity," emphasizing conventional gender roles, with women staying at home to raise children and men going out into the public realm to provide political leadership and to earn money for their families.[91]

It is interesting that many of the women mentioned in this chapter, especially in the CCF, had husbands who were either very much in the background or absent altogether. This was true, to varying degrees, in the case of Gretchen Steeves, Eve Smith, Effie Jones, and Laura Jamieson. Steeves and Jones had husbands who largely kept out of politics and quietly supported their spouses' political careers. Eve Smith was divorced a number of times, while Jamieson's husband died at a relatively early age. Educated women from relatively privileged backgrounds assumed a dominant role in their marriages and, in turn, took on a public political role. Although they valorized the male-breadwinner ideology, and men's roles as leaders in politics, in practice many political women did not see men as important figures in their lives. This may have reflected the influence of independent women from the suffrage era – women such as Agnes Macphail, who never married and who did not valorize relationships with men. In other cases, most notably those of Mona Morgan and Grace MacInnis, both the wife and the husband played a key role in politics, and the two marriage partners functioned as political equals.

The idea of place is also relevant in explaining the political worldview of left-wing women. British Columbia, and the city of Vancouver in particular, was a place where radicalism flourished. Both Laura Jamieson and Dorothy Steeves moved from other locations – rural Ontario and the Netherlands, respectively – to settle in Vancouver. Left-wing individuals saw the North American west coast as an area that would be hospitable to radical viewpoints. The particular communities in which political women resided shaped the politics of leftist (and rightist) women in indelible ways. Mollie Crowe's story shows how a left-wing atmosphere could emerge in areas where resource development – mining, forestry, and fishing – was strong. The absolute power of bosses and owners in areas like the Kootenays, Skeena, and Vancouver Island led to the rise of strong labour and left movements. The wives, sisters, and daughters of miners and loggers, as well as independent single women from these communities, became a key part of this left-wing trend.[92]

In this chapter, I suggest that women's choice of political parties resulted from their class, ethnic, and religious backgrounds. I also show that the particular locations in which women lived and worked played a role in their choice of political movement. Perhaps most important, I show that family backgrounds profoundly influenced women's political choices. These factors all contributed to the optimistic, even statist, attitude of left-wing women. It is clear that there were populists and elitists among left-wing women. These divisions also existed among right-wing women.

2

Ladies, Let Us Hold High the Banner of Social Credit!

Women on the Right

Social Credit Party women held special meetings and conventions in a manner similar to their counterparts in the Communist Party of Canada and the Co-operative Commonwealth Federation. Speaking at a convention of the Social Credit Women's Auxiliaries (SCWAs) in 1968, Ethel Smith, a prominent member of the SCWA and the Alberta Social Credit League, offered a rallying cry for SCP women: "Ladies, let us hold high the banner of Social Credit!"[1] Smith argued that conservative women had to bring their virtues of femininity and caring outside the home to reform a corrupt and morally impure modern society. This encapsulates SCP women's ideology quite well. By 1968, the SCP in Alberta was in decline as an electoral force, still strong in rural areas but increasingly out of touch with younger, urban voters in Calgary and Edmonton.[2] This strong statement and the convention itself were part of an attempt to buttress the fortunes of a flagging political party.

This chapter is a mirror image of its predecessor: in it I offer a series of biographies of SCP women. SCP women's ideology was contradictory. On the one hand, many SCP women endorsed reactionary views on a number of issues. They suggested that marriage, motherhood, and child-rearing were part of a woman's sacred duty to themselves and to the Canadian nation. They asserted that the time in which they were living – the postwar period – was to blame for modern social problems like the decline of the traditional family, the increase in the number of working women, and the rise of juvenile delinquency.[3] On the other hand, Social Credit ideology was also technocratic and modern in its support for economic development, technological progress, and women's advancement. As the quote in the title of this chapter – "Ladies, Let Us Hold High the Banner of Social Credit" – implies, SCP women did endorse an increased role for women within the SCP, although with the proviso that their participation would lead to the entrenchment of conservative values in Canadian society. The SCP argued that conservative women should come out of the home to promote their party's ideology. Ironically, SCP women's support for women's advancement – albeit narrowly defined – paved the way for women's increased involvement in public life in the 1960s and in subsequent decades. Contrary to SCP women's intentions, the presence of women like Rose Wilkinson and Cornelia Wood outside the home implied that women, even those of the right, should be more involved in the public sphere. One cannot deny that SCP women disdained feminism and everything that the left stood for. By the late 1950s and early 1960s, however, even women of the right were increasingly moving outside the home, and this helped to pave the way for more and more women to enter the public sphere in later decades (if sometimes only indirectly).

Place is also key to explaining conservative women's choice of political party. SCP women were largely from rural areas and small towns in Alberta and British Columbia. Many came from working-class and poor backgrounds and lived in areas with strong traditions of evangelical Christianity and religious conservatism.[4] SCP women supported conservative branches of the Baptist, Methodist, Presbyterian, Pentecostal, and Nazarene churches as well as other similar Protestant sects. Some of these women migrated from small towns and rural areas in the United States while others came from similar areas in Alberta and British Columbia. In other words, they came from places with traditions of "rugged individualism" – places that were suspicious of, even hostile towards, the bureaucratic welfare state and socialism, liberalism, and communism. These areas of western Canada helped to produce a right-wing vision of society, even as the urban and resource-based areas of British Columbia produced a left-wing vision.

Like left-wing women, many right-wing women came from families with strong traditions of political involvement. Many of the SCP women whom we will meet had male relatives who were involved in the party, although the women were strong activists in their own right. Like left-wing women, right-wing women used the ideology of maternalism, and notions about women's innate ties to care and nurturance, as a spur to political activism. Also like left-wing women, right-wing women sought to remake the public world of politics and economics in the image of the home (albeit this image differed significantly from that of their counterparts on the left). Finally, again mirroring the situation on the left, there were divisions in the SCP between elitist (or pro-business) conservatives and populist (or traditionalist) conservatives. Women made up a disproportionate number of the traditionalist faction, which included a large number of devout evangelical Christians.

As with the left-wing women discussed in Chapter 1, I chose these particular SCP women because of their prominence in the party and because there were enough primary sources to enable me to draw a basic portrait of their lives. Most of the women profiled here were leaders in the party, not rank-and-file supporters, perhaps because the SCP's grassroots supporters tended to be from less educated backgrounds and did not leave behind as large a source base from which to draw biographical details.[5]

Thus, my conclusions about SCP women are based upon a relatively small number of leading and mid-level activists. I discuss the most prominent women and those who were representative of all SCP women. Unfortunately, detailed membership lists giving the precise number of women who were active in the party do not exist. As with most political organizations, the number of members in the Alberta SCP fluctuated over the years of its existence. From a peak membership of forty-one thousand in 1937, the number of members dropped to only eight thousand in 1944. Before the 1971 election, the membership stood at thirty thousand.[6] The scholarly literature is less developed for the BC branch of the SCP, and, consequently, it was not possible to find membership numbers for the BC party.

There were, however, Social Credit Women's Auxiliaries in virtually all communities, large and small, in Alberta and British Columbia. SCWA president Ruth Landeryou estimated that there were 727 women in the auxiliaries in 1968. In both provinces, substantially more women were passive supporters and sympathizers of the SCP movement. Landeryou claimed that there were forty-five SCWA branches in Alberta and two SCWA provincial councils, one in Calgary and one in Edmonton.[7] The auxiliary executive in each community sent one representative to its local constituency association as well as two delegates for every six members and one delegate for each additional ten members to the provincial SCP convention. The Annual Convention of Women's Auxiliaries, held in the same location as the SCP convention, elected the delegates who attended subsequent auxiliary and party conventions.

There were provincial executives for all of the SCWAs in Alberta and British Columbia. The provincial executive of the women's auxiliaries in both provinces appointed representatives on the Board of Directors of the Alberta and BC Social Credit Leagues.[8] The number of women in the SCP movement was relatively small – perhaps, at most, 30 percent of the total membership of the party in both provinces – but the women's auxiliaries had an official status within the party and auxiliary women had an inside view of party policy.

From 1935, when the Socreds were first elected, until 1966, seven women were elected under the party's banner at the provincial level. Ethel (née Knight) Wilson was one of the SCP's most prominent public figures. Elected to Edmonton City Council in 1951, Wilson, a former seamstress, had worked for a packing firm for seventeen years.[9] In this capacity, she became secretary-treasurer of the Edmonton Labour Council; she also sat on the city's library board. Wilson was first elected to the Legislature in 1962 and was the only woman to achieve cabinet rank during the Socred years in office. She was the driving force behind the establishment of the Alberta Women's Bureau in 1966. The government inaugurated this institution on the fiftieth anniversary of Alberta women's attainment of voting rights, and its purpose was to conduct research into female lives and concerns. Initially, it was mostly ineffective with regard to offering any practical help to Alberta's women. During the 1980s and 1990s, however, the Alberta Women's Bureau did provide assistance for feminist activities: it addressed issues such as sexual harassment, violence against women, and poverty as well as concerns particular to Aboriginal women. Although it was not the intention of the Socred government (or later Conservative governments), the Women's Bureau became an important vehicle for the advancement of women in Alberta. Wilson had a foot in both the populist and the elitist camps in the SCP. In her attacks on modernity, she was a traditionalist conservative. As a strong supporter of the evangelical Pentecostal Church in Alberta, she criticized modern forms of media, notably television and "crime" comic books, as corrupting influences on children and youth. She was also adamantly opposed to smoking and to drinking alcohol, especially among young people. As a former trade unionist, she identified with working people in Alberta and sometimes spoke out against big business, saying that it had too much power in the province. Otherwise, Wilson was a staunch supporter of the party's hierarchy. She did not express anti-war views or criticize capitalism as a system. Although the Socred hierarchy claimed that Wilson's induction into cabinet was evidence of the party's commitment to women's equality, in practice all members of the party's leadership spoke out against women's advancement.[10]

Perhaps even more than Wilson's, Ruth (née Gemmill) Landeryou's personal history provides a capsule version of a Socred woman's life. Landeryou's husband, like those of other political women, was involved in politics. Ruth and John Landeryou were SCP supporters in the city of Lethbridge, where a significant proportion of the populace espoused conservative religious views.[11] John was the MLA for Lethbridge from 1944 to 1971 and was a strong supporter of Ernest Manning during Manning's tenure as premier. Previously, from 1935 to 1940, John had been the SCP federal MP for the riding of Calgary East. Ruth Gemmill was born in 1915 in Humboldt, Saskatchewan, and came from a family with deep religious roots. Her father was a United Church minister, reflecting the rural Protestant background of many SCP and CCF members. The family moved to Edmonton when Ruth was a young girl and remained there. Ruth Gemmill worked for the Hudson's Bay Company for twenty-six years, retiring while holding the position of merchandise manager. She married John Landeryou in 1959, inheriting four stepchildren and twelve grandchildren.[12]

Ruth Landeryou's family had a strong influence on her political perspective: her husband and father were both religious and both held conservative political views, as did she. She was involved in many community organizations, notably the Rebekah Lodge, during her years in Lethbridge, indicating her strong commitment to public service. She stated that she was an "honorary Indian princess of the Pegein Tribe" and that she had been given the name "Princess Blue Bird."[13] She was a prominent member of the SCWA, serving as its president from 1966 to 1968.[14]

Ruth Landeryou's views enable us to see a Socred woman's perspective in microcosm. At an SCP convention in 1968, SCWA president Landeryou commented on the strength of the auxiliary movement. She praised the Socred provincial regime in Alberta, suggesting that the province was "a living example of a Government and a people dedicated to the principles of true democracy."[15] She argued that the individual was the fundamental building block of society: individual rights, she stated, should be paramount in western Canadian society. Alberta was "making a sound and effective effort to keep the light of civilization burning brightly" against the threat of socialism and communism.[16]

Landeryou's comment on individual rights reflects a key aspect of Socred thought. The party was, at least rhetorically, against state intervention and opposed the policies of leftist parties like the CCF and the CPC; even the federal Liberal Party faced SCP scorn for its statist views. The SCP supported what it saw as free enterprise, individual initiative, and the capitalist ethic. It argued against the establishment of a welfare state in Canada even though, in practice, it brought in many welfare state measures and used the state to foster big business and large capital (particularly in the oil business). Nonetheless, SCP women reified the idea of the individual and the nuclear, heterosexual family as opposed to the supposedly all-powerful state. Support for the individual and the traditional family was a key part of right-wing women's ideology, even if SCP governments in both Alberta and British Columbia did little to forestall capitalist modernity's attacks on these institutions.[17] Given her support for the party's leadership, Ruth Landeryou must be categorized as a member of the elitist, pro-business faction of the SCP. She never spoke out against capitalism or war, and she and her husband were strong supporters of Ernest Manning's pro-business policies.

Landeryou's colleague, Cornelia Lucinda (née Railey) Wood was perhaps the most outspoken of the elected SCP women. Born on 14 April 1892 on a farm in Boxford, Missouri, a young Cornelia Railey had trouble obtaining formal education since her family moved frequently.[18] In 1904, the Railey family moved to Stony Plain, Alberta, a rural community west of Edmonton. Cornelia Railey attended Calgary Normal School and was a member of its first graduating class in 1908. After having taught for four years, she tried her hand at acting. Working under the stage name Dorothy Vernon, she appeared in a number of productions for the Orpheum Stock Company in Edmonton.[19]

In 1912, Cornelia married Russell Edgerton Wood on Christmas Eve. Russell was from a farm family that had migrated from Maple, Ontario. The Wood family had come to Alberta in 1906, initially as homesteaders in Sangudo.[20] Cornelia's father, Henry Newell Railey, who claimed descent from Sir Walter Raleigh and Thomas Jefferson, was an ardent "political fan." A telephone call from the Alberta Liberal Party, which needed good public speakers to support its candidates at election time, served as Cornelia Wood's introduction to politics. Wood argued that, if she could help to elect Liberal candidates, then perhaps she could win election as well. She soon became a prominent member of the Alberta Women's Institute: from 1931 to 1935 she was provincial supervisor of its girls' club and was the organization's president from 1937 to 1941.[21] In 1933, under the influence of William "Bible Bill" Aberhart, she embraced Social Credit ideology.[22] This was a common theme in the personal narratives of SCP women: many attributed their involvement with the party to Aberhart's influence and personal charisma. This plays into the individualistic orientation of SCP women: SCP members often remarked that a "great individual," usually Bible Bill, prompted their involvement in the Social Credit movement.

Cornelia Wood subsequently helped to organize SCP study groups in the Stony Plain area. She was first elected as an MLA in 1940 and would remain in the Legislature until 1966, excepting a brief interregnum from 1955 to 1958. She ran unsuccessfully as an independent in the 1967 provincial election, asserting that Social Credit had strayed too far from its monetarist, anti-banking heritage. She was later elected mayor of the town of Stony Plain.[23] Wood was a strong anti-communist and a follower of the views of C.H. Douglas. Like Douglas, she held a conspiratorial worldview. Wood suggested that a small group of male financiers controlled the world and the banking system. Unlike some male SCP supporters, notably Patrick Ashby and federal SCP MPs Norman Jaques and John Horn Blackmore, Wood did not believe that this small group of men was Jewish.[24] There were a number of anti-Semites under the Social Credit banner, but Cornelia Wood was not one of them, nor did any of the most significant SCP women possess openly anti-Semitic views.[25]

Cornelia Wood parlayed her anti-communist views into strong support for the anti-fluoridation cause, a key concern for many SCP members. This was connected to her conspiratorial worldview and was a common perspective among right-wing populists. Commentary on the fluoridation issue was nearly ubiquitous in Socred publications and pronouncements. In keeping with the party's strong support for Cold War anti-communism, many prominent SCP members opposed the fluoridation of Alberta's and British Columbia's water supply on the grounds that it was a communist plot. At a 1966 SCWA convention in Calgary, the "Library" Auxiliary moved a motion regarding fluoride. The motion read, in part: "The prescribing of medicinal agents for the prevention of disease is a personal and exact procedure governed by medical authorities." Using language that was common in SCP publications, the auxiliary argued that the protection of individual rights was an essential element of Western democracy. A provision might be made to introduce fluoride treatments into "specially marked commercially marketed milk and/or other liquid by choice of the individual," but the government should not legislate the fluoridation of the country's water supply.[26] This comment reflects the conservative concern with individual choice: advocating the use of measures like the initiative, the referendum, and the recall became part of this ideology. Interestingly, the debate over fluoride brought together people of different political stripes: some leftists and union activists also opposed fluoridation because they saw it as an example of the state's unwarranted influence on the lives of working people. Opposition to new forms of medicine and to new forms of technology had a long history in Europe and North America, and the anti-fluoridation campaign in western Canada is in keeping with this.[27]

Cornelia Wood suggested that fluoridation would make the people of Alberta and Canada easy prey for a foreign power, which could introduce a mind-controlling substance into the province's and country's water supply. Wood's concern with this issue reflected an anxiety, present in many sectors of society at this time, regarding the effects of modernity, science, and technology on the public.[28] A concern about expert knowledge, especially in the health and psychiatric fields, also played a role.[29] This was particularly important in the context of the Cold War, with its atmosphere of fear and paranoia. There was much worry in capitalist societies that unhealthy minds would lead to a communist takeover: citizens of Western societies had to be morally upright and of sound mind or communism would seep in.

SCP women heavily supported this view, and they attempted to alter public policy in order to implement their ideological program. Members of the Edmonton branch of the Local Council of Women, of which Cornelia Wood was a member, asked city council to hold off on the implementing of fluoridation until more research had been done. Drawing on her Manichean worldview, Wood argued that "the fluoridation movement" had a great deal of money, power, and influence and that its opponents did not.[30] She drew an explicit link between the fluoridation of water and civil defence: "[The] mechanism for fluoridation of water supplies in any community would provide the perfect weapon for saboteurs." Moreover, she commented, fluoride "is tasteless and odourless. The damage would be done before it could be detected." Wood said that she was proud that "Alberta [led] in civil defence" and, to that end, she argued that the province should make "civil defence really work by keeping [its] water supply free from being used by saboteurs using fluorides."[31] Opponents of fluoridation had a good deal of success: referenda on the implementation of fluoride failed several times in Vancouver and Calgary during the 1950s and 1960s, and a referendum on introducing fluoride into Edmonton's water supply only narrowly succeeded in 1966.[32]

Women played an important role in shaping SCP ideology and public policy on the fluoride issue. SCP women's opposition to fluoride, and their ability to galvanize public opposition to it, assisted in the defeat of referenda on fluoridation. They were also able to make anti-fluoridation part of SCP's public agenda, against the wishes of SCP men. Fluoridation was not an issue for Ernest Manning or W.A.C. Bennett; however, it was for Cornelia Wood and Lydia Arsens. This was one, fairly rare, area in which women had a clear and present impact on the policies adopted by the party hierarchy.

The focus on fluoride reveals the division within the SCP. As I have noted, this division can be seen as that between populists/traditionalists and elitists/modernizers. Leonard Kuffert suggests that the SCP contained a variety of different ideological groupings under its umbrella and that different groups within the party endorsed various modes of conservative thought. One Socred faction distrusted urban life, secularism, and modernity and longed for a return to the "island communities" of a preindustrial society, where immigrants, working women, communism, and atheism could not trouble them.[33] Ironically, this branch of the party also disdained modern corporate capitalism and war, seeing these phenomena as having played a substantial role in the decline of rural values and traditional families. This was the populist/traditionalist branch of the party, consisting of "social conservatives" and many evangelical Christians. However, the dominant branch of the SCP in both Alberta and British Columbia, influenced by the prosperity that came to western Canada in the post-Second World War period, was composed of right-wing technocrats, precursors of the neoliberal ideologues of the 1980s and 1990s. These individuals, the elitist/modernizers, favoured the use of the provincial state to foster economic modernization and growth through corporate mergers and the expansion of government.

The elitist/modernizers ultimately gained control of the SCP: for example, SCP administrations in Alberta did not pass laws to help farmers or to restrict access to abortion, yet they did bring in policies to help the oil business and to facilitate urban and suburban growth. Male party leaders like Ernest Manning, W.A.C. Bennett, and Orvis Kennedy, despite paying "lip service" to socially conservative values, were members of the elitist wing of the party, as was Ruth Landeryou. Cornelia Wood was perhaps the most prominent member of the populist wing of the party. There were others, like cabinet ministers Ethel Wilson and, in British Columbia, Philip "Flying Phil" Gaglardi, who had a foot in both camps. As Lisa McGirr notes, it was ironic that some conservatives failed to see that rampant capitalism, an aspect of the modernity that they deplored, assisted in destroying the small-town and rural values that they upheld.[34]

It is not surprising that many SCP supporters, including many women, subscribed to an anti-modern perspective. As several scholars point out, evangelicals have often mobilized politically in times of crisis, particularly when they feel that their values around small towns, the family, and the church are under threat. The Cold War era was certainly a time when life seemed uncertain, especially due to international concerns. The post-Second World War era was also a period of increasing secularization and urbanization: many conservative Christians, including many of the women studied here, suggested that the church was in decline because of the changes resulting from the postwar era.[35]

SCP women's views borrowed from first-wave maternal feminism as well as from prominent women from the pre-Second World War era. For example, Liberal senator Cairine Wilson – the first Canadian woman to be appointed to the Senate – supported a kind of Gladstonian, Christian liberalism that upheld women's natural superiority as the way forward for women in politics. This was similar to Socred women's ideology, even if Wilson's pro-welfare statist views did not fit with the former's perspective.[36] Older women's organizations like the Women's Christian Temperance Union and the Imperial Order Daughters of the Empire also argued that a woman's maternal nature could change society. Both organizations tried to foster a Canada that adhered to white, Anglo-Saxon, British values.[37] SCP women's anti-statist viewpoint echoed nineteenth-century liberalism, in much the same way as did the viewpoint of Old Right female conservatives in the United States, who argued for a return to limited government, an isolationist foreign policy, small-town values, and individual rights. Had they known about Social Credit, Old Right women like Rose Wilder Lane and Isabel Patterson may have looked to SCP women as sisters in arms.[38] Ironically, traditionalist SCP women also had much in common with male "Tory" conservatives, largely centred in Ontario, such as George Parkin Grant and Donald Creighton. These men decried industrialization and modernization and looked to rural and Christian values as a salve to the wounds caused by modernity; however, their anti-Americanism and pro-British ideology did not figure in SCP women's views.[39] All of this suggests that SCP women borrowed from earlier (female and male) conservative viewpoints. Right-wing women in Canada were part of an international, or at least continentalist, context that was conducive to gendered conservatism.[40] Yet SCP women created a uniquely western Canadian vision of conservatism.

Cornelia Wood's focus on fluoride had national ramifications. Indeed, the SCP's concern about fluoride was not limited to Alberta, it being shared by many BC supporters. SCP MLA Lydia Arsens, for example, also subscribed to a conspiratorial view of fluoride. Arsens favoured temperance concerns and job training for women as well as anti-war campaigns, but she opposed women working after marriage and the fluoridation of water. She lasted only one term in office, from 1953 to 1956, perhaps because of her anti-establishment perspective. Little is known of the details of her career. She was born in Sunny Slope, Alberta, in 1906, and her brother and sister-in-law still lived in Alberta at the time of her death in 1983. Arsens became a teacher and founded the first PTA in Sunny Slope. Later, she moved to Victoria to run a restaurant; subsequently, she was elected as one of three members for the Victoria constituency in the 1953 BC provincial election.[41]

In a speech before the BC Legislature in 1955, Arsens argued that leaders of the community were being misled into thinking that fluoride was a good idea. Like Cornelia Wood, Arsens cited expert advice to buttress her position. The Canadian Dental Association and Public Health Service had come out against fluoride, while the US Federal Security Agency had favoured it. In Arnses' view, the Federal Security Agency supported fluoride because doing so would enable American elites, through "mind control," to force their views upon an unsuspecting populace. "Poisoning" the country's water supply was a means towards this end. Interestingly, several diet faddists, vegetarians, and naturopaths attended a rally at which Arsens spoke. She believed that the "big aluminum companies" were "in on" the conspiracy to introduce fluoride. She described herself as "a country girl brought up on rolled oats and good whole wheat bread and cream and eggs."[42] This belief in purity, which could easily be given a reactionary twist given the Cold War emphasis on conformity, helps to explain her views. It also foreshadows 1960s-era New Left concerns about returning to the land and environmentalism.[43]

At times, Arsens expressed contradictory viewpoints. She supported temperance and opposed the establishment of more bars in Victoria, implying that they corrupted youth. Similarly, she spoke out against "the entry of women into such fields of work as driving buses," suggesting that this was unfeminine and harmful to women's reproductive organs.[44] She had a strong populist streak, not only speaking out against corporations but also arguing for socially conservative views, notably her antipathy towards working women. We can definitely place Lydia Arsens within the traditionalist, anti-establishment faction of the SCP. Arnses' position reflected her roots in western Canada, with its populist opposition to state control and big business. The right-wing circles in which Arsens ran, and the conservative focus on conspiracy theories pertaining to fluoride and bankers, also helps us to understand her ideas. Conspiracy – the idea that an unseen, malevolent force controls the destinies of righteous people – was a key notion in left-wing and, especially, right-wing political movements. Conservative groups in the United States, notably the John Birch Society, argued that communists and "liberal" capitalists worked together to destroy the traditional values of the family, Christianity, and individual rights.[45]

While their ideology was often reactionary, Socred women did express support for the advancement of women. SCP women possessed a very particular attitude towards women's roles in society. Although they argued that women needed to come into the public sphere to "clean up" politics, they had an individualistic conception of women's rights. A statement by SCP member Rose Wilkinson, a Calgary MLA from 1944 to 1963 and one of the few Roman Catholic SCP members, stands as an example of the conservative woman's view on the issue of female advancement. In 1945, Wilkinson warned delegates at an SCWA convention of the existence of a national crisis. Arguing that the world was "suffering from the want of women's brains," she urged women to work together to "obtain a wider knowledge before accepting public office."[46] She endorsed an increase in women's participation in the SCP, in the public sphere, and in politics. Given the "crisis" that was nearing, the world needed women outside the home, in politics and society. Wilkinson did not specifically describe this crisis; however, her statement offers evidence of the anxious, arguably paranoid, worldview of many Socred supporters. Wilkinson was likely anticipating the onset of the Cold War, which would only exacerbate feelings of anxiety among SCP supporters.

Like many SCP women, Wilkinson had come to the party through her friendship with William Aberhart, and she endorsed his vision of monetary reform as well as the Douglasite anti-banking tradition. Wilkinson had been involved with the SCWA since its inception and was a nurse by profession.[47] Proud of her Irish heritage, she was a key public face for the SCP, often giving voice to the party's conservative positions on motherhood and the family.[48] Wilkinson, like most other SCP women, asserted that her successes in public life resulted from individual strengths and initiative. SCP women often seemed to see themselves as living in a Horatio Alger story: they spoke of overcoming poor family backgrounds by being morally upright and then finding success in the public arena. In her strong anti-statism and support for Douglasite ideology, Wilkinson fits into the populist wing of the SCP.

Another prominent SCP woman, Elizabeth Robinson, also expressed her ideas on the possibility of women's advancement.[49] Robinson's husband, a medical doctor, had been the Socred MLA for the constituency of Medicine Hat. Upon her husband's death in 1953, Elizabeth Robinson became the sitting member for the party in that riding, a fairly common point of entry into politics for women of various ideological stripes.[50] Robinson was re-elected twice and remained the MLA in Medicine Hat until her death in 1960.[51] In a 1955 speech, she addressed the women at an SCWA convention and noted that "there [were] only two women in the legislature to represent 135, 500 in the province,"[52] referring to herself and Rose Wilkinson (Cornelia Wood had been defeated in the previous election). Robinson cited the statistic that, in the 1948 Alberta provincial election, women provided 43.6 percent of the total vote. She used this statistic to argue that Alberta needed more women representatives. She was concerned that, through indifference, women might lose the privilege of voting. To ensure that this did not happen, they must "value this fundamental right and responsibility of citizenship." In her support for female advancement, Robinson observed that women were capable of accomplishments that were beyond imagining. She held that "there [was] a feeling that women should be playing a more active life in public affairs."[53]

In a later speech, Robinson invoked Canada's British heritage, still a strong point of pride for many Canadians in the 1950s.[54] She asked whether women had forgotten the example of Emmeline Pankhurst and the early suffragettes in Britain, drawing a direct line between Social Credit and maternal feminism. She celebrated the "Famous Five" suffragists, particularly Emily Murphy, Irene Parlby, and Louise McKinney, who were strong proponents of a white Canada and a strong British Empire. Robinson argued that these women were models for SCP women. In a further comment, she cited Canada's British heritage as a spur to Canadian women's political activism: the "best known and loved woman in the world today is our own Queen Elizabeth II." Although she celebrated women who were involved in public activities, Robinson also lauded women who stayed in the home as mothers and wives. Thus her view of women in public life was two-sided. She argued for women's increased participation in public life but, in the same breath, suggested that women ought to be fulfilling their traditional roles in the home. In commenting that Socred women needed "an unseen hand" to guide them while the "great Christian spirit" filled their lives, she reflected the religious focus of the party.[55]

Elizabeth Robinson later advocated for more government assistance to women whose husbands had been killed or incapacitated while working in industry, picking up on issues that her late husband had supported. In 1955, Robinson's views on women and state assistance were hardly radical;

however, her statements offer evidence that at least some women during the 1940s and 1950s – previously seen as a time of retreat for the women's movement – supported the further (albeit narrow) participation of women in public life. For the SCP's female supporters, only certain kinds of women – those who endorsed conservative values – were considered equal to the task of participating in the public realm. Robinson had a foot in both populist and elitist camps. She rarely spoke out against the party hierarchy and, like her husband, strongly supported the leadership. Yet she also spoke in support of women's increased rights – a key characteristic of the populist camp. SCP men, especially during the Manning years, almost never spoke in favour of women's increased participation in public life. For their part, SCP women used maternalism, and support for conservative maternal feminism, to endorse a wider role for women in public life.

SCP supporters in British Columbia expressed similar views. In particular, Lydia Arsens argued in favour of women's advancement. In addressing a Socred rally in North Vancouver, Arsens stated: "Women can stand shoulder-to-shoulder with men. Not only [the] home but all phases of life are more balanced in thought and action if both sexes have exerted influence." She clearly believed that women needed to play larger roles in society and in the party: "We need honourable men and women of strong character, strong in will and desire, to persevere, to unselfishly serve, and to wage a ceaseless campaign in our march to Ottawa." Part of her speech comments on her childhood on an Alberta farm. As part of a family of ten children, she was "blessed with God-fearing, industrious, and thrifty parents."[56] Like other conservatives, notably Rose Wilkinson, Arsens saw herself as living in a Horatio Alger story. She emphasized how her personal initiative and individual abilities enabled her to become involved in politics. This personal narrative is indicative of the individualistic focus of reactionary women. In its endorsement of a more public role for women who subscribe to conservative Christianity and to an individualistic brand of liberalism, SCP women's ideology might be called "Christian liberalism."

In other ways, however, Socred women's view of a new society reflects that of male conservatives. In one particular case, Lydia Arsens expressed admiration for the party's founder William Aberhart, remarking that he was "a big man with a big heart, full of love and compassion for the people." Arsens saw Aberhart as an example that men should emulate, arguing that he regularly "called on God for strength and guidance. He believed in the sanctity of the individual and always defended the democratic rights of the individual." She called Social Credit "Mr. Aberhart's dream" and presented him as the benevolent father figure of the SCP; in particular, she suggested that Aberhart was a father figure to SCP women.[57]

Here, we have one small example of how SCP women sought to portray a man's proper role in society. SCP women's perception of men was somewhat contradictory. On the one hand, they praised men as strong political leaders, patriarchal father figures, and benevolent, Christian, and humane individuals who ruled the party, the province, and the family in a strict, but gentle, manner. On the other hand, they borrowed from first-wave feminism the idea that men had done a poor job of running society and government: men's rule had allowed for foolish wars, economic and familial collapse, and the rise of secular modernity. Thus, righteous women had a responsibility to promote "social housekeeping" – that is, to advocate for white, Christian, conservative women's role in returning society to the traditional values of the home, the Christian church, rural living, and the family. Although not often stated publicly, SCP women's position on men was two-sided: they both endorsed conservative men's domination of the party and society yet cited men's incompetent leadership as a rationale for the increased role of conservative women in public life.

As the example of Lydia Arsens suggests, SCP supporters in British Columbia held many of the same views as did their Alberta colleagues. Tilly Jean (Cameron) Rolston was perhaps the best known of the female SCP members in the Pacific province. Her parents, originally from New Brunswick, came to British Columbia in 1887, the same year that a fire destroyed much of Vancouver. The family lived above a rented store on Water Street and later moved to Georgia Street. Tilly Cameron was educated at Vancouver Normal School and spent two years at the University of British Columbia. In 1909, she married Fred Rolston; the couple later had three children. Fred Rolston died in 1945 at the age of sixty. Originally from Ontario, he had lived in Vancouver for fifty years. Tilly Rolston was an active member in the BC branch of the Canadian Society for the Control of Cancer. She was also involved with the Canadian Club of Vancouver and the Vancouver Symphony Orchestra. Rolston was superintendent of primary classes at the First Baptist Church before it delegated her to the Vancouver Council of Women.[58]

Tilly Rolston first ran for public office in 1938 for a Parks Board seat. She was elected on the Non-Partisan Association ticket and remained on the Parks Board until 1947. Her first foray into provincial politics came in 1941, when she won the Progressive Conservative nomination for a seat in the Vancouver-Point Grey riding. She was elected and held the seat until June 1952, when she retired because of cancer.[59] As has been well documented, a Liberal-Conservative coalition, established to keep the "socialist hordes" of the CCF out of power, ruled British Columbia from 1941 to 1952. The Non-Partisan Association fulfilled a similar function at the municipal level in Vancouver from 1937 onward.[60] In 1952, Rolston joined W.A.C. Bennett in crossing the floor of the BC Legislature to join the SCP. She remained an SCP member until her death on 12 October 1953.[61]

Like other conservative women, Tilly Rolston expressed support for women's advancement. She spoke out against poor working conditions for women in factories and on farms during the Second World War. At the same time, she supported the "glamorization" of the farm in order to entice recruits to return to rural areas. This was part of her belief in the conservative "back-to-the-land" ideology, established to lessen the appeal of left-wing radicalism during the Depression and the Second World War.[62] Tilly voted for the Women's Equal Pay Act, initiated by Laura Jamieson but claimed as its own by the SCP government, indicating that she had some sympathy for working women. Nevertheless, she opposed not only the idea that housewives should work outside the home during peacetime but also the introduction of public money for childcare for working mothers. Reflecting an ideology of domesticity, she often stated that "a woman's place is in the home."[63] Like CCF and CPC women, she supported a maternalist ideology and used it to fight for lower prices for such staple goods as milk (although this met with little success). Tilly denounced delinquency among teenagers and youth, arguing that mandatory army service would curb youth crime (thus reflecting a conventional right-wing perspective). Rolston disliked party lines and rigid discipline, a major factor in her defection to the Socreds.[64] She had a foot in both populist and elitist camps in the SCP. She saw herself as an "outsider" and, on many issues, took positions that were contrary to those of the party hierarchy. Yet she was a close friend of W.A.C. Bennett's and, on most issues, supported the ideas of big business.

Other SCP women expressed entirely different ideas. Indeed, not all populist SCP women held to the traditionalist, evangelical views of Cornelia Wood and Lydia Arsens. Edith Rogers possessed a liberal, even social democratic, position. Rogers was born Edith Blanche Cox on 20 September 1894 on a farm in Eastville, Nova Scotia, and was of conservative and Presbyterian parentage. She left her family at age eighteen in 1912, coming to Alberta to teach public school. She later worked at Edgerton as a bank teller before moving to Killam. In 1923, she married W.W. Rogers, a local high school principal. Soon after, the family moved to Calgary, where Edith Rogers and her husband became associates of William Aberhart. In 1930, Rogers received her introduction to politics when she served as a member of the campaign committee for R.B. Bennett, then the federal leader of the Conservative Party. As friends of Aberhart, Rogers and her husband left the Conservative Party shortly after the election and became followers of the SCP. Clearly, family played an important role in the shaping of Edith's political consciousness. Both she and her husband joined the SCP at the same time and both were distressed by the suffering caused by the Depression. Both argued that Social Credit might offer solutions.[65] Significantly, in discussing her introduction to public life, Rogers emphasized both individual factors (the influence of Aberhart) and societal factors (the impact of the Depression). This may account for her populist, libertarian perspective, which would eventually result in her moving from the SCP to the CCF – a political journey that most SCP women did not make.[66]

Edith Rogers's political life tells us a great deal about how Social Credit changed over time. In January 1933, Rogers attended the first meeting of what became the SCP in the basement of Aberhart's Prophetic Bible Institute. She soon became a key supporter: in preparation for the 1935 provincial election, the party gave her the task of organizing all Social Credit groups in the northern part of Alberta, while her comrade, Edith Gostick, organized the groups in the southern portion of the province. Rogers undertook a rigorous speaking schedule, which paid off for the Socreds in their 1935 landslide election victory. Rogers was elected in Ponoka, defeating former United Farmers of Alberta premier John Brownlee. During her time in office, from 1935 to 1940, she tried to help not only women whose husbands had deserted them but also widows. She attempted to include Alberta widows in the Mothers' Allowance Act. Rogers also dealt with education and was instrumental in introducing an act that established teaching as a profession in the province. She would later, as a member of the CCF, sit as a school board trustee in Edmonton from 1959 to 1974.[67] After Aberhart's death in 1943 and Ernest Manning's subsequent ascendancy as premier of Alberta, Rogers became disillusioned with the party's rightward trend. She defected to the CCF in 1944, throwing her considerable energy into the CCF Women's Council, serving as president of the Edmonton branch for part of 1947.

Edith Rogers died in 1985, the same year as Cornelia Wood. The SCP's early radicalism and anti-capitalism seem to have attracted her to the party. She supported monetary reform, advocated for women's rights, and criticized bankers and large monopolies. In fact, her views were similar to those of other populist SCP women from later eras, like Cornelia Wood and Lydia Arsens. We can definitely categorize Edith Rogers as a member of the anti-elitist SCP faction. When more conservative SCP leaders took over the party, Rogers moved to a political party that more consistently reflected her views.[68] Given her suspicions of capitalism, it is not surprising that she attacked the banking system in the same manner as did later right-wing populist SCP women. Thus, we might think of the SCP as moving from a situation in which left-wing populism dominated the party (from 1935 to 1943) to a situation in which, given the dominance of pro-business conservatives in post-1943 Social Credit, right-wing populism was a minority position (from 1943 to 1970).

Edith Rogers was a supporter of Douglasite economics. In a speech before the Alberta Legislature in 1937, in which she offered support for a bill designed to tax the banks, Rogers argued: "It has been through the weapon of taxation that the financial oligarchy has been able to impose their will upon the people." Banks were exploiting farmers, then in a majority in Alberta: "The bulk of provincial, municipal, and dominion taxes go to pay interest to the financial institutions. They do not want the land but they want the farmer on the land to pay taxes and interest. The slaves go with the plantation."[69]

Rogers continued with her critique of the banks, noting that they "create money out of nothing and lend it to the nation through the agency of loans, war bonds, and other national securities." In other words, the banks bought the war debt for nothing. "We pay them," she remarked, "for having created and appropriated for their own use the national debt." Using a "producerist" argument, she called out banks for not creating credit "by the sweat of their brow but by skilful education and propaganda." Banks had led the masses to believe in the "dawn to dusk" ideal of work; it was time to turn the tables and make the bankers pay all of the taxes.[70]

Edith Rogers's libertarian views came out more forcefully in other sections of the speech. She commented on "freedom," a key SCP concept. According to her, freedom was "probably the most abused word in the language of man." Social Credit rhetoric and print publications often argued in favour of the ideology of "security with freedom." They suggested that Alberta needed security in the form of strict controls on harmful societal elements. Initially, this took the form of anti-banking statements, but later, when the SCP took its conservative turn, the emphasis on security resulted in a crackdown on the supposed communist threat. Freedom initially implied the right of farmers and workers to be free of the control of unscrupulous bankers (who had caused the Depression), and, indeed, populist SCP members like Cornelia Wood and Lydia Arsens continued to use freedom in this context. In the atmosphere of the 1950s and the Cold War, however, "freedom" came to mean adherence to the "free market" system and opposition to Soviet Communism and other kinds of left-wing or socialist economic systems. Still, the ideology of freedom and opposition to the "World Slave State" remained key ideas in SCP discourse throughout the party's history.[71]

Given her later support for social democratic tendencies, Rogers's support for the notion of "security with freedom" reveals much about the views of the early SCP. Like many women in the party, Rogers argued against the state's role in the economy and society. Among her comments on this issue, she once noted: "Freedom of economic security is something which has never been granted to any but a chosen few in the previous history of the world." Economic security included "freedom of speech, educational and health facilities, religion and culture, not for the few but for the many. This is the freedom which this government seeks for its people."[72] This view is very much in keeping with the ideology of the American Old Right, thus indicating similarities among different groups of right-wing women.[73]

Particularly when compared with Cornelia Wood and Lydia Arnses' views, those of Edith Rogers indicate some of the changes in the SCP between 1935 and 1943. Rogers's worldview was similar to that of more populist SCP women from later decades. Both left-wing populists like Rogers and right-wing populists like Cornelia Wood criticized capitalists and bankers. Banks were, and continue to be, key cogs in the capitalist state. Rogers suggested that the banks were part of an unjust system that taxed farmers and working people unfairly while allowing wealthy people access to the privileges of the system. Cornelia Wood agreed with this perspective but added the socially conservative argument that capitalism introduced modernity in the form of increased urbanization, mechanization, and secularization. This, in turn, destroyed the Christian, familial traditions that had made western Canada a great society. Still, Wood and Rogers had more in common than one might think, and, indeed, both were critical of the influence that elites and businesspeople had on the SCP and on society in general.

The contrast between Rogers's and Wood's theories suggests something about the presence of evangelical Christianity in the SCP. While always present in some form, the influence of the religious right became more pronounced upon Aberhart's death. When Manning came to power, many of the left-leaning supporters of the SCP, most notably Rogers but also Ethel Baker and Leona Barritt, left the party, and evangelical women such as Wood and Ethel Wilson came to dominate.[74] Like other fundamentalist Christians, William Aberhart asserted that humanity had to prepare for the "last days," when Christ would return to earth in order to redeem those thought to be worthy. Later, however, after Aberhart became premier, his radio broadcasts and public activity in support of using religion to foster social reform were anathema to Alberta's conservative evangelicals.[75] John Stackhouse contends that Aberhart had little influence on theological doctrine in the church but that his methods of transmitting his beliefs – most notably radio and his speeches at Calgary's Prophetic Bible Institute – set the standard for later North American evangelicals.[76] After Manning came to power, the activist aspect of Aberhart's rule was downplayed, although right-wing populist views continued to reside in the party, especially among women. Still, in a very basic sense, Alvin Finkel's argument that the SCP hierarchy increasingly adopted a more conservative position rings true.[77]

In many ways, SCP women were representative of North American right-wing women. The views of SCP men and women cohered on a number of issues, notably the importance of evangelical Christianity and the need to suppress communism. Yet, as we have seen, many SCP women held populist positions that manifested themselves in their support for women's advancement. Cornelia Wood and Ethel Wilson, drawing on ideas espoused by first-wave maternal feminists, asserted that white, Anglo-Saxon women needed to come out of the home and to enter the public sphere. In doing so, they would use their female virtues to clean up politics and to save it from unscrupulous communists, socialists, bankers, and federal government bureaucrats who had little idea of what was going on in western Canada. At the same time, SCP women asserted that motherhood was a woman's sacred duty in life. For men in the SCP movement, and for some women, a woman's role in Canada involved raising children so that they would follow the Socred ideal of individualism, evangelical Protestantism, and anti-communism.

In a number of important areas, however, SCP women held views similar to those of left-wing women. Both groups argued that, because of their maternal virtues, women had a role to play in society. Both asserted that women needed to bring their special powers into the public realm to save the world's children not only from juvenile delinquency but also from a potential nuclear holocaust. Furthermore, both had a sense that their respective political parties were trying to forge a new world order. Women's special role in this struggle emerged, they argued, in large part because of their domestic and maternal functions. They were also connections between the populist wing of SCP women and the anti-elitist wing of CCF women: all were critical of capitalism and its exploitation of human beings and resources, albeit in very different ways.

Thus, the ideologies of these different groups of women were not as different as they might seem at first glance. We have seen that the geographical origins of right-wing women played a substantial role in shaping their political choices: the conservative religiosity of places like Lethbridge, Medicine Hat, and the Fraser Valley formed the ideology of SCP women in the same manner that urban life and resource areas shaped the ideology of left-wing women. The west's antipathy to central Canada and the federal government also played a role, if a smaller one, in shaping right-wing women's views. As we have seen, biological family ties played a significant role in right-wing women's political choices, just as they did in those of left-wing women.

Above all, perhaps, SCP women argued that their organization was not simply a political movement but, rather, "a way of life." Scholars dispute the role that women have played in right-wing movements. Some suggest that women were less reactionary than right-wing men and so played lesser roles in right-wing movements.[78] Others argue that women have been key players in reactionary groups and have strongly benefited from their part in the right-wing movement.[79] In the case of the SCP, some women did play important roles in the party – as leading spokespeople, as MLAs, and, in the case of Ethel Wilson, as a cabinet minister.

Bob Hesketh's argument that the 1948 purge of the party's anti-Semitic Douglasites led to the sudden collapse of women's activism is incorrect. Hesketh argues that the wives of prominent SCP men formed a majority of SCP women activists in the 1930s and 1940s.[80] During the late 1940s, the 1950s, and the early 1960s, other women became SCP supporters, many of whom lacked direct familial connections to the party. Their activism can hardly be dismissed: SCP women played key roles in election campaigns, charity work, and in relentlessly promoting the party's ideology. Moreover, some SCP women, both before and after 1948, were activists in their own right: they were not "simply" the wives of SCP men. The ideology of SCP women was not just backward-looking and reactionary.[81] Many SCP women genuinely identified with the small person in society – the small-business owner and his wife and farming men and women – and criticized the effects of capitalism and modernity on these people. In this light, it might be helpful for writers and commentators to rethink their notions of what constitutes "right-" and "left"-wing politics.

It was not until the mid- and later 1960s, with the onset of second-wave feminism and the slow decline of maternalist ideology, that women lost their power within the SCP, and the party itself began to wither. A delegate to a 1961 Socred convention commented: "The part which can be played by the ladies in our national organization is as great as their role in the homes of our nation."[82] This reflects, as much as any statement could, the gender ideology at work in the SCP. While Socred "ladies" held their party's banner high, they did so in the hope that they could use their role in the home as a model for the reformation of society in the public sphere. As we see in the next chapter, women of both the left and the right argued for a change in the way notions of "home," "work," "private," and "public" were constituted in post-Second World War Canada.

3
Peace Is the Concern of Every Mother

Communist and Social Democratic Women's Anti-War Activism

I now move on to a series of case studies that demonstrate the similarities and differences in right- and left-wing women's ideologies. I discuss peace and anti-war concerns, women-only organizations, and juvenile delinquency. In particular, in both this chapter and the following, I show that both left- and right-wing women expressed opinions on the issues of peace, the Cold War, and nuclear disarmament. When Communist Party of Canada member Dorothy Lynas stated that "peace [was] the concern of every mother,"[1] she expressed a view that crossed ideological boundaries: CPC, CCF, and SCP women all argued that women's positions as mothers led them to support peace and anti-war activities, even if left- and right-wing women fought against war to achieve different goals. A shared sense of gender identity led women from different political parties to support an anti-war perspective; however, where left-wing women sought to abolish war as part of their campaigns towards a stronger welfare state and the decline of capitalism, right-wing women did so in order to strengthen local communities and individual freedom. In short, left-wing women opposed war on an outward-looking, internationalist basis, whereas right-wing women opposed it on an inward-looking, localist, and isolationist basis.

Women in all three parties – the Communist Party of Canada, the Co-operative Commonwealth Federation, and the Social Credit Party – used maternalism as a "strategically essentialist" argument. The use of maternalist language was an effective strategy for political women: it allowed them to make a broad-based, cross-class appeal to different groups of women, many of whom were otherwise uninterested in public life and in joining political parties. Maternalism served as a useful recruiting tool, enabling women to appeal to non-political people. Although substantial numbers of men in the CPC and the CCF also opposed war,[2] women of all political stripes argued that their status as mothers made them especially able to lead anti-war campaigns. SCP men rarely mentioned issues related to peace and war, unless it was in the context of defeating communism or condemning the Soviet Union. Political women used motherhood as a justification for political activism outside the home.[3] CPC, CCF, and SCP supporters all argued that women needed to bring their maternal virtues of caring and nurturance out of the home in order to reform a world that was run by men and that had turned towards war, violence, and nuclear destruction. This was a kind of "social housekeeping" – an idea borrowed, in part, from first-wave feminism and the activists from the Progressive Era – whereby women organized to defend homes and the public sphere from the problems associated with the effects of uncontrolled capitalism and war.[4] In this endeavour, political women of the left and the right sought to break down the divisions between the private (domestic) sphere and the public (workplace) sphere.[5] In effect, political women used maternalism as a mechanism and not simply as a discourse: left- and right-wing women used maternalist language as a tactic to appeal to different groups of women and men. CP, CCF, and SCP women all endorsed maternalism in order to highlight their femininity and their status as mothers. Left-wing women used maternalism in order to appear "mainstream" and respectable to more conservative members of society. They also used maternalism to highlight the hypocrisy of capitalists and political leaders who outwardly exalted motherhood but privately supported wars and killing, both of which destroyed families.

There were differences among left- and right-wing women's views on maternalism and anti-war activism. All three groups of women saw the possibility of war as a moral issue. For left-wing women, immoral wars cost money that might have put food into the mouths of hungry children. For right-wing women, wars took men away from their homes and towns, thereby destroying traditional families and rural and small-town communities. Yet, for the most part, left-wing women saw war as an economic concern: socialist or social democratic societies would eliminate war and use the money this saved to benefit society through better health care, housing, and education. In contrast, right-wing women asserted that an end to war would engender a return to traditional values associated with the home, family, rural communities, and traditional Christianity.

Clearly, there were differences in the views of left- and right-wing women. Yet, in maternalism, both used the same gender ideology. In fact, if other groups of political women had used maternalist strategies, this might have opened up more space for women in all political movements.

Although the Cold War heightened public concern over the issues of peace and war, women's involvement in anti-war movements was not new. Women had been involved with groups and movements that opposed war since the early part of the twentieth century. Much historical writing concerning women and peace in the North American context concerns either the pre-Second World War period or the 1960s.[6] Still, left-wing women's involvement in the peace and anti-war movement of the late 1940s and 1950s was a key part of their vision of the New World Order. Indeed, CPC women's anti-war activism appeared shortly after the end of the Second World War and took on a particular resonance in the late 1940s, when the Cold War began to heat up.[7] Maternalism emerged as a key theme in left-wing women's anti-war discourse almost immediately. On 6 May 1949, the CPC published an article by prominent member Viola "Vi" Bianco concerning Mother's Day and its implications for left-wing and working-class women.[8] Bianco argued that Mother's Day "should be a day of peace and happiness," a time when mothers could view their children growing up "with confidence at what the future holds in store." This situation, she stressed, was merely an ideal: it did not exist in reality. The prospect of nuclear war and annihilation weighed heavily on her.

In the peace movement, Bianco excelled both as an activist and as a writer. Continuing her remarks on this subject, she offered a more explicit connection between anti-war activism and gender: "Women, the spokesmen of life, given a vision of their strength and their responsibility, can be the greatest force for peace." Pressing her point, she linked anti-war and anti-capitalist activism to Mother's Day: "On this Mother's Day and V-E Day when we gather to salute our mothers and our victory over fascism let our slogan for the future be: 'not poppies, not crosses, but life.'" She further argued that Mother's Day should have a political aspect. On Mother's Day, she argued, "[Left-wing people should] pay tribute to the working-class mothers who have sacrificed so much in the struggle to bring up their families. Let's demand a stop to the mad armament race. Let's demand a foreign policy based on trust and friendship. No one wants war except those who make money out of it." She held that working women, specifically mothers, had a special role to play in stopping war since it meant death to their husbands, brothers, and children. One of Bianco's comrades, commenting on a peace conference in Vancouver in June 1950, noted that women were concerned that their husbands, brothers, friends, and, especially, their children "should no longer be brutalized and murdered." The writer, explaining CPC women's anti-war politics, summed up their activism with the claim that "it was the love of life that moved them."[9]

Ideas about the use and misuse of Mother's Day became an important part of left-wing women's discourse regarding peace and war. In one instance, an anonymous CPC supporter concluded that, despite its commercialism: "The idea of holding a mother's day is a good one. The common possession of the living world is a mother. Mother's Day should be every day, for mother love is constant, unchanging and universal, the greatest force for peace and against war."[10] This point was apt, given that nineteenth-century socialists and feminists initiated Mother's Day as a time of anti-war and pro-woman protest.[11] In another issue of the party newspaper, "C.H." of Vancouver asks, rhetorically, "Who are the Peace Builders?" The response is that "every mother who bears children, every father who carries hope for his sons and daughters, every boy and girl who wish someday to become useful citizens" could be considered peace builders.[12] These comments suggest that a specifically female kind of radicalism emerged on the left, one that presented women's particular virtues – nurturance, caring, and mothering – as being innately anti-war. Of course, this sort of argument represents the very essence of maternalist thought. According to left-wing women, these female qualities needed to be brought into public discourse in order to foster a "culture of peace."

Maternalist discourse offered left-wing women an avenue into radical action that had not previously existed.[13] As Todd McCallum suggests, Marxist radicalism was often portrayed as innately male and as existing only on the factory floor and outside the home.[14] CPC women's anti-war radicalism was in a different vein. Left-wing women portrayed themselves as existing solely in the home; however, they attempted to redefine the domestic sphere as a positive space for women. During the 1940s and 1950s, political women did not see the home as a place of female submission or inferiority. Indeed, it was the public world of men that needed to change and to take on the nurturing and caring virtues of the home. Both left- and right-wing women argued that, while women ruled the domestic sphere, they needed to come out of the home in order to remake the public sphere in the image of the domestic. All three groups of women were ambivalent in their portrayal of men, even though the latter were the leaders of society and headed all three parties. CPC and CCF women argued that men of the left – "their" men, so to speak – supported anti-war views and would help to bring about a socialist society. For left-wing women, the problem was that *elite* men, those of the capitalist and business class, were the ones who held power. SCP women, in contrast, borrowing from ideas connected to first-wave maternal feminism, suggested that men were fiercely competitive and less virtuous than women. Men had led the world to the brink of ruin through their support for war and violence. It was up to (relatively privileged and educated) women to remake society in the image of the domestic sphere. So political women differed regarding the potential role of men in the anti-war movement. Both left- and right-wing women used maternalism to argue against war, but in very different ways.

Left-wing women's anti-war campaigning embraced a sensitivity to class politics in conjunction with a pro-peace stance. "Mrs. Raymond Lang," secretary of the Lake Cowichan Women's Auxiliary to the communist-led International Woodworkers of America, expressed her organization's opposition to war in 1945. In a letter to George Brown, a high-level official with the Congress of Industrial Organizations, the left grouping of US unions, Lang asked if organized labour could "afford to sit on the fence and leave the question of world peace and employment to be dictated by big business[.]" She also condemned "the American press who reflect[ed] the views of rank isolationism and semi-fascism in the United States through seizing every opportunity to attack the Soviet Union."[15] Lang was opposed to simplistic Cold War anti-communism. She also connected the question of peace with the issue of jobs, indicating that CPC women's concern with class and a secure standard of living for working people was closely connected to their anti-war campaign. CPC members like Lang recognized that, whereas a war economy might create temporary jobs, in the long run a third world war would destroy Canada's environment, economy, and civil liberties.

Elsewhere, Canadian CPC women spoke of the danger of using maternalism to argue against war. In one instance, party member Hilda Loving expressed her strong hostility to war: "The average Canadian man and woman doesn't want war. We have no quarrels with the peoples of any other country."[16] In making reference to Ilse Koch, a female guard in a Nazi concentration camp whom a US judge had recently freed, Loving remarked: "This will be a warning to Canadian women, the widows of a future war."[17] Loving suggested that racism and fascism could easily arise in the right context and that even women, supposedly nurturers and mothers, might readily support fascist ideology. Her mention of Ilse Koch implicitly points to the dangers of the unfettered use of maternalist arguments: clearly, not all women were hostile to war, violence, and fascism. Accordingly, Loving attacked pro-war views by associating war with fascism. As part of an attack on far right viewpoints, she argued that women should hold meetings and protest against Western intervention in Europe, which would only lead "to fascism and away from democracy."[18] She recognized that Western governments were supporting former fascists in such countries as Italy and Germany, and she concluded her letter with an exhortation to "fight this drive to a third world war that none of us want."[19]

CPC women like Loving were concerned with the rising tide of right-wing extremism after the "official" defeat of fascist governments.[20] For this reason, CPC women sometimes expressed anti-war arguments that did not rely entirely on maternalism. Some left-wing women linked anti-war activism with class and anti-poverty issues, thus implicitly critiquing maternalist arguments for failing to account for those women who did not identify with anti-war politics. Still, remarks like these were uncommon: for the most part, left-wing women's maternalist focus emerged strongly.

As part of their peace activism, CPC women campaigned heavily against the nuclear bomb. Claire "Kayla" Culhane, member of a left-wing Vancouver family of mixed Russian-Jewish and Irish extraction,[21] spoke out against the fear-mongering that many "Cold War Warriors" promoted in schools. Civil Defence Bulletin No. 10, an item issued by the municipal government, stated that Vancouver schools had to conduct A-bomb drills similar to "Duck-and-Cover" exercises in American cities.[22] Culhane challenged the school board, the PTAs, and teachers themselves to "insist that they make every classroom a classroom for peace by teaching our children to respect and honor children of other countries, and not to be concerned only with the safety of our own people."[23] In keeping with the CPC's support for the international communist movement, and for the Soviet Union in particular, Culhane argued in favour of international cooperation. CPC women and men alike often agitated for cooperation among different countries in the East and West, especially countries that had communist governments such as those in Eastern Europe, China, and (later) Cuba.[24] For some Canadian left-wing women, maternalism extended to include mothering the children of other, sometimes non-white, nations. Continuing her critique of the school system, Culhane stated that parents did not want to have their children pushed into the war makers' plans of preparing their lives so that they would "accept war as an inevitability."[25] In the US context, as scholars like Amy Swerdlow note, anti-war women were undertaking similar activities to convince children that war was not the answer to society's problems.[26]

Culhane's remarks drew on older CPC traditions of combatting militarism in schools. During the 1920s, as Joan Sangster and Margaret Hobbs show, the CPC-led Women's Labour Leagues fought against the spread of pro-war ideas among school children.[27] CPC women's organizations, in the 1920s and after, largely disagreed with the pacifist stance of other women's peace groups, notably the Women's International League for Peace and Freedom, notwithstanding that organization's position that it would work with anyone who shared its beliefs, communists included.[28] The CPC argued that wars and violence perpetrated against repressive capitalist nations would sometimes be necessary, especially to safeguard a socialist revolution.

As the example of Claire Culhane suggests, communist women's anti-war activism drew on internationalist sentiments. Ethel Clark of Vancouver similarly argued: "[Women must] take the lead in this fight against the threat of war and have the courage of our conviction to protest against anyone in our midst who has the nerve to say 'I hate Jews' or any other race."[29] Betty Griffin challenged women to speak out against the pretense of "defence expenditures," which were, in reality, promoting the drive towards another war. Female-led communist organizations like the women's auxiliaries to trade unions represented the means through which women could challenge war makers and capitalists. Griffin also argued that left-wing women should speak out against conscription and, especially, against "the fascist mentality that regards women as fit only for the tasks of bearing children and slaving in the kitchen."[30] This comment suggests that women constituted a neglected resource upon which the left could draw.

Beryl M. Wheeldon of Departure Bay, British Columbia, further exhibited the CPC's brand of maternalism, her comments echoing the rhetoric of women's earlier anti-war pronouncements. Like Griffin, Wheeldon maintained that the CPC had not made sufficient use of women in the battle against capitalism and war: "Women constitute a world to educate and develop in the fight for world peace and in the general progress of working conditions."[31] She addressed "the mothers of the soldiers of capitalism."[32] "Wars," she noted, "mean not flags and bands and excess profits but broken bodies, divided homes and general frustration of the purposes of their lives."[33] Wheeldon asserted that left-wing women, because of their maternal roles, were ready learners as well as natural students of the anti-war cause. Griffin's and Wheeldon's comments suggest that some believed that women, *as mothers,* were a resource upon which the left could draw to promote its arguments against war. Here, we can see the blurring of the lines between the public and the private worlds for women of the 1940s and 1950s. These left-wing women presented the home as something positive that could actively help the left, not as a place of retreat.

Left-wing women also expressed their maternalist perspective through anti-war and pro-peace organizations both in Vancouver and province-wide. The communist-led Congress of Canadian Women (CCW) was one such group. The CCW supported initiatives surrounding gender, consumption, and women's work inside and outside the home. At a CCW convention in May 1952, the organization passed a resolution asking that the Canadian government act to bring an end to wars that were killing children in Korea, Vietnam, and Malaya.[34] The CCW further asked that all bacteriological stations operating in Canada be dismantled. As part of the same campaign, the organization came out against military training and the introduction of atomic defence drills in schools. This reflected long-held beliefs among CPC women and other pro-peace women's organizations.[35] The CCW made an effort to have all stores sell "decent toys" for children instead of war-themed toys.[36] As the *Pacific Tribune* noted: "A letter is to be sent to the Kellogg Company, manufacturers of breakfast foods, protesting their use of toy weapons as gifts to induce youngsters to use their products."[37]

In this example, the CCW drew clear links between women, child-rearing, and consumption. It presented these issues as key elements of women's unpaid work and then used them to stimulate CPC women's political consciousness. In this way, CPC women connected anti-war activism to class issues: working-class women purchased products for the home, including children's toys. This being the case, working women could use their purchasing power to strike a blow against war. By refusing to buy war-themed toys for their children, women could attack the manufacturers of war toys at the point of consumption. Left-wing women combined maternalist arguments with other aspects of the left's ideological repertoire, such as anti-poverty issues and internationalism. As Deborah Gerson notes, left-wing women often used family-centred rhetoric in radical ways. CPC women in the United States argued that such anti-communist laws as the Smith Act were destroying families and children's lives.[38] This led to a particular version of women's activism: in upholding the family, motherhood, and marriage (themes often utilized by political conservatives), left-wing women turned these ideas in radical directions.[39] Canadian CPC women were doing much the same thing when they invoked motherhood and family as a vehicle for anti-war activism.

Perhaps paradoxically, the anti-war rhetoric of CPC women contained within it a strong element of support for Canadian nationalism. One particular instance illustrates this trend. During a 28 June 1958 protest in Vancouver's East Side, a group of communist women distributed leaflets against nuclear-armed US bombers undertaking flights over Canadian airspace. CPC women established the primacy of women as pro-peace activists, denouncing "this insane policy that constantly threatens our lives and the lives of our children."[40] The leaflet demanded restoration of Canadian control over the country's armed forces.[41]

CPC women, like some members of the CCF, supported a "left nationalism," expressed in anti-American terms. They argued that the US military-industrial establishment threatened Canada's airspace and independence. They linked this point to the idea that the United States represented the "highest stage" of postwar capitalism. Leftists in Canada rejected American domination along with the elite American ideology of manifest destiny in foreign policy and racism and segregation at home. Several years later, Progressive Conservative prime minister John Diefenbaker became a foe of American encroachment on Canadian affairs. Indeed, in general, the years around 1960 and after saw a rise in Canadian nationalism and anti-Americanism. As Stephen Azzi argues, the rise of the New Left in the 1960s and early 1970s only increased anti-Americanism among the nationalist left.[42] The long, sometimes troubled, history of Canadian-American relations no doubt played a role in stimulating anti-Americanism. Ostensible Soviet antipathy to American foreign policy was also a factor.[43] The CPC's support for anti-Americanism was part of its attempt to seem mainstream and non-threatening to Canadians who otherwise distrusted communist ideology. This, too, can be seen as a form of strategic essentialism, although it did not prevent the decline of the CPC after 1956.

Anti-war activists were, at times, willing to use patriotic celebrations for their own ends. In one particular case, communist women used the Remembrance Day ceremonies as a vehicle for political action against war and fascism. The 1949 celebration of Remembrance Day in Vancouver's Victory Square occasioned an anti-war protest by CPC members Katherine Marsh, Viola Bianco, and Effie Jones. The three women, members of the communist-led Women's Committee for Peace Action, placed a wreath on the cenotaph. Following this, they read a statement on the fight for peace, while other members of the committee distributed copies of the statement to citizens attending the ceremony. As part of the protest, Effie Jones read the following passage: "In the name of our heroes who died that there might be a better world, let us form a common front, [and] eliminate any differences which can only benefit the war-makers who profit from the bloodshed of war."[44]

This statement, with its invocation of heroic soldiers, sounds somewhat accepting of militarism. Communist women could use quasi-militaristic rhetoric with conservative overtones even when claiming to critique war and capitalism. Indeed, rather than protesting against the glorification of war, these CPC women used their participation in the celebration as an occasion to oppose war preparations. Jones's British background, along with a lingering sense of English identity not only within her but also within other female communists, may also have contributed to this more conservative language. Similarly, many in the CPC asserted that their support for the Allies and the Soviets during the Second World War had put them on the right path towards defeating fascism. As James Naylor convincingly argues, the Second World War, both during and afterwards, was depicted positively by the left as well as by most other sectors of Canadian society.[45] The use of pro-militaristic language may also have been an attempt on the part of these CPC women to prove that they were patriotic Canadians and not tools of the Soviet Union. Conservatives in Canada and elsewhere often tried to portray those on the left as being subservient to Moscow, and the CPC's use of pro-military language was no doubt an attempt to challenge this view.

Many different themes emerged in CPC women's discourse regarding the threat of nuclear war. Communist women presented themselves as the mothers and wives of soldiers who would be killed in a third world war. This was connected to Canadian communists' support for the Soviet Union as many assumed that any foreseeable wars would be waged between the West and the Soviets. CPC women also expressed their concern that money that could have been used for schools and parks for children was going towards war preparations.

The use of maternalist language was a complex issue for the left. In some instances, maternalism played into the hands of right-wing foes of women's equality because it posited that a woman had an essential nature that was inextricably connected to her ability to bear children. This notion could be used to argue against women's access to equality in employment and in other areas of society. While left-wing women used maternalism strategically, in order to gain sympathy for their cause from people in the political mainstream, doing so sometimes allowed foes of women's equality, including patriarchal male CPC members, to argue that women were not qualified to step outside their roles as mothers and wives. Many left-wing women did not see themselves as feminists but, rather, as socialists who opposed the capitalist system.[46] Thus, they emphasized that class was the most important factor in determining oppression: in a socialist society, women's oppression would automatically disappear, along with other forms of hierarchy.[47] As we have seen, however, political women did not see the home as a place of retreat; rather, they wanted to see the public world of high politics and foreign policy remade in the image of the nurturing and gentle home. Ultimately, this use of maternalist arguments provided CPC women with an entry point into dominant discourses. It provided them with a mechanism through which to attempt to change, or at least to modify, dominant discourses surrounding a woman's role in society.

Along with CPC women, female activists in the CCF also played important roles in the anti-war movement during the 1940s and 1950s. CCF women's support for the peace movement in British Columbia was less explicit than was that of their CPC counterparts. Indeed, social democratic activism surrounding issues of war and peace took on a different political tenor, given the anti-communist views of many in the CCF. Nonetheless, a large number of CCF women were vociferous opponents of Cold War dogma, even if the CCF as a whole endorsed anti-communism. CCF members became interested in anti-war activism when the Cold War started to heat up in 1947–48. During these years, Czechoslovakia emerged as a Soviet satellite, the Truman Doctrine highlighted a new phase of American imperialism, and the Marshall Plan came into effect. The battle between capitalism and socialism, and the consequences that might result from this fight, were foremost in the minds of many political people. Many CCF women were strong activists for peace, and this was linked, in part, to the social gospel tradition in the party, which emphasized pacifism.[48]

Nevertheless, CCF women's pronouncements surrounding war and peace were frequently contradictory. In certain instances, the party's anti-communist stance lessened CCF women's criticisms of warmongering capitalists and politicians. Some CCF women even identified maternalist rhetoric with communist propaganda. "Mrs. B." MacLean of the Burrard CCF expressed her offence at attending a meeting of an organization called Mothers Against War and learning that many women in attendance were members of the BC Committee for the World Congress of Mothers, a communist-led organization. These women wanted MacLean to sign a "Peace Scroll," a petition that the committee planned to send to the World Congress of Europe. The Women's International Democratic Federation, which MacLean viewed as a "Communist front," sponsored the petition.[49] MacLean commented: "If I wanted to help the Communists, I'd join the LPP but I don't and neither do the women I meet."[50] She argued that it was dishonest for the communists "to try to put something over on mothers because they want peace so desperately."[51] It was ironic that MacLean castigated CPC women when her own party often used a similar maternalist discourse to advance anti-war perspectives. This anti-communism among the Canadian social democratic left was not unique. In the United States, too, as Robbie Lieberman shows, liberal anti-war women, such as those involved in the Fellowship of Reconciliation, expressed opposition to communism and the Soviet Union.[52] These anti-communist pronouncements had the effect of pushing the political spectrum to the right in both Canada and the United States. With the communists eliminated as a major political force by the end of the 1950s, elitist right-wingers were able to focus their energies on defeating liberals and social democrats.

Thus, while some BC social democratic women strongly opposed collaboration with conservative political leaders, others did not. Indeed, CCF women sometimes expressed fairly mainstream views of war. Writing on Halloween in 1951, prominent CCF member Elizabeth Kerr called on women to assist on "poppy day, Saturday, November 10."[53] The Vancouver CCF Women's Council assisted with the poppy drive in order to raise money for impoverished veterans of Canada's wars. Ostensibly, this brief item in the party press represented a class argument since war veterans, who were often from working-class families, needed money that CCF women could raise. Nonetheless, it is indicative of the more conservative views of many CCF women. Left-wing women's anti-war rhetoric and activism, at least in some instances, encompassed support for working-class Allied veterans as well as for pacifism, anti-imperialism, and, especially, maternalism.

Like the CPC, which sought acceptance in conventional society by employing a maternalist discourse, the CCF moved towards the centre by joining in practices such as supporting veterans by selling poppies and laying wreaths on war memorials. Like the CPC's use of seemingly pro-military language, this was an attempt to appear "respectable" among mainstream commentators who often accused left movements of being linked to the Soviet Union. The move towards seeming mainstream and respectable was even more of an issue for the CCF than it was for the

CPC since it sought to change the political system by working within it and electing people to public office.[54] The repressive atmosphere of the Cold War and the 1950s only exacerbated the trends towards conservatism and conformity in the CPC and the CCF. By 1961, left radicalism in mainstream Canadian electoral politics was largely dead.[55] Nonetheless, the experiences of activist women in the 1950s taught CPC and CCF members valuable lessons, which they passed on to their comrades, thus helping to sow the seeds for the second wave of feminism in the 1960s and afterward.[56]

The use of a maternalist strategy showed that left-wing women had learned important lessons regarding the kinds of messages that society found palatable. While far less common than in the CPC, maternalist rhetoric was not absent from CCF women's anti-war statements. The January 1960 edition of the *CCF News*, the party newspaper, published a letter written by W. Dahlberg of Golden, British Columbia, which states:[57] "Every thinking man and woman is fully aware of the real danger inherent in the Cold War and armament race." Due to their role as mothers of male children who would later fight and die in wars, women were willing to risk more than men to save their offspring from a nuclear catastrophe. Dahlberg appealed to leading CCF women to organize a campaign that would pressure governments to hasten the end of the Cold War. The "useless and wasteful" armaments race had to be eliminated as well. The CCF, Dahlberg argued, should support the possibility of peace and co-existence among all people.[58]

Other CCF women expressed even stronger ideas regarding war and violence. Mildred MacLeod, who wrote a bi-weekly women's column for the *CCF News*, gave voice to the anti-war views found in the party. In 1951, MacLeod, like her comrades Dorothy Steeves and Colin Cameron, joined the CCF's Socialist Fellowship. In one column, written when the Korean War was at its height, MacLeod commented on "the ghastly fate of thousands of Korean little ones, bombed and burned and homeless."[59] Responding to charges that international events were irrelevant to Canadians, she argued: "The conditions of millions of the world's children is our business. Do we not spend nearly 90 cents of every tax dollar on war?"[60] As part of her opposition to war, she appealed to women's maternal nature: the world had become too small to ignore any part of it. For this reason: "To protect our own darlings, we must consider the fate of every child, everywhere."[61] The Vancouver CCF Women's Council passed a resolution on nuclear testing in October 1958 that reflected MacLeod's concerns. The resolution stated: "We continue to hear from scientists' warnings of the dreadful results of these tests, already certain to affect the unborn children."[62] The Women's Council expressed approval of a resolution passed at a recent CCF national convention asking for all countries to abandon and ban nuclear testing.[63] Like Claire Culhane, Mildred MacLeod used internationalist as well as maternalist arguments to buttress her pro-peace views. The anti-imperialist focus of Canadian left-wing women, downplayed by some earlier historians, is here evident.[64] Christina Nichol argues convincingly that a strong left-wing, anti-imperialist tradition existed within the broad Canadian left, especially in British Columbia; however, more conservative social democrats succeeded in defeating this tradition.[65] Prior to this Cold War-era defeat, however, Canadian left-wing women advanced arguments that supported maternalist concerns around protection for women and children.

In another example of the CCF's maternalist discourse, long-time member Grace Worth attacked British Columbia's municipal "duck-and-cover"-style drills. "The purpose of their antics is preparation for war, which is a cruel insult to motherhood and a disgrace to humanity," she argued.[66] Worth expressed the perspective, common among both liberal and reactionary first-wave feminists, that women were morally superior to men: "I have concluded that it is the fathers and not the mothers who have led the world to the brink of extinction where it stands today."[67] In linking women's moral superiority to the anti-war campaign Worth was presenting a common feminist argument: she exhorted women of the world to "awake and arise and in an ever-increasing flood demand righteousness."[68] Like CPC women, many left-wing women saw themselves as being particularly suited to "cleaning up" the world's problems, a legacy borrowed from maternal feminism. As Carol Bacchi convincingly argues, female suffragists held that women needed to bring their particular virtues of nurturance and caring into the public sphere in order to save it from men, who had done a poor job of administering society and politics. First-wave feminists, especially, criticized male politicians who started foolish wars that resulted in the deaths of many young men.[69] Grace Worth's comments are part of this tradition: left-wing women from the 1950s argued that their particular virtues could save society from men, who had started pointless and bloody wars. Left-wing women used maternalism as a spur to increased political activity outside the home, much as did some first-wave feminists.

CCF women's anti-war pronouncements sometimes exceeded the beliefs of the more moderate members of the party, presenting a perspective that was similar to that of the CPC. In one particular case, members of the BC CCF Women's Council urged the Canadian government to speed up the production and distribution of essential goods because "peace [could not] be built on empty stomachs."[70] These women expressed concern for the material well-being of people in Canada and elsewhere. This implicit connection of unpaid caring, labour, and child-rearing with concern about the world order suggests a worldwide identification with women as mothers and homemakers similar to that expressed by CPC women. At the same time, their analysis addressed extreme global inequality: social democratic women, like members of earlier women's peace organizations such as the Women's International League for Peace and Freedom, believed that peace could only be built in a world premised on social and economic equality. Like CCF men, social democratic women held differing views on anti-communism and other issues. As women and maternalists, they believed that females had special responsibilities, particularly as mothers, in fighting against war for the sake of future generations of children (notably sons, who could expect to be conscripted or killed). A common anti-war ethic, based on female opposition to combat, sometimes produced an uneasy, temporary alliance between CPC and social democratic women. As in the case of their CPC counterparts, for CCF women, the use of maternalist ideology was a mechanism: it represented a means by which they could argue, strategically, for an increased role in conventional Canadian society.

As we have seen, the CCF had a spectrum of viewpoints on war, the bomb, and international relations.[71] Both radical and more conservative social democratic women used maternalist language to make their cases. The CCF became more conservative as time passed. During the 1950s, the party's right wing ousted the left wing from positions of power, and the CCF began to support such mainstream foreign policy organs as NATO and the United Nations. Many young left-wing members, who might have been the CCF's next generation of intellectuals and activists, left the party at this point. The more conservative CCF members who took over the party's leadership did not object to American imperialism or American control of Canadian resources. The creation of the New Democratic Party in 1961 only exacerbated this trend. The CCF-NDP's male leaders marginalized the views of female party members, a process accompanied by the decline of maternalist discourse. Even though the decline of maternalism was not the cause of the CCF's increased conservatism, it did coincide with the temporary decline of women's organizing within the party. Female social democrats had to wait until the late 1960s for a new generation of feminist leadership to emerge within the NDP.

The same was also true with the CPC, although, with the late 1950s and the increase in Cold War anti-communism, party membership for both men and women declined, and the party never again attained prominence in Canadian society. Some CPC and CCF women from the 1940s and 1950s played important roles in second-wave feminism, which arose during the 1960s. And second-wave feminist groups like the Voice of Women borrowed much of their rhetoric and ideology from earlier women's maternalist groups.[72]

Maternalism was a fundamental idea in left-wing women's discourse. The use of this discourse was ultimately positive for radical women; in particular, it led them to a clearer understanding that women's mothering role should be recognized as work. These leftists applied a materialist analysis to women's role in the home and were concerned about issues of wages, equal pay for equal work, and childbearing and childcare. In this sense, British Columbia's left-wing women saw the home and family as a site of radical activism, *not* as a place of conservatism, domesticity, and retreat. Home and family were key parts of their daily labour experiences (many CPC and CCF women were married, had children, and undertook domestic and paid work) and thus part of their ideology. Maternalism offered women a route into radical activism and a way of shaping their "feminine" traits in a radical manner. As scholars like Joan Sangster and Linda Kealey note, left movements offered women more space for activity than did more mainstream, right-wing movements.[73] The 1950s-era activism of these left-wing women, as Kate Weigand and others note, functioned as a bridge to the more radical views of the 1960s.[74] As Dorothy Sue Cobble and Meg Luxton argue, working-class women, both liberal and leftist, largely took over leadership of the North American feminist movement in the 1945–60 period.[75] I agree with these arguments, but I would add that the actions of right-wing women also helped to, albeit indirectly, foster second-wave feminism – even though most right-wing women were highly suspicious, if not hostile, towards the goals of the New Left and second-wave feminism.

Feminist scholars are, rightfully, suspicious of ideologies that seek to portray women as "naturally" mothers and wives. However, the use of maternalist arguments allowed left-wing women to challenge capitalism and to offer radical critiques of war, imperialism, and the possibility of nuclear destruction. Home and family meant different things for left-wing women than it did for liberals and right-wing women. Left-wing women subscribed to a version of "social feminism," as Naomi Black and others define it: these women maintained that their differences from men stemmed not only from a biological basis but also from the different gendered experiences of the two sexes.[76] Studying male experiences could not solve what many saw as women's unique dilemmas, notably juggling childcare and paid work outside the home.[77] Many left-wing women asserted that they needed to use "feminine" traits associated with the private sphere to transform the public sphere of politics and international relations. They believed that bringing women's particular virtues into the world of men would result in a more nurturing public sphere that would be able to function without war and violence. This would result in the blurring of the public and the private and a reconceptualization of both spheres.[78] Arguably, some also sought, in their women's auxiliaries and councils, to carve out a separate "female sphere" free from patriarchal norms. For all of these reasons, left-wing women's "social" or "maternal" feminism may be seen as operating as a form of radical social and political critique and practice.

Maternalism was a useful and necessary tool for left-wing women in British Columbia. Because of their efforts, a vibrant, if short-lived, anti-war and anti-nuclear movement emerged in Canada during the 1950s.[79] The strategic use of an essentialist vision of a woman's role allowed for a politics and language of opposition to war that re-emerged with the anti-war movements of the 1960s.[80] These women carved out space for themselves in a time when women's roles were restricted, even if not to the extent that previous historians have argued. There were many pockets of activism, including feminist, leftist, and anti-war activism, during the 1950s, even if the general atmosphere of the period was conservative. Similarly, the Cold War experience in Canada during the 1950s was not as constricting as it was in the United States, a situation that allowed for marginally more vibrant leftist and feminist movements to emerge in this country.[81] CCF women who endorsed the anti-war perspective were largely members of the populist wing of their party. Elites in the CCF – those who argued for top-down control of decisions and disliked internal democracy in the party – were far more likely to support war and governmental action against foreign enemies than were the populists. The same distinction – between populist and elitist women – was even more dramatic in the case of the SCP.

4
Traveling Bags for Their Trip to Russia

Social Credit Women Campaign for Peace

Cold War anti-communism played a significant role in Canadian provincial politics, and Social Credit Party women were an important part of this. Anti-communism was closely connected to international issues, particularly the possibility of war with the Soviet Union. The prospect of domestic subversion, as well as invasion from without, preoccupied SCP women, as it did anti-communists elsewhere. SCP women and men sometimes portrayed social democrats and other domestic leftists as being hostile to free enterprise and democracy, which they associated with American-style capitalism

Ruth Hilborn, who would become president of the Social Credit Women's Auxiliary, wrote that she had visited SCWA members in Saskatchewan and then went on to equate social democracy with Soviet-style communism; retiring Commonwealth Co-operative Federation cabinet members in Saskatchewan were given "traveling bags for their trip to Russia," implying that CCF members supported the Soviet Union and its supposed anti-Western, anti-capitalist perspective.[1] Her observation linked domestic Canadian provincial politics with foreign policy issues. This chapter, which is the obverse of the preceding chapter's look at left-wing women and the peace movement, discusses SCP women and their views on foreign policy and Cold War international relations.

SCP women, like those on the left, used maternalist ideology as a spur to political involvement. They argued that conservative women had a duty to reshape public society in the image of the home; this, for many SCP women, meant opposition to war and violence. The Cold War, and wars in general (because they took husbands, brothers, and sons away from families for long periods), meant the destruction of traditional institutions like the home and the nuclear family, small towns and rural areas, as well as traditional Christianity. As the wives and mothers of soldiers, SCP women suggested that their husbands, brothers, and sons should not be fighting in conflicts that damaged western Canadian society. In keeping with their connection to first-wave feminism, some SCP members asserted that, if women held more power in overseeing foreign policy, then the violence, killing, and loss of economic opportunity that resulted from war would not occur. Socred women implied that they represented the potential mothers of a new and better order. Maternalism was a mechanism for right-wing women as well for left-wing women: the former used the idea of women as "natural" mothers to support many aspects of their conservative worldview. It was also a method of attracting women and those who were otherwise not interested in SCP ideology. Yet the idea that women were fundamentally mothers and wives was much more of a core belief for SCP women than it was for their left-wing counterparts. While maternalism was certainly important for Communist Party of Canada and CCF women as a strategy, SCP women saw it as fundamental to a woman's role in life. For the right, motherhood was an undercurrent in virtually every statement by and about SCP women, whereas for the left it was not. This is an important distinction between the two groups.

In general, SCP women used conservative arguments to oppose war. Wars meant increased industrialization, technology, and modernization, all aspects of post-Second World War Canada that traditionalist SCP women disdained. Wars also meant increased taxation, the growth of the state, and the loss of individual freedoms. SCP women, at least rhetorically, favoured lower taxes, smaller provincial and federal state structures, and individual rights. Their anti-war activism came from a conservative, even a reactionary, place. The SCP women who endorsed this anti-war ideology came almost exclusively from the populist, evangelical wing of the party.

SCP women hoped for a return to an earlier period (the timeframe for this period was never precisely indicated) before the onset of urbanization, secularization, and the rise of the welfare state. These women saw the New World Order as consisting of peaceful Christian agriculturalists, free from the constraints of the all-powerful state. This was one area, among many, in which right-wing women had a view that was somewhat similar to that of left-wing women (even though the former's opposition to war had a very different basis than did that of the latter). This was also an area in which SCP women differed from the men in their party: SCP men were strongly in favour of using the state to combat communism, and they were willing to pass laws that trampled on civil liberties in order to do so.

Here it is necessary to offer a brief word on the views of male SCP leaders regarding issues of peace and foreign relations since these views became the official policy of the federal SCP and its provincial branches. During a leadership convention in July 1961, the federal SCP outlined its official position on a variety of issues related to Canada's Cold War policy. Part of an official document outlining the SCP's foreign policy position stated: "Canada is a peace-loving nation." The same document also argued that Canada should keep a well trained reserve army, even in times of peace. The SCP insisted that practical plans needed to be developed in order to ensure Canada's survival in the face of a possible nuclear attack by the Soviet Union or one of its allies. Presenting a common conservative viewpoint, the party noted: "Eternal vigilance is the price of freedom so preparedness is the secret of survival." Having asserted the need for defence against nuclear attacks, the SCP policy document promised that, under an international agreement, a Socred government would do "all in its power to bring about world-wide abolition of all nuclear weapons." Nuclear testing would be restricted to "such uses and tests as are possible without creating radiation hazards" since "self-preservation is the first law of life."[2]

Clearly, official SCP policy surrounding the Cold War and the possibility of international peace was ambiguous. Rhetorically, the party based its foreign policy on "love of our fellow man." According to the statements of party leaders, Canada had to carry its share of responsibility in the Western hemisphere and elsewhere in the world. Canada's role was that of an "independent nation dedicated to the cause of world peace rather than as a member of power blocs and military alliances."[3] This position ignored the fact that Canada was already tied into the US military alliance in the form of NATO and, as of 1958, in the form of the North American Air Defence Command, the latter an attempt to integrate Canadian and American responses to a potential Soviet air attack. During the Cold War, SCP leaders, and some male members, whether knowingly or not, provided uncritical support for American foreign policy. In various issues of party newspapers, Social Crediters offered support for right-wing, anti-communist dictatorships (notably South Korea's Syngman Rhee) and strongly criticized Third World politicians who were, however haltingly, supported by the Soviets, particularly Egypt's Gamel Nasser.[4]

Alberta premier Ernest Manning made frequent comments on issues related to the Cold War. At an SCP convention in Edmonton in 1950, Manning delivered a speech that encapsulated the official position of Socred elites on the Cold War. "Man's problem today," he argued, "is one of survival itself." Here was see the sense of crisis present in much Cold War rhetoric. Manning expressed his disappointment that many people were not participating in church-centred events, and he cited a statistic stating that 9 million out of 140 million American citizens took no active role in the church. "Is there any wonder," he went on, "that there are ears receptive to the wiles of atheistic Communism?" Like others in his party, Manning suggested that only a return to conventional Christianity could save the world from the communist menace. If SCP supporters failed to challenge the lack of religious belief in the general populace, then "the entire world" would fall "under the enslavement of godless tyranny."

Manning later remarked that communism was an evil that could potentially lead to the "annihilation of the human race." He went on to argue: "If man is to continue to survive, he must retrace his steps to God." Speaking in a style that highlighted the crusading appeal of the SCP, he urged all Socreds to "prepare for leadership in the crucial hour."[5] Manning connected anti-communism to the SCP's conservative religiosity and its messianic sense of purpose. The world had to be saved from atheism and communism, and the SCP was the only party that could effect a new order of Christianity and family values. This was an idea common to all Socred discourse. In practice, and in spite of the noble rhetoric (e.g., love of one's "fellow man"), Manning endorsed Western military interventions into other countries, particularly if they resulted in the weakening, or downfall, of communist or left-wing governments. Ernest Manning was an elitist, in spite of his populist-sounding rhetoric: he was willing to use laws and corporations to expand the powers of government in order to fight communism and to develop the economy.

An unpublished document dealing with the subject of "Defense" offers further evidence of the official Socred position on Cold War foreign policy. This item makes reference to a speech given by Robert N. Thompson, then the leader of the federal SCP. Thompson presented his vision of the Cold War: Canada, as a member of NATO, was obligated to support the United States and to make the North American air defence system work. As we have seen, many in the SCP subscribed to a conspiratorial worldview. For Socreds, communism was an unseen force that promised to destroy all that the capitalist West had built. "Russia," Robert Thompson noted, "spends two billion dollars a year on spreading the

Communist message around the world." Further: "Five children study the principles of communism for every one learning the principles of Christianity." The climate of the 1950s and early 1960s, with its emphasis on security and the lack thereof, was ripe for the onset of such paranoid-sounding language. Thompson continued in the same vein, arguing that SCP members needed to support the United States and other Western nations in fighting communism and socialism in the "Third World." "The works of Khrushchev and Mao, not the Bible, threaten soon to be the world's best seller," Thompson argued. "Should we really be surprised when illiterate nations, subjected to the barrages of this type of pressure, succumb to communism so easily?"[6]

The foregoing statement tells us much about the foreign policy position of SCP elites. Thompson expressed a colonialist viewpoint, which, in the context of the Cold War, took on an assimilationist tone. As Franca Iacovetta argues, during the postwar period, many people of various ideological stripes suggested that, in order to fight off the perceived threat of leftist extremism, non-Anglo-Saxon immigrants to Canada needed to be educated to become moral, non-communist, English- or French-speaking Canadians.[7] For SCP members, the solution to the communist threat was to accept the messianic mission of bringing Western civilization and "Christian principles" to these supposedly backward peoples. Social Credit needed weapons "of the spirit and of the mind" to defeat communism and socialism. According to the SCP: "[Christians have] a far superior armoury to that possessed by communism – if we will but orient ourselves to use it." To that end, conservatives were obliged to take the message of "freedom and democracy" to less advanced nations in order to stop the spread of leftist ideals. SCP leaders alleged that the world was engaged in a life-or-death struggle between the West, with its ideology of "free enterprise and the free way of life," and leftist totalitarianism.[8] Thompson, like virtually all SCP leaders, was a classic "humanitarian interventionist": that is, someone who argued that Western nations' invasions of other countries could help those places to advance – economically, culturally, and socially – while at the same time defeating anti-capitalist ideologies.[9]

Robert Thompson, borrowing from the Douglasite perspective that was so much a part of early SCP thinking, further asserted that the democratic way of life had been "placed in jeopardy by a system of distribution that the Western countries – all of them – have been unable to make work." Unscrupulous bankers were out to control the world's money system and install a slave state. The only answer was to institute a monetary system based on Social Credit principles.[10] This would still be a capitalist system, but it would be one based on a vision of evangelical Christianity, anti-modernism, and anti-communism. SCP men endorsed peace-making principles in theory, but, in practice, almost all of them consistently supported American-style, Cold War anti-communism.

Socred women's views on nuclear war and the Cold War were far more nuanced than were those of Socred men. In fact, we can safely characterize SCP women's views as "anti-war." An example from a 1961 SCWA convention serves to illustrate this point. The convention passed a resolution condemning nuclear testing. The testing of weapons resulted in "deadly fallout covering the world," which would be detrimental to the living and, especially, to "generations of unborn children." With the stockpiling of nuclear weapons, people would "abandon normal common sense instead of reasoning."[11] This is a clear example of how right-wing women used a maternalist perspective to argue against war. The auxiliary explicitly noted that nuclear bombs, and a future nuclear war, would have a negative impact on unborn children. These SCP women spoke to women's status as mothers and called upon women to speak out against war and violence *as mothers*. These comments also reveal SCP women's anti-abortion and anti-birth control views – an aspect of SCP women's thought that was not often expressed publicly. Still, this demonstrates how a conventionally right-wing perspective – opposition to abortion – dovetailed with an anti-war perspective. War, especially nuclear war, killed children, including unborn children. SCP women, then, sometimes combined a conservative, even a reactionary, view with what we might see as a leftist view: opposition to war.

Cornelia Wood also expressed a perspective on peace and international issues that deviated from that of the party's male hierarchy. During the course of a speech made directly after the Second World War, she remarked that Canada needed peace and prosperity. Having won the franchise after the end of the First World War, Canadian women had followed men in allowing the world to spin out of control and to become impoverished and war-torn. Wood argued that women needed to unite in order to "demand the abolition of want and poverty and war." Expressing a perspective that would not have looked out of place in a CPC or CCF publication, she asked: "Who is affected more by war than women, who give their sons, husbands, sweethearts, fathers and, in the last war, their daughters?" Women had to challenge war, according to Wood. "Ladies," she asked, "do you notice women are called upon to do much toward winning the war, but no one calls upon us to prevent war?"[12] This was an unambiguous anti-war statement by one of the most prominent SCP women.

Wood's remarks suggest that this anti-war impulse among right-wing women spanned several decades when the SCP was in power: the anti-war statement made by the women's auxiliary occurred in 1961, while Wood's statement was made during the 1940s. Clearly, many years in political office had not blunted SCP women's anti-war opinions. This speaks to the stranglehold that Social Credit had over Alberta's political life from the 1940s through to the late 1960s: during this period, aside from the SCP, there were no other realistic political options for Alberta residents. This meant that SCP MLAs and spokespeople were free to express varying opinions, even if the party's leadership did not act on their views. Indeed, while a large number, perhaps even a majority, of SCP women opposed war, SCP men did not feel the same way. Still, a substantial minority of SCP members and activists held anti-war views.

We have seen that SCP women were ambiguous about a man's role in society. Borrowing from first-wave feminism, SCP women often portrayed themselves as more virtuous and moral than men, even men in their own party. This was part of the justification for conservative women to come out of the home: they needed to save society from unscrupulous elements in public life and wanted to reform the public sphere through exposing it to maternalism. This view of men became particularly important to SCP women's anti-war position: populist right-wing women blamed war and violence on stubborn men who started wars and then expected women to "clean up" the mess. Thus, while SCP women often lauded exemplary men, particularly male SCP leaders – notably Premiers Ernest Manning and W.A.C. Bennett as well as SCP founder William Aberhart – they expressed concern, even disgust, at other groups of elite men who started wars and left society in poor shape. In its portrayal of men as the major problem with contemporary society, we might see this view as a precursor to some branches of 1960s and 1970s radical feminism.

Anti-war activism crossed ideological boundaries. Those on the left were often opposed to war but so, too, were traditionalist conservatives like Wood and Old Right politicians and activists in the United States. Indeed, many isolationist conservatives in the United States – some of whom would likely have rejected the label "conservative," seeing themselves instead as representatives of nineteenth-century laissez-faire liberalism – were strongly anti-communist yet opposed expansionism and combatting communism abroad. These conservatives, notably John T. Flynn, William Jennings Bryan, and Senators Robert Taft and Robert

LaFollette, as well as women like Elizabeth Dilling and Kathleen Norris, supported the small-town, "Main Street" values of decentralization, local government, and freedom from unjust laws. They focused on improving society at home in North America rather than on dealing with issues overseas.[13] SCP women had much in common with these conservative isolationists. SCP ideology must be seen as part of a continentalist, North American vision of conservatism that emphasized small-town values, populism, Christianity (usually of the evangelical variety), local control, and the family. This was distinct from European brands of conservatism, which were often elitist and based on support for monarchy and aristocratic traditions. It is interesting that SCP women's anti-war activism continued into the 1950s and 1960s, while the Old Right isolationist activism declined during this period in the United States, particularly among right-wing women. Many conservative women began to support US international adventures during the 1950s and in subsequent decades.[14]

Elsewhere, the anti-war focus of SCP women is displayed in even stronger terms. Drawing on images used to foster maternalist arguments, Cornelia Wood stated that women needed to accept responsibility for preventing future wars. In particular, they had to come out of the home and save society from men's folly: "Surely we must agree that there is something radically wrong with these man-made systems that bring about such destitution with accompanying sorrow."[15] For Wood, the answer to the world's ills, including war and violence, lay in establishing a money system based on C.H. Douglas's vision of economics. Women, according to Wood, needed to bring their maternal virtues into the public sphere to save it from men who had started needless wars that, in turn, had resulted in economic and social calamities. The Cold War and the looming possibility of war and nuclear destruction made it even more imperative that conservative women take on leading roles in Canadian society.

SCP member E. Vera Hattersley's stance on international affairs offers further evidence of the reactionary impulse implicit in SCP women's anti-war position. In an early edition of the *Canadian Social Crediter*, Hattersley offered a critique of nuclear weapons. Reflecting the religious focus of the SCP, she remarked: "We all have a duty to our home, to our church, and to our community" to save society and to "purge it of war and violence." Presenting an analysis of the Cold War situation, Hattersley argued that "the world in which we live in is very sick." It was up to SCP women to cure the world of its ills for the sake of future generations. As part of her remarks concerning the international situation, she asked: "Is it to be a lifetime spent under the shadow of the hydrogen bomb, or of some other weapon of mass destruction more terrible still?" This was a clear criticism of war and violence, and of the politicians who started wars. Like others in the party, Hattersley suggested: "Only Social Credit offers a future that can be faced without horror. Only Social Credit has the answer. Let us help to spread the good news." Hattersley's answer to the problems of the nuclear age, unlike that of left-wing women who focused on economic concerns, was to emphasize a return to spreading what Social Crediters termed the "good news" of traditional Christianity. SCP women's opposition to nuclear weapons was based on their vision of "freedom, individualism, and liberty." This was not the kind of opposition that left-wing women expressed towards war and violence (theirs was based on an anti-capitalist position). Indeed, Socred women suggested that wars occurred because of decisions made by men *as individuals*. Moreover, Hattersley suggested that male politicians and planners started wars because they did not sufficiently adhere to a laissez-faire vision of economy and society. In her view, laissez-faire capitalism involved removing the state from as many parts of society as possible, including foreign affairs. Wars meant higher taxes, crackdowns on civil liberties, and, above all, increased state intervention, something that doctrinaire conservatives like Vera Hattersley opposed.[16]

J.A. Wyatt, president of the Calgary Council of the SCWA, expressed a view that differed somewhat from Hattersley's. Wyatt argued against war, but from a perspective that borrowed from religious sects such as the Quakers, Amish, and Mennonites.[17] When commenting on the Cold War, particularly the battle between the Soviet Union and the United States, Wyatt asked: "Why do these conditions prevail?" Expressing disdain for the rivalry between the two great powers, she answered: "It is a disregard for God's commandments."[18] Wyatt expressed disgust at the state of the world, particularly regarding issues of violent human conflict. Her opposition to war came out of a religious ideology, not unlike the opposition of members of the CCF who subscribed to pacifism and the social gospel. Wyatt asserted that humans needed to return to God and the Bible and that doing so would salve the wounds of the modern world. Wyatt's vision of an anti-war world was not based on a maternalist ideology or on a belief in laissez-faire individualism but, rather, on the hope of a return to a biblically ordered society.

SCP women's anti-war activism, then, had a variety of origins, but maternalism was the most important. We can see this in the pronouncements of other well known SCP women. Muriel Manning, wife of the provincial premier, rarely spoke out publicly on political issues. She tended to play a "behind-the-scenes" role, supporting her husband in his political career. Manning did, however, offer some commentary on the international situation, and this was in keeping with the anti-war views of other Socred women. Reflecting the anti-communist position, she noted: "To save the world we must have greater knowledge [of military and scientific technologies]." To save Western democracy, Manning argued, "our knowledge must equal Russia's." This Manichean view of the Cold War – seeing it as a competition between the capitalist West and the totalitarian East – was standard issue for SCP women and men. What Manning followed this up with, however, was different. In a section of her speech addressing war, she remarked that it was a "horrible word to mother, wife, sister, sweetheart." Men, Manning argued, "think that their scientific knowledge applied to perfection and bigger bombs is the way to peace. Women know deep down that this is not so. Their understanding of human nature tells them that this is only increasing international tension, which leads to war. There must be another way." In this same speech, she condemned "economic insecurity," which resulted in family breakdown and emotional problems for children. Chastising men for focusing too much on technological advancement and material wealth, Manning asserted that women had a stronger understanding of what would lead to a good life for families: "freedom, opportunity for cultural development and spiritual growth." These are what would help both the nuclear family and the Canadian nation. Women and men had to work together in order to eliminate trade wars, which engendered economic insecurity, as well as genuine "bombing wars." Manning's maternalist leanings are front and centre in her remarks.[19]

Manning's comments typified SCP women's anti-war views: it was "spiritual growth" and cultural opportunities that would end war. While she commented on the problem of economic insecurity, Manning did not advocate government intervention or any kind of collective response to this problem. Instead, she held that ideas of "freedom and cultural and spiritual liberty" would save the day.[20] Manning's argument reaffirmed a conservative, anti-war perception of the New World Order. The solution to problems found in democratic nations, it seemed, involved intensifying conventional, Western-style democracy and returning to an older rural and Christian vision of Canada – to a time when the federal state and, consequently, militarism was weaker. Although they proposed different solutions to the problems engendered by war and violence, SCP and left-wing women both employed a similar anti-war discourse.

Yet Cornelia Wood and her SCP colleagues were not sympathetic towards a peace movement that included socialists and communists. Social Credit also opposed most mainstream attempts at international cooperation, or "peacemaking." Wood expressed hostility towards the United Nations and efforts at creating a postwar global community, equating these overtures with collectivism and communism. In the United States, a similar situation emerged: anti-communists accused elite supporters of the New Deal, "liberal internationalism," and the UN (like Alger Hiss and Harry Dexter White) of passing on secrets to the Soviets, while Old Right conservatives like Senator Robert Taft opposed the UN, fearing that it would draw the United States into more and more international conflicts.[21] Social Credit possessed broadly similar views towards supporters of internationalism. During the Second World War, American diplomat Clarence Kirschman Streit proposed a federal union between the United States and all British Commonwealth nations. Wood responded that such a situation would remove "sovereign power" from Canada. In keeping with her conspiratorial view of the world, she remarked that the proposal would result in "a large totalitarian state in which all effective power, including armed forces, would be centralized in a financially dominated international authority." She also dismissed the Four Freedoms proposed by Franklin Roosevelt. She asserted that people lacked these freedoms owing to a lack of money caused by the machinations of an international conspiracy, which had a monopoly on the world's finances. Until that monopoly was broken up, Wood clamed, "all talk of the Four Freedoms [would be] idle chatter.[22]

SCP women's opposition to internationalism, which they equated with leftist values, came out more forcefully elsewhere. As part of an argument against international banks, Wood suggested that electing the CCF to power would play into the hands of "finance."[23] The SCP even opposed the federal Liberal and Progressive Conservative Parties, seeing them as too moderate and overly interested in using the state to solve societal problems. In a 1949 speech, given in support of an SCP candidate for Parliament, Wood argued that the Progressive Conservative Party offered "no remedy against socialism and communism." Similarly, she suggested that the Progressive Conservatives had no solution for "the system that leads to these 'isms.'"[24] In an earlier speech, Wood had linked communism in Canada and the Soviet Union to the establishment of the "World Slave State," a theme that she often mentioned in her writings and speeches. Calling communism a "creed," she argued that the CPC had "decided to gain control of labour unions in order to support the CCF. Their plan

[was] that once in office through the CCF, the Communists, under Russian international control, [would] take over."[25] Like most SCP members, Wood supported the conventional Cold War view that CPC and CCF members were tied to Moscow. This view of the CCF ignored the fact that many social democrats were staunch anti-communists. SCP members argued that the introduction of communist and socialist regimes inevitably resulted in slavery and the loss of individualism and freedom.

Wood further remarked that Stalin, like Hitler, was "built up by International Finance to undermine all the so-called democracies and build the one world slave state," again reflecting the views of traditionalist conservatives. Many anti-modern conservatives around the world have argued that bankers and capitalists supported left movements with money and moral backing in order to undermine the "permanent values" of order, tradition, family, and Christianity.[26] Wood's arguments here mark her as one of these traditionalists. And, indeed, this kind of argument was common among populist right-wingers in Canada and internationally.

The SCP's overall perspective, from 1943 – the year of William Aberhart's death – until 1970, remained fairly constant in most areas. The party's male hierarchy, which emphasized winning elections, economic development, and increasing corporatism, maintained a strong hold over the party's election platforms and internal and external policies. Cornelia Wood, in fact, chose to run as an independent in the 1967 Alberta provincial election, arguing that the party had strayed too far from its Douglasite, anti-monopolist heritage. From the 1940s until the 1960s, in an effort to stay in power, the SCP somewhat moderated its mainstream opinion – for example, the party's male hierarchy did not object strenuously to the introduction of Medicare. Technocratic, pro-statist conservatives in Alberta became the voting base of Peter Lougheed's Progressive Conservatives. The latter appealed to young urban and suburban voters in Edmonton and Calgary as well as to those who had felt left out during the SCP's time in power. The Progressive Conservative Party replaced the SCP as Alberta's ruling party in 1971.

As we have noted, many women remained committed to the SCP's anti-modern, evangelical wing, even as this faction of the party declined during the late 1960s and 1970s. In 1966, three female Socred partisans penned a letter, addressed to all party members, arguing that the SCP had become too liberal. Lois McDearmid, Ivy Bourcier, and Verna Cole wrote: "The iron hand of socialism seems to have gripped the very heart of Alberta and the pulse of individual liberty and Christian principle grows ever more faint." The women expressed disillusionment with the direction that the Socred government was taking, alleging that it was "no longer greatly concerned with the teachings of its founding father, Major C.H. Douglas." They posed the question: "Because Russia, China, Hungary, Poland, Cuba have a condition of state enslavement, does this imply that such Satanic systems are RIGHT?" They used maternalist language to support a conservative position: state-sponsored programs, particularly those that they perceived to be a result of the welfare state, had a negative effect on families. Using a gendered argument against fluoride, the three women stated: "We are mothers, and we believe we are ENTITLED to the care of our children's health and well-being without the bogey of 'GOVERNMENT INTERVENTION.'"[27] Women, in this perspective, had certain rights based on their positions as mothers of children who would later become citizens. These three women claimed the right to ask for private health care, administered without the state's involvement, for their children.

The views of McDearmid, Bourcier, and Cole reflected the anti-war perspective of many SCP women. They were also opposed to "bombing wars" overseas, even as they expressed strongly anti-communist views. Along with maternalism, they turned to patriotic rhetoric, remarking that men had died during two world wars and Vietnam while "thousands more [were] willing to die for ONE REASON ONLY ... to ensure freedom of choice and individual liberty, as opposed to STATE COMPULSION AND STATE APPROPRIATION of fundamental and god-bestowed rights." These women appealed to conservative religion in the fight against communism and the welfare state. They asked: "Shall we have Jesus Christ or Karl Marx?" They further asked their readers: "[Do you support] Divine revelation or Human philosophy? Love and forgiveness or hatred and cruelty (class warfare?) Private property or government ownership? Free enterprise or state monopoly? Freedom of movement or Berlin Wall or Bamboo Curtain?" According to them: "[The answer] lies with every individual Christian who has lost the vision of his faith, and his belief, incarnated into the reality of action, truly 'making the word flesh.'" The letter concluded with an appeal to the Alberta government: "May God guide you in your very difficult work in the days ahead."[28]

McDearmid, Bourcier, and Cole expressed concern that men had fought and died in two world wars, as well as in Korea and Vietnam, to preserve "freedom" and to combat the spread of communism. Their letter asserted that a return to traditional Christian belief was necessary to forestall any future wars and to hold back any increase in liberal and left-wing thought in Canada. Rather than going to war, they argued that people had to take an individualistic approach to combatting the problems of the modern world. If individual men and women could return to the church, and to the values of freedom and individualism, then the move towards the "World Slave State" could be stopped. This was in keeping with the populist SCP vision of the new world as consisting of peaceful Christian agriculturalists. The comments of these three women suggest that traditionalist conservatism, as well as Douglasite economics, continued to be important within some factions of the SCP, even after many members had ceased to follow Douglas's teachings. It is, of course, impossible to know whether or not the letter was actually transmitted to all members of the SCP. Nonetheless, its existence suggests that, as late as 1966, some Socred women held to a strong, unrelentingly populist anti-war ideology.[29]

Clearly, although traditionalist SCP women were anti-war, they held strong anti-communist views. They took notice of events occurring in Europe and elsewhere. E. Vera Hattersley, for example, commented on the 1956 Hungarian Revolution. Calling the rulers of Hungary "professional thugs," Hattersley offered a vitriolic denunciation of communism. She remarked that Hungarian refugees from the revolution were "entering the free world, most of them for the first time," and continued: "We are ambassadors to these people for the free way of life." This was typical SCP rhetoric on this issue. During the course of making her argument on the need to help Hungarian refugees, Hattersley suggested that Canadians should fear a potential communist takeover. "We have to help these people," she stated, "and while we do it let us pray that the lot of the refugee fleeing before the Communist colossus may never be ours. Can we even be so sure of that?" She followed up this point by charging that "kill, kill, kill!" was the credo of Hungarian communism but that "kill Communism [was] the credo of enlightened youth."[30]

The events of 1956 in Hungary had a profound impact on conservatives, as they did on social democrats. Many conservatives and liberals in the West expressed shock at the brutal suppression of the Hungarian revolt. This, in turn, led to an increase in anti-communism in Western nations, even though anti-communists in the United States and elsewhere offered little practical help to the 1956 revolutionaries. Hattersley's comments on communism stemmed from her reaction to events in Hungary. Given her earlier expressions of disgust with war, and with the male politicians who waged it, we can assume that when Hattersley talked about killing communism she meant as an ideology – something that was to be killed by a superior ideology, not through "bombing wars." This was a common stance among populist conservatives in the United States as well as in Canada.[31]

Provincial cabinet minister Ethel Wilson also offered commentary on the Cold War and anti-communism. In a CBC telecast in June 1966, Wilson remarked that during the Second World War, as well as during conflicts in China and Vietnam, "the free world paid the price for victory" and "[was] engaged in no less a struggle today" against "the spread of Communism."[32] Canada needed to take a more aggressive approach in its foreign policy in order to counteract this threat. Wilson believed that Canada needed to support NATO and the United States in the Cold War by increasing the amount of money it invested in its armed forces. She noted: "There are sinister forces at work, the purposes of which are as clear and as potent as were the forces against us twenty some years ago [during the Second World War]." These evil entities were "undermining national unity," destroying moral and social standards, and damaging faith in the democratic process and "Christian principles." Wilson linked these events to the spread of juvenile delinquency among Canadian youth. Malevolent individuals were responsible for "corrupting youth and bankrupting our nation financially and morally."

Picking up on ideas of decline prevalent in Western history, Wilson remarked that, of the "22 civilizations which have existed so far in world history, 10 have fallen from within." This fact fit well with the SCP view of life: "History tells us that people of those eras became lovers of pleasure, taking no personal responsibility for moral standards or political ethics."[33] This type of language, implying a conspiratorial attitude towards the causes of perceived social and political ills, was typical of SCP women, and the atmosphere of the Cold War only enhanced their Manichean views. Wilson argued that a moral, rather than an economic, change was necessary to lessen the problems of modernity. It is significant that Wilson, one of the few women who had any real influence on official SCP policy, did not utilize a maternalist or an anti-war discourse but, instead, presented views similar to those of SCP men. Indeed, as we saw earlier, Wilson had a foot in both the elitist and the populist wings of the SCP. Here, she expressed views that were in keeping with those of traditionalist conservatives; however, she was also sympathetic to the use of state and military power to challenge communism internationally.

Wilson asserted that, if communism could be defeated internationally and militarily, then this might lay the groundwork for the defeat of secularism, welfare statism, liberalism, and socialism in Canada. This, again, was a common view among SCP women and men: putting more material and ideological resources into anti-communist actions overseas, most notably in Vietnam, would help to defeat communism, thereby arresting the decay in Canadian society. In this way, SCP women linked international and domestic concerns.

The Cold War and nuclear issues were equally important among Social Crediters in British Columbia, and SCP MLA Lydia Arsens was particularly interested in ideas pertaining to the Cold War. Arsens voted in favour of a resolution in the BC Legislature, submitted by the CPC-led BC Peace Council, advocating nuclear disarmament. Yet, like her colleagues in Alberta, Arsens's anti-war stand was rooted in a conservative political orientation. She connected her anti-nuclear stance with opposition to the fluoridation of water. "No state, government, or group of individuals" had the right to force citizens to take medicine without their consent. This was totalitarian and contrary to the will of "freedom-loving" people, Arsens argued. The fluoridation of water would open the door to other forms of mass medication as well as to nuclear weapons and war without the consent of the people. The introduction of fluoride would be the perfect ploy to enable "an enemy" – that is, members of the Communist Party – to take over a city without loss to industry or property: "atomic bombs or civil defence [would] not be needed." Arsens, like Cornelia Wood earlier, cited expert advice, specifically that of Harold Deith Box of the University of Toronto and Charles Eliot Perkins, a biochemist and physiologist. Both had argued that the introduction of fluoride would lead to cancer.[34]

In other statements, Arsens expressed similar ideas. She employed the image of men dying to save the "free world" from some unknown menace, usually the vaguely defined "totalitarian state." The notion of "totalitarianism" was very strong during the Cold War years, and many conservatives and "Cold War liberals" used it to discredit left-wing movements. Instead of far left or far right totalitarian movements, they asserted, the West should subscribe to "vital centre" liberalism, which would bring in New Deal-style social programs to ensure the exclusion of communism.[35] Arsens, too, subscribed to Cold War orthodoxies; however, her opposition to communism, like that of other SCP women, came from a different place than did liberal opposition. Indeed, SCP women argued that New Deal-style social programs were part of the problem: they led to socialism and communism. Traditionalist conservatives like Arsens argued for a return to values associated with individualism. Still, like Cold War liberals, including many in the CCF, Arsens suggested that a battle between good and evil was being waged in the world. Like McDearmid, Bourcier, and Cole (the three women who addressed the SCP in Alberta), Arsens, in her fight to keep the world free from totalitarianism, drew on the image of brave soldiers dying in two world wars. This image from the Second World War seems to have been quite portable: the left used it to argue for more state benefits and a peaceful world.

The SCP used the Second World War to argue against communism. According to Lydia Arsens, a third world war "[was] brewing and brewing fast." "Communism," Arsens stated, "is rapidly spreading because millions are still starving, naked and dying of disease." She was not critical of Western racism: she did not link worldwide starvation and poverty to the policies of wealthier nations. She did, however, strongly critique anything that smacked of socialism. Reflecting a Douglasite position, Arsens remarked: "Our free enterprise democracy has fallen down badly only because its monetary system is as outmoded as the scythe, the buggy and the foot messenger." Arguing that Socred provincial regimes in Alberta and British Columbia had made great strides in improving economic conditions, Arsens asserted: "Our economy is suffering because our federal government has not yet had the intestinal fortitude to regain the control of credit and currency from the banking institutions so it can inculcate enough purchasing power to balance the demand and the output."[36] She also criticized the banking system and suggested Douglasite economics as a solution to the world's problems, including communism, which, she suggested, would collapse of its own weight when presented with a feasible alternative.

Foreign policy concerns could be found elsewhere in Arsens's language around the economy. She argued that Social Credit supporters had to "form a solid army of men, women and children such as was never known before." This army would not seek to "kill or slaughter"; rather, it would seek "to feed the hungry, clothe the naked and restore life and joy into the hearts of men."[37] This foreshadows the rhetoric of American conservatives during the Vietnam War, with their talk of defeating communism by fighting for the "hearts and minds" of colonized peoples. Rather than a physical war, which would be instituted without the people's consent, Arsens, using a libertarian perspective, advocated for a propaganda war against communism. When presented to people in communist-led countries, such propaganda would win them over to the capitalist point of view.

Instead of supporting "hot" wars around the globe, SCP women argued for directing a peaceful propaganda campaign against communism. Arsens's anti-war perspective was closely related to her attack on the central state, a key part of her libertarian vision. She alleged that federal government warehouses stored millions of pounds of butter at the taxpayer's expense. She also charged that Ottawa intended to offer this butter to foreign countries at a great loss to Canada. Rather than do this, she and other SCP members suggested, the government should distribute any excess butter to war veterans, pensioners, and/or welfare recipients.

In criticizing the federal government, Arsens gave voice to an anti-statism, and a sense of western alienation, in the SCP that paralleled conservative anti-war attitudes in the United States. A significant number of SCP members, including populist women, viewed the federal government as a tool of vested interests. Socred supporters particularly disdained central Canadian elites, who, they argued, had little sense of what farmers, workers, and small business owners in western Canada experienced. Moreover, traditionalist SCP women presented the federal government, and its allies in the Toronto–Ottawa–Montreal business alliance, as modernizing warmongers whose policies destroyed traditional values associated with family and church by getting young men to leave their families and small towns. Arsens's accusations against the federal government stand as a fairly rare instance of an SCP woman specifically referencing regional disparities. This was something that was far more common among SCP men.[38]

In the United States, too, anti-war conservatives from outlying regions (i.e,, regions outside the orbit of New York City and Washington, DC, where foreign policy decisions were usually made), like Senator Robert Taft of Ohio, Senator Kenneth Wherry of Nebraska, Senator Charles Percy of Illinois, and (later) Congressman Eugene Siler of Kentucky, expressed suspicion of Wall Street and warmongering power brokers in DC. These conservatives valorized small business owners and farmers. They argued that war was destroying rural and isolated regions of the United States, just as SCP women argued that modernity and centralized power were doing the same in Canada.[39] Conservative Christianity played a role in both Canadian and American conservatism. American conservatives advocated opposition to communism based on the allegation that communist nations were anti-religious. If anything, Social Credit supporters went even further, expressing their dislike of the federal government – and, by extension, welfare statism and socialism – by advocating a return to Christianity. God and the Bible, they suggested, not the secular state and its laws, should be the basis upon which society should be run. Traditionalist SCP women argued that God's law, which mandated against war and violence, transcended all human laws.

In this chapter, I show that SCP women used maternalism as a spur to political activism. Like women on the left, women on the right organized against anything that they thought might threaten the home and family – in this case, the prospect of war – and sought to bring their particular virtues outside the home for the purpose of reforming public society. SCP women's opposition to war came from a conservative, even a reactionary, place. War, they argued, was a product of the modern state, with its high taxes and assaults on freedom and traditional values. For SCP women, war was "the health of the state."[40] SCP women suggested that if Canada could return to the traditional values associated with home, family, and church, which they believed existed before the Second World War, then this might forestall the drive towards war and the growth of state coercion. Thus, some SCP women used laissez-faire capitalism as an ideological mooring for their anti-war position: modern warfare meant a huge increase in the powers of the impersonal federal state, something that principled laissez-faire conservatives opposed. With the notable exception of Ethel Wilson, this anti-war perspective was the exclusive domain of populist SCP women. Elitist, pro-corporate SCP women, along with virtually all SCP men, endorsed the Cold War and the bombing wars of Korea and Vietnam that were concomitant with it. A common maternalist ethic, based on anti-war principles, united right- and left-wing women on this issue, although the former argued against war from a traditionalist laissez-faire perspective, while the latter argued against it from an internationalist welfare statist perspective.

It is worth asking how much impact SCP women's anti-war pronouncements had on SCP policy as a whole. The answer has to be, at least in the short term, "very little." Ethel Wilson, the one SCP woman who held a cabinet post, largely went along with male SCP ideas about the Cold War. Women like Cornelia Wood and Lydia Arsens, who did present ideas that differed from those of men in the party, had little influence on SCP policy. The Alberta and BC Socred parties, as provincial entities, did not have a massive influence on Canadian foreign policy, in any case, nor did the federal SCP, with its relatively small, and regionally based, contingent of MPs. Still, the SCP functioned as a strong repository of right-wing ideas that produced a particularly western Canadian kind of conservatism – one that was much more influenced by evangelical Christianity than was any other brand of Canadian conservatism. The conservative ideas that SCP women and men presented with regard to foreign policy resonated with a significant number of western Canadians. Indeed, in the late 1980s and 1990s, we can see echoes of the SCP's traditionalist, small-town perspective in the Reform Party of Canada.[41] SCP women activists should receive some recognition for having played a significant role in inculcating conservative views in Alberta and British Columbia. Furthermore, and like left-wing women, SCP women's anti-war perspective prefigured the increase in anti-war activism among various groups on different points of the political spectrum during the 1960s.

Populist SCP women's use of maternalist arguments led to an increase in women's visibility and activism in the party. Like their counterparts on the left, Socred women's maternalist musings allowed them to make an argument that supported women leaving the home to remake society in their image. In effect, SCP women's rhetoric may have been conservative, but its result was not. Indeed, SCP women's use of maternalism led to their increasing the appeal of Social Credit to women who were otherwise not interested in politics. When maternalist language began to decline during the late 1960s with the onset of second-wave feminism, women's roles in the SCP, and the party itself, also declined. If other Socred women beyond the traditionalist faction had used maternalist arguments and tactics, it may have allowed for a larger, more independent voice for SCP women. This, however, was not to be: "separatist" strategies and actions for women – that is, having women-only groups as part of male-dominated organizations – led to an increase in women's activity in the CPC, the CCF, and the SCP.

5
The Well-Being of the Home Depends on the Well-Being of the Union

Women-Only Organizations

In this chapter, I discuss "equality versus difference" in the context of right- and left-wing women-only organizations such as the Social Credit Women's Auxiliary branches and the women's auxiliaries of left-wing trade unions such as the International Woodworkers of America and the International Union of Mine, Mill, and Smelter Workers. The issue of equality versus difference has been a key one in feminist studies for many years. Scholars who write on this subject present two contrasting arguments. On the one hand, Estelle Freedman claims that commitment to feminism and women's advancement often languishes in ostensibly progressive organizations that lack subgroups to specifically advocate for women's equality.[1] There is much validity to this claim. On the other hand, some argue that creating "special interest" groups within political movements leads to a marginalization of the causes that these groups hope to advance.

There is no easy way of squaring these circles. Feminist scholars suggest that there is a difference between "separate organizing" and "separatism." Separatism argues for an explicit refusal to work with men and a focus on building alternative female communities, as is indicated in the term "lesbian separatism." Separate organizing, by contrast, represents a strategy for empowering women, a key part of the struggle to alter political and economic configurations. Women and men might, for instance, organize a committee in a trade union that focuses on women's issues in the union and the workplace; this would be an example of organizing separately in order to raise the profile of women and their concerns.[2]

I suggest that separate organizing, if not separatism, is a necessary strategy for advancing the goal of women's empowerment. Advocates of separatism often portray it as a goal in and of itself: that is, women's choosing to remove themselves from patriarchal society. Conversely, feminists who advocate separate organizing do so as a means to an end: that is, increasing the number of women's voices in the public sphere. I support the latter position.

Separate organizing for right- and left-wing women had a positive effect on women's advancement in the Social Credit Party, the Communist Party of Canada, and the Co-operative Commonwealth Federation. The establishment of women-only groups in all three political parties introduced women to new ideas and brought them out of the home to engage in political activism and, at least theoretically, to be trained for leadership positions within these movements. Often, only the most educated and prominent women became movement leaders; yet this does not blunt the overall point that separate women's groups led to an increase in women's activism for both right- and left-wing women. Both the SCWA and women's union auxiliaries used ideas about maternalism and motherhood as a spur to women's political involvement. One prominent union leader noted that "the well-being of the home depends on the well-being of the union."[3]

This speaks to the idea that women did not see the home as being inferior to the public sphere of the church, the union hall, or the workplace. Indeed, women wanted to reform the public sphere so that it would reflect the nurturing values of the home. We might see this separate organizing of women in the late 1940s and 1950s as a prelude to the women-only "consciousness-raising" groups of the 1960s and afterwards.[4] While the vast majority of right- and left-wing women from the period between 1945 and 1961 would likely have rejected the label "feminist" – indeed, women in these three parties hardly ever used this word – SCP, CCF, and CPC women's political involvement helped to lay the groundwork for the rise of second-wave feminism. Women's activity played a crucial role in advocating for the positions of their respective parties. It was not until the 1960s, with the decline of women-only groups and maternalist language in the CCF and the SCP, that women's activities in these parties decreased. Interestingly, this downturn in women's activities corresponded with a decline in the electoral fortunes of both parties.[5]

There were a large number – a minority to be sure, but a substantial minority – of women activists of the right and the left whose maternalist pronouncements helped to keep women's concerns in the public eye during the late 1940s and 1950s, and this led to an explosion of women's activity during the 1960s. With few exceptions, women who supported the advancement of women were members of the populist faction of the CCF and the SCP. Elitist male members of these parties, wanting to keep power for themselves and being ill-inclined to expand the voting (or membership) base of their parties, were generally not enthusiastic about recruiting women.

I respectfully take issue with the view of earlier historians who argue that women's activism in trade unions declined during the 1950s. The CCF takeover of unions from the CPC during the late 1940s did not automatically translate into an immediate downturn in women's participation.[6] I also take issue with the views of historians like Benjamin Isitt and Joan Sangster, who emphasize the small number of women who fought for explicitly female concerns in trade unions and left-wing movements.[7] Clearly, there were many women – and these were not simply those who subscribed to left-wing views – who pushed for an increased role for women in public life.

As we have seen, the SCP contained many women who supported female advancement. A July 1961 address by SCWA president Marion Smith offers a capsule version of SCP women's work within the auxiliary. Smith noted: "[Women are becoming] alarmed about the future of their children, and they are becoming increasingly dissatisfied with the negative approach of the present administration in Ottawa." As I have mentioned, the regionalist appeal of the SCP was an important part of its overall ideology and platform. "Ottawa" represented a sort of Sodom and Gomorrah for SCP supporters: they saw the virtuous, Christian west as standing against the immoral, secular centre of Canada. Yet Smith couched her opposition to the federal government in maternalist language: it was the negative impact that state control would have upon women's children that truly concerned her. This type of statement was typical of SCP women: they offered support for their parent party's viewpoint (e.g., hostility towards federal government control) but did so by employing maternalist language (e.g., women as the mothers of children who would be hurt by the negative policies of the federal government). The SCWA gave women space to formulate these kinds of positions. As previously stated, among SCP women maternalism was both a discourse and a deeply held belief, and employing maternalist language made it more acceptable for them to take on public roles in a conservative post-Second World War Canada.

As for women's equality, Smith noted: "[A] woman's place is no longer confined to the home. Women are taking their places in all fields of skill and endeavour and will continue to play an ever-increasing role in determining the direction of change in public affairs." For this reason, Smith exclaimed, "WOMEN ARE A FORCE TO BE RECKONED WITH!"[8] She reasoned that, because women could vote, they could determine the results of elections. Socred women sometimes paid tribute to women's ability to influence the course of electoral politics. Like some of the more conservative first-wave feminists, these SCP women wished to utilize women's voices to change the public sphere so that it would reflect women's concerns.

Smith's address continued, with her noting that the goals of the SCWA were to educate women in the principles and policies of Social Credit and, in an attempt to gain "financial freedom," to promote the SCP throughout Canada. The SCWA was established to assist SCP constituency organizations at all times, and particularly during election campaigns, by having members work at party headquarters and at the polls. She also remarked on Socred ideology and its ultimate goal: the party was nearing the "grand climax" of the "greatest crusade for economic democracy [that] a free people has ever known."[9]

The focus of Marion Smith's address shifted from the potential benefit of increasing women's roles within the SCP to the perceived benefit of Socred ideology for women. The idea of a "great Social Credit crusade" comes up many times in SCP imagery and rhetoric.[10] The SCWA provincial organizer, Stella Baker, had previously remarked, at a conference in 1954: "Each one of us can be a missionary and try for new members in our own district, and help to spread the gospel of Social Credit by letters to friends, sending pamphlets to other provinces and helping on the 'On to Ottawa Drive.'"[11] Baker's statement suggests the messianic appeal of the SCP and its attempt to make links with other provinces in order to win power federally. In particular, Baker emphasized that *women* had a key role to play in getting SCP governments elected at the provincial and federal levels. She further insisted that women-only groups – especially the SCWA – were a perfect vehicle through which to accomplish this task. Though not often acknowledged by men in the movement, SCP women saw themselves as fulfilling a key role in the party (which they certainly did).

An anonymous author, obviously a member of the SCWA, wrote a paper on Socred women's organizing that further demonstrates the quasi-messianic view of many SCP women. She made a comment on the auxiliary theme song "Win Them One by One" and noted that this was "the task [to] which we, the Social Credit Women of Alberta, must set our hands." Women, the author makes clear, could be a key part of spreading the party's message. SCP members were obliged to present "the good news of Social Credit" to every woman in the province via personal contact and conversation. Then, the author notes, the auxiliary could feel that it had done everything in its power "to give Alberta the chance to show the rest of Canada we mean business."[12] The woman's vote was important to right-wing parties, and SCP women activists were expected to bring that out in provincial and, to a lesser degree, federal elections.

Later, this same anonymous author made an even stronger statement about Social Credit, its crusade to save Canada, and women's role in this crusade: "Here we are after ten years of magnificent effort and achievement – at another crisis hour in the struggle, and what do we find?" What SCP members found was this: "Hundreds of our staunch Social Crediters, mainly men, [are] absent from us – having joined in the magnificent military struggle to drive back the forces of dictatorship, state domination and tyranny" (this is a clear reference to the Second World War). She goes on to argue that women needed to "assist [their] leaders in waging the same struggle here at home." They needed to help their men by prosecuting "the battle on the home front to drive back these same sinister forces of dictatorship, state control and tyranny, which [sought], behind their backs, to force upon them, after their return, the self-same things they ha[d] gone to vanquish." She concludes: "This, ladies, is our task! This is the torch, which they have thrown to us! Be ours to hold it high!" Here she alludes to John McRae's patriotic poem "In Flanders Fields" in an effort to exhort women, on the home front, to support men against enemies both foreign and domestic.[13]

Clearly, SCP women's groups could be used to promote women's advancement in public life, with the explicit goal of forwarding the views of the SCP. In particular, SCP women sought to portray the welfare state as a threat to financial and personal liberty. At a 1963 SCWA convention in Calgary, the Sylvan Lake Women's Auxiliary proposed a motion stating that too many people depended on public welfare: "We feel that this could become destructive to the recipients." This reflects the idea of "less eligibility," a prominent notion in conservative circles.[14] Socred women argued that social workers should encourage welfare applicants to show self-reliance in solving their financial and family problems. The Sylvan Lake Women's Auxiliary proposed that the Alberta Department of Public Welfare exercise more control over welfare costs because "much abuse [was] made of this assistance by the recipient." The Alberta government, these women argued, must consider an amendment to curtail welfare recipients' use of cars and/or trucks.[15] We might see this as indicative of a libertarian view of society. As populists, SCP women argued against the all-powerful bureaucratic state and for a return to neighbourhood, community, and church-based solutions to society's problems. This position was, of course, profoundly conservative, particularly in its argument that people on welfare should face punitive measures. Yet it cannot be denied that SCP women were sincere in their belief that the state should not intervene in any aspect of the economy, including through the implementation of welfare measures.[16] As I show in earlier chapters, unlike many elitist SCP males, SCP women were disproportionately against the use of the state, even for economic development.

Right-wing women's views on welfare, as on other issues, were at times paradoxical. In one particular instance, the Edmonton-based Mill Creek Women's Auxiliary asked the delegates at an SCP convention to petition the provincial government to assist "older people." The auxiliary was particularly concerned about those citizens receiving pensions who wanted to continue to live in their own homes. It asserted that property taxes were becoming a burden for senior citizens; therefore, it called upon the government to lower property taxes for pensioners.[17] On the surface, this seems inconsistent: Socred women wanted less government assistance in the case of welfare recipients but more in the case of old age pensioners. In fact, this view is in line with the central tenets of right-wing thought. Many conservative thinkers argued that older citizens, particularly those of white Anglo-Saxon background, had "paid their dues" to society through work and military service. In keeping with this, right-wing ideologues sometimes argued that seniors were more "deserving" of state largess than were welfare recipients, reflecting older, nineteenth-century ideas of the "deserving" and the "undeserving" poor.[18] Following this mode of thinking, the Alberta SCP often made concessions to older people in its platforms and proposals. The SCP's use of the state, in practice, was not anti-statist; rather, the party simply used the state in slightly different ways than did left-wing parties in order to advance its ideology. Nonetheless, SCP women's view of the state was very different from that of left-wing women, who were unambiguous in their support of an increased welfare state.

We can see SCP women's support for varying uses of the provincial state in other public pronouncements. At one convention, the SCWA passed a resolution supporting recognition of the principle of "equal pay for equal work" for women who held jobs similar to those held by men. Moved and seconded by two women from Calgary, the resolution requested that the

Alberta government consider providing women with equal opportunity to work. It also stated: "[No employer] shall discriminate between his male and female employees by paying a female employee at a rate of pay less than the rate paid to a male employee employed by him for work of comparable character."[19] In statements like these, Social Crediters advocated using the state to help individual women and to support female advancement. By the 1950s, when this resolution was adopted, women had been involved in activism outside the home for nearly a century.[20] This resolution was in keeping with SCP women's general viewpoint in that it encouraged women's individual initiative as well as their ability to participate in the workforce. Implicitly, it supported SCP women's belief that women had to come out of the home in order to shape society in positive ways.

Party politics, and the SCP's electoral ambitions, also played a role in statements such as that contained in the above resolution. In both Alberta and British Columbia, the party had to appeal to large groups of voters, including women, if it wished to remain in power. SCP leaders and party activists needed to attract voters and supporters who were not always as conservative as they themselves. This willingness to compromise and to be pragmatic on certain issues no doubt played a role in keeping the SCP in power in these two provinces for long periods. The above resolution on women's roles helped to bring in, and to create space in the party for, women who otherwise might not have supported SCP ideology. It also undercut the left in both Alberta and British Columbia by promising to support a policy – equal pay for equal work – that could be seen as being part of the platform of Liberal or CCF/NDP administrations. The rhetorical support for women's rights, however, did not always translate into practical state support. Successive SCP governments in both provinces failed to enact legislation to ensure that working women received equal pay for work of equal value.[21] Populist women within the SCP supported pro-women policies, but the party hierarchy did not.

Like left-wing women, SCWA members put on events and raised funds to assist the party. In this sense, the political women's organizations on both the left and the right fulfilled similar functions. In order to facilitate this kind of activity, the party forged links among various Socred groups in Alberta and British Columbia. At times, BC Socred women expressed their admiration for their allies in Alberta. Florence Gresty, president of the BC SCWA, stated that Socred women on the coast owed "a debt to Alberta women for the pioneer work done ... [T]hey visualize[d] the progress as that of Alberta women carrying the torch from which BC ha[d] lighted their torch and the march [was] on with one light going on to others." At an earlier SCWA convention in Alberta, Lydia Arsens offered greetings from BC Social Crediters and told of how BC women received encouragement from their Alberta counterparts. She remarked on "the exchange of ideas that results from working together." Arsens displayed a cookbook prepared by members of the BC SCWA branches and expressed hope that the Alberta auxiliary would buy copies. BC Social Crediter Evelyn Fingarson of Vancouver spoke at the same conference, urging women from both provinces to take a more active part in politics. She also argued: "Whatever we achieved would prove an inspiration to others working along in the same direction."[22] This link between the BC and Alberta women's auxiliaries suggests that the two provincial branches possessed a broadly similar ideology.[23]

Thus, BC SCP women assisted their party in ways similar to those displayed by their Alberta colleagues. A letter from Zena M. Wright, secretary of the North Vancouver Socred constituency association, noted: "We are holding a garden fete on the evening of Saturday, July 17th in Mr. Pinkess's lovely garden ... commencing at 6:00 PM. Invitations are going out to all members of our constituency Executive, so perhaps you will find friends to come with."[24] Socred women also helped to organize public meetings and supported male Social Crediters, especially during election campaigns but at other times as well. A letter from Marjorie Davies, president of the West Vancouver SCWA, to Carole Caponero, secretary of the North Vancouver SCP constituency executive, commented on a potential venue for a public meeting: "It is the opinion of the West Vancouver Social Credit WA that it is desirable to have a small hall well filled." Davies noted that, if necessary, the West Vancouver SCWA would be willing to give a small donation of five dollars if the collection taken did not cover expenses.[25]

While both Alberta and BC Socred women supported their parent parties in similar ways, there were differences between the level of involvement of the two provincial women's branches. In Alberta, the SCWA, as well as the SCP itself, had a far stronger financial and demographic base than did the SCWA in British Columbia. This meant that BC SCP women had to play a much larger fundraising role. The minutes of an auxiliary meeting mentioned that BC SCP women were "serving coffee during intermission and after the meeting this evening."[26] The auxiliary council further recommended that a social fund be set up to sponsor garden and Christmas parties. The profit realized from these events would go towards funding provincial election campaigns.[27] In Alberta, the more established SCP had somewhat stronger resources, although both provincial branches were, by the end of the 1950s, receiving support from big business, including the oil, timber, and mining industries.[28] The BC SCP, however, was not as powerful in the urban centre of Vancouver as it was in the more conservative interior of the province. As previously seen, the BC Socreds also had the disadvantage of facing a relatively strong opposition party, which was not the case for the Alberta Socreds.[29] Because of all of these factors, the BC Socreds needed any funds, however small, that could be raised through events like garden parties.

SCP women in British Columbia, at least during the party's earlier years from the 1940s to the 1960s, seem to have been somewhat more marginalized and less involved with their party's inner workings than did their Alberta colleagues. Initially, SCP women in Alberta had a lot of messianic, evangelical zeal. The presence of Women's Institutes in Alberta, as well as the example of the "Famous Five" suffragists in that province, may have played a role in inspiring women activists in Alberta.[30] It should be noted that much of my information on the BC Socreds comes from the latter years of the 1950s and the early years of the 1960s. If BC SCP women were not a strong a presence in their party in the 1940s and early mid-1950s, then a change occurred in later years. Bob Hesketh's argument that women became progressively less important to the Alberta party's platform and ideology during the 1950s and afterward does not apply to the BC SCP.[31] If anything, BC SCP women became more prominent in the party in the 1960s and 1970s, as evidenced by the increasing presence of grassroots women supporters as well as MLAs like Grace McCarthy, Agnes Kripps, Patricia Jordan, and Isabel Dawson.[32]

In their auxiliaries and women's groups, then, SCP women played an important role in the functioning of the SCP. It would have been hard to imagine that Social Credit could have enjoyed such success in Alberta and British Columbia without the support of women. Women-only groups were key to the significant female influence with the male-dominated SCP. These female-only groups provided women with a route into politics and with training in political leadership, even if very few women ended up having any influence on the party hierarchy. The use and influence of arguments borrowed from maternal feminism loomed large among both right- and left-wing women. Women in all three parties – the CPC, the CCF, and the SCP – often stated that they were more virtuous and nurturing than were men and that, for this reason, they needed to leave the home and enter public life in order to save it from men.

CPC women's organizations were explicitly based in class politics. In this, their organizations differed from SCP women's groups, none of which used class as an organizing principle. CPC women were especially prominent in the auxiliaries of male-dominated trade unions. The International Union of Mine, Mill, and Smelter Workers was a union in which communists were prominent: the leaders were mostly communists, and many rank-and-file members were also CPC supporters. In 1949, the Canadian Congress of Labour, led by anti-communist CCF member Charles Millard, used illegal and undemocratic tactics to expel Mine-Mill from its ranks. Despite this, communists remained important in Mine-Mill, and rank-and-file workers in the mining industry continued to support communist-led locals. Mine-Mill counted many women among its champions. Although they did not work in the mines, the mothers, sisters, and wives of miners, as well as many other women in mining communities, became part of, or formed, auxiliaries to support their men.[33] In other areas of work, most notably in the service and retail industries, women did engage in front-line work and, at times, attempted to organize unions and to fight in radical struggles.[34]

A draft constitution of the Mine-Mill Ladies' Auxiliary, dated 1955, offers evidence of the nature of women's auxiliaries in left-wing trade unions. The preamble to the constitution reads: "We hold that there is a class struggle in society, and that this struggle is caused by economic conditions." As part of their mandate, the women offered support for men in trade unions: "We affirm the economic condition of the producer to be that he is exploited of the wealth which he produces, being allowed to retain barely sufficient resources for his elementary necessities." The document presents a radical denunciation of capitalist society, arguing that only the working class could achieve its own emancipation. Mine-Mill's radicalism was heavily gendered. Article 1, section 2, of the Mine-Mill constitution sets out the expected role of women in a radical trade union: "The objects of this organization shall be to educate and train the women in the labor movement, to teach them the correct channels in which to spend the union-earned dollars, and to assist their local unions in time of need and labor disputes."[35]

The union, through the women's auxiliary, asserted that women needed to be taught "correct" trade union principles. The women's auxiliary promised to support the union in all of its legislative efforts and to provide educational and cultural activities for the children of left-wing families. Some male leftists suspected that women were inherently conservative and that they lacked knowledge of political matters. The unstated assumption was that women had been confined to the home for so long that they needed to be taught the ways of the public sphere, particularly with regard to radical politics and economics. This belief regarding women's conservatism was a concern for male leftists before the Second World War and continued to be one, albeit to a lesser extent, after the war. The CPC view, which endorsed woman's role as a support for the family and as a mother and helpmate, reflected mainstream perceptions of gender.[36] But, whereas CPC men argued in favour of women staying in the home, CPC women argued the opposite.

As part of their activity in left-led, male-dominated unions, CPC women faced a conundrum. Left-wing women were expected to participate in traditionally female tasks related to child-rearing and nurturing. They were also expected, given their presumed lack of political sophistication, to learn about politics, trade unions, and radical activism. CPC women argued strongly for an increased role in the business of reshaping society. A resolution put forward by Mine-Mill Auxiliary 133, from Britannia Beach, British Columbia, at an auxiliary convention offers evidence of this. According to this resolution, the union would require its auxiliaries to support schools for the education of working-class women: "The educational program of our Auxiliaries should provide the opportunity for union sisters to learn and study economics, labor legislation, [and] trade union history." Left-wing women were also expected to study the struggle for women's emancipation as well as childcare and home-management. The auxiliary argued that having women study these subjects would enable them "to fight for the rights of the working people in the public field and improve their lot in the home and for the family."[37]

As can be seen, auxiliaries offered CPC women a presence in the union movement and, through this, a way into political action (just as, albeit with a different goal, SCWAs offered Socred women a path towards political action). They served the function of drawing women out of the home, including many working-class women who were otherwise uninterested in politics, and educating them as leaders. Auxiliary activities were usually connected with emphasizing women's mothering roles as nurturers and caregivers. The report that Dorothy McDonald, "chairman" of the administrative committee of the auxiliaries, gave to the Fourth Annual Convention of the Mine-Mill Auxiliaries illustrates this. All union auxiliaries in Canada, McDonald stated, adopted wards in veterans hospitals. At Christmas, some auxiliaries took baskets of food and gifts to old-age pensioners in British Columbia's resource-based communities.[38] "Parties have been held for the children of union members especially at Christmas time. In Western Canada, the Auxiliaries took a special interest in crippled children's hospitals," noted McDonald.[39] Mine-Mill auxiliaries supported drives by the Red Cross, the Children's Aid Society, and the Salvation Army as well as by the March of Dimes and fundraising organizations for cancer, TB, and heart research. Auxiliaries raised funds for their unions through bazaars, teas, bake sales, bingo, card parties, rummage sales, and tag days.[40] Families and children were often the focus of CPC women's activism outside the home.

Left-wing women combined the above activities with actions that offered explicit support to union men. Dorothy McDonald noted that the auxiliary provided strike relief and donations to locals that needed assistance. She commented on the situation of the union, noting that "the CCL and STEEL ha[d] raided locals in Trail, BC," a reference to the attempt of more conservative CCF-led unions to steal members from Mine-Mill.[41] As a result of McDonald's comments, each women's auxiliary of District 8 offered to contribute at least fifty dollars to fight the raiders. The same report remarked on another aspect of auxiliary life: "It is usually the Auxiliaries who are in charge of entertainments put on by the locals which help to bring the families of Mine-Mill together and also aid in a financial way."

As we see, the role of women in left-wing organizations and auxiliaries was complex. Mine-Mill auxiliaries engaged in activities that emphasized women's traditional roles as mothers, wives, and helpmates; however, they also engaged in activities that brought union women into new worlds. In particular, the Mine-Mill auxiliaries were concerned with municipal work, especially street and sidewalk repairs: the union supported better lighting and sanitation in BC municipalities on Vancouver Island and in the BC interior. The auxiliaries took on these issues in cooperation with other women's groups. They backed local projects like community swimming pools, cancer and VD research and care, and health clinics; they also helped to collect clothing and other essentials for war-torn countries. Union women demanded that wartime day nurseries be allowed to stay open,[42] especially in overcrowded areas or in instances in which mothers had to work outside the home. Mine-Mill women fought to improve conditions for all working-class and poor women.

In fighting for swimming pools, health care, and wartime day nurseries for local communities, veterans, and working women, CPC women pushed the traditional conception of women as caregivers in a more radical direction. Women saw themselves as fulfilling their traditional role but doing so outside the home and as part of a left-wing movement. They did not see the home as inferior; rather, this view was an extension of the tradition that was started by the Women's Labor Leagues of the 1920s and that continued with left-wing and union women in the 1930s and 1940s. It is also significant that most of the women discussed here were married and had children. That married women with children were taking on more active roles outside the home is a testament to the changing nature of women's work after, and because of, the events of the Second World War. In many ways, left-wing women were moving beyond their traditional roles. CPC women's activism outside the home, like that of SCP women, was part of political women's attempt to reshape public society in the image of the home.

Communist women's activity in auxiliaries could also be seen as part of the left's strategy to appear mainstream and respectable in the post-Second World War period. The anti-communist context engendered by the Cold War is key here in that it severely limited the options for radical activity on the part of left-wing parties and movements. More mainstream, non-communist unionists were even more willing than were their CPC peers to avoid appearing radical. As Shirley Tillotson notes, during the early Cold War years, many unions were involved with community organizations like the United Way. Unions used such organizations to promote their presence in communities – in essence, to publicize their agenda in a subtle way – and to construct an image of themselves as good community citizens. For conservative, liberal, and social democratic unionists, this sort of activity was closely connected to the Cold War and anti-communism: "respectability," as defined by 1950s standards, included opposition to godless, totalitarian communism. Even CPC unionists wanted to appear respectable: their actions in supporting organizations like the Red Cross and community swimming pools were part of a concerted effort to avoid offending mainstream public opinion. As Julie Guard and Mercedes Steedman show, even members of the RCMP, who spied on left-wing women and men during the 1940s and 1950s, could find little evidence of any actual communist or, indeed, left-wing insurgency. Left-wing women's involvement in rummage sales, Red Cross fundraising drives, and Tupperware parties seemed innocuous and spoke to the mainstream orientation of many of them, especially regarding gender roles.[43] Left-wing women supported these efforts to appear mainstream and to attract new female members into their movement; however, their actions also spoke to their genuine desire to reshape the public sphere in the image of the home.

Women involved in other CPC-led unions supported similar initiatives. In particular, auxiliary members of the International Woodworkers of America were active in relation to a variety of issues. As previously noted, control of the IWA, the largest union in British Columbia at the time, involved a particularly hard-fought battle between communist and social democratic trade unionists. Anxious to demonstrate their anti-communist credentials, CCF-led unionists connived with employers to push CPC trade unionists out of the IWA. In response, the communists formed another group, the Woodworkers Industrial Union of Canada, in October 1948. This union lasted for several years, but the vast majority of its members returned to the IWA within months of its founding. A similar situation occurred in other Canadian unions, like the Steel Workers Organizing Committee, the United Automobile Workers, and the Canadian Seamen's Union. Pitched battles took place between CPC and CCF unionists; social democratic unionists used illegal and immoral, but ultimately successful, methods to expel communists.[44] IWA women were perhaps the most vociferous in supporting their parent union against the CCF takeover.

During the 1946 strike of BC woodworkers, auxiliary women – all CPC members – played a crucial role in supporting striking men. A district officers' report to an IWA convention remarked that active auxiliary members contributed enormously prior to, and during, the strike. "Aside from visiting our sick and injured brothers," the women "occupied themselves with improved hospital conditions, community problems, and have spearheaded the drive against skyrocketing prices and for the maintenance of government price control," the report noted. The issue of high prices became particularly important during strikes, when wages were lower or non-existent. According to this report, as far as union men were concerned, the women in the auxiliary were "an inspiration to [them] all." Furthermore: "[The union's power] can be enhanced with the added strength of many thousands of our organized women-folk into the powerful arm of women's auxiliaries."[45]

CPC publications contained regular commentary on the strike, and women's roles in it. The *Pacific Tribune* remarked on IWA auxiliary women's heroism in participating in the "Trek to Victoria" to petition the provincial government to raise wages and lower prices. The author commented that the women of the IWA "were in the long march from up-island to join with their men folks in Victoria in demanding wage increases to meet the price raids of monopoly capital." The women also pushed for a shorter working week to ensure more leisure time for their male relatives. IWA women fought for union security: they wanted to change provincial law to guarantee that timber barons could never deprive woodworkers of the right to their jobs or to the right to join a union. CPC women battled to "win the peace" for labour through their campaign against high prices and through their fight against discriminatory labour legislation.[46]

Union women's work was crucial to whatever success CPC-led unions had across North America. In one particular instance, the Vancouver women's auxiliary established a coffee canteen for the workers at headquarters, and a social committee planned dances to raise funds for the strike. "Coffee must be made. Sandwiches must be made. Entertainers are needed," noted the *BC Lumber Worker*, quoting a member of the auxiliary. The author of the piece argued: "Every picket line must have a coffee canteen. For a coffee canteen at any of the mills it would take at least three women each shift ... these canteens must be established at once." Exhorting women to help their union in the strike, the newspaper urged: "Every grocery store must be canvassed. Every dairy, bakery, pharmacy. We need MONEY. Our strike fund won't last forever." This, the writer noted, was an "Auxiliary job."[47] June Olsen, a member of the women's auxiliary, noted that the auxiliary women went to Victoria to show that they supported their husbands.[48] Lil Godfrey, an IWA stalwart from Lake Cowichan, commented: "It was really inspiring when we were all out there on the lawns with [IWA leaders] Harold Pritchett and Nigel Morgan and the returning soldiers."[49]

Like other women's groups, the IWA auxiliary undertook such "Jimmy Higgins" style jobs as providing coffee and sandwiches for strikers and union meetings, visiting workers in hospitals, and adopting crippled children.[50] Jeanne Ouellette, an auxiliary member, noted that women "were there as helpers." Women were called on to cater picnics, dances, and socials. They also did most of the visiting at hospitals and took gifts to IWA members who were incapacitated as a result of workplace injuries.[51] At a women's auxiliary conference, the IWA auxiliary announced that hospital visiting should be its members' chief function. Members visited workers in hospital once a week and distributed cigarettes, chocolate bars, and copies of the *BC Lumber Worker* to them. On one occasion, the *BC Lumber Worker* announced that auxiliary members "outdid themselves in the serving of a bounteous and appetizing supper of salads, cold meats, cake and coffee." In 1946, the paper praised auxiliaries for their hard work on various union bazaars, which were held to raise money for a children's solarium at a hospital.[52] Lil Godfrey noted that the auxiliary had an annual sports day for children, which was held on Labour Day. The auxiliaries also regularly sponsored a parade for the children of IWA members.[53] CPC, later CCF, women played crucial roles in maintaining left-led unions. CPC and, to a lesser degree, CCF women portrayed their activism as being part of a larger struggle for better wages and working conditions for men and for a more just society for all. In the case of the 1946 strike, left-wing women also argued that they were organizing and fighting for their children and families against hard-hearted bosses and governments who had little interest in the plight of the working class. Left-wing women fought against anything that they thought would harm their families and homes. This provides us with another example of how left-wing women employed maternalist ideology as a strategy to fight against bosses and capitalists and to present themselves as the true protectors of the family and home. In this way, they turned the often conservative rhetoric of familialism in a more radical direction.

The "female consciousness" that animated women's activism enabled (especially) left-wing women to see themselves as the protectors of the home and family and even of men. This was also true of right-wing women, although within the SCP there was more of a tendency to portray men as foolish – even incompetent – and in need of women's housekeeping skills that would help them to remake society. This contributes to the broader discussion of how political women saw men and masculinity. Left-wing women presented men and boys – and sons and brothers – as comrades and relatives who needed women's help to gain higher wages and better working conditions within society. They saw the home as "their" domain, an area within which men and boys were subordinate to women. Like those on the right, left-wing women wished to remake public society in the image of the home. For CPC women, the male-dominated workplace was the area that they most wished to reshape, in a nurturing manner, through better wages and working conditions. This perspective, as we have seen, borrowed much from women from the Progressive Era and first-wave feminists who endorsed the ideology of "social housekeeping."[54]

Of course, the actions of union men had a significant impact on left-wing and union women. Indeed, the ouster of CPC unionists from the IWA was a conscious decision on the part of social democratic and right-wing unionists in the Canadian Congress of Labour (CCL) and their counterparts in the strongly anti-communist American Federation of Labor. At a 1947 CCL convention, conservative unionists decided that Bill Mahoney, a close associate of CCF supporter Charles Millard, would head up a two-year campaign to rid CCL unions across Canada of communist influence. CCF leaders M.J. Coldwell and David Lewis approved this plan, as did anti-communist trade unionists in the United States, notably former American CPC leader Jay Lovestone. The ousting of the IWA from the CCL took place in September 1948 in the aftermath of the BC Federation of Labour's annual convention. At this convention, Mahoney and his supporters physically bullied wavering delegates to vote against the CPC-supported slate of candidates for election to the union executive. On 20 September, Mahoney addressed IWA members over the radio, remarking, inaccurately, that CPC members in the IWA's leadership wished to take the BC IWA out of the international woodworkers union and move them into a "strictly Canadian" union, which would isolate BC woodworkers from their comrades in Canada and the United States. After this, the CCF-led IWA decided, ironically, to leave the International and the CCL. This ended the left's hold over the woodworkers' union.[55]

Women in communist-led trade unions did not give up their tradition of protest even in the face of anti-communist propaganda and activity. CPC women and men in the IWA vociferously attacked the anti-communist, CCF-affiliated "White Bloc" of woodworkers' unionists, which was based in the New Westminster local. The CPC accused the CCF of denying "the fundamental civil and democratic rights of women to participate in the economic, political, and social life of our country on an equal basis."[56] An earlier issue of the *BC Lumber Worker* quoted James Fadling, who became president of the new CCF-led IWA: "It's a disgrace. We have endorsed the Marshall Plan and here the Auxiliaries come out against it. They have failed us."[57] The paper argued that the IWA auxiliary had been disbanded because CPC women "wouldn't goose-step to Fadling's orders" – namely, to support the Marshall Plan and the founding of NATO, both anti-communist measures.[58] In fact, CCF women set up new auxiliaries after 1948, and this resulted in animosity between CPC and CCF women.

CPC women joined with their men in the new Woodworkers Industrial Union of Canada, and rivalries ensued between CPC and CCF women's auxiliaries. For example, IWA Local 92, Ladysmith, a CCF auxiliary, rejected an "insidious request" from wayward Woodworkers Industrial Union of Canada sisters that the auxiliary funds, obtained from bake sales, be given over to the communist women.[59] As the *BC Lumber Worker* put it: "The loyal women said that certain members who decided their allegiance lay elsewhere were trying to put on pressure that the funds should be donated to some charitable organization." Ladysmith Sub-Local 1–80 supported its CCF "sisters" by "advising them to disregard altogether the childish threats."[60]

Historians often assume that the CCF dismantled the women's auxiliaries in left unions at the same time as they expelled communist unionists. Owing to this, many argue that women's activism in the IWA decreased after the 1948 split in the union. There is some valid evidence for this belief. The *BC Lumber Worker* quoted Carl Winn, international secretary of the IWA and a member of the White Bloc, as saying: "[Women] are good for only two things: to work in the kitchen and to service the American navy."[61] CPC women accused the White Bloc, particularly James Fadling, of being unwilling to work with auxiliary women and of trying "to Taft-Hartleyize them" – that is, of trying to remove their power by getting rid of the auxiliaries.[62]

Communists themselves promoted the idea that women's activism in the IWA significantly decreased after the CCF takeover.[63] Evidence from the 1950s, however, casts doubt on this assertion. The CCF-supported IWA auxiliary continued to put on dances and to sponsor bazaars to which each member would bring an item that could be sold to raise money for the union. Continuing with the focus on maternalism, the women's auxiliary also adopted a Nanaimo child who was a patient in the Queen Alexandra Solarium. Later, the auxiliary reported: "Michael ... responded well to treatment," and "he was allowed to return home after a few months."[64] A January 1953 issue of the *BC Lumber Worker* indicates that the women's auxiliary for Local 1–80 in Chemainus had held numerous socials in October and November of the previous year, involving whist, bingo, and quiz contests.[65] While these examples present women as being domestic, home-centred people, the same can be said of examples taken from the time when the CPC ran the newspaper and the union. CCF women, as well as CPC women, supported a maternalist ideology and sought to remake public society in the image of the home.

An article by prominent IWA supporter and CCF member Peg Stewart is indicative of the union's interest in gender issues after the 1948 split. Her article on female organizing asserts: "Women organize fast enough when they're convinced there's a job to do. Look at all the church groups and home and school, and Red Cross sewing sessions, and the way women get together when there's a picket line to feed and keep in coffee." She offers a comparison between men and women's organizing efforts: "I'm not trying to pretend that union organization is the same thing, but I do think the same motives can be used – the same feeling that there's a job to be done, and the girls have to get together and do it, for everybody's sake."[66] Stewart is referring especially to white-collar unions, but her comments certainly apply to more proletarian organizations like the IWA. Clearly,

CCF women, like CPC women before them, continued to be important union supporters after 1948. The similarity between the CPC and CCF agendas is, in fact, remarkable. Political opportunism on the part of the CCF leadership – as well as the overarching influence of Cold War anti-communism in both the United States and Canada – resulted in the ouster of communists from various areas of Canadian society during the late 1940s and 1950s. The CCF wanted to be the only political force on the Canadian left. It largely succeeded in taking on this role, but with the result that, over time, the mainstream political spectrum became more and more conservative.

Women-only organizations fulfilled a positive role in their respective parties and in advancing women's activism during the late 1940s and 1950s. Women's auxiliaries and councils offered women a chance to become involved in political life; they also trained women to be political leaders, at least theoretically, and many women in all three parties emerged as prominent voices. The similarities between women's organizations of the right and left, in their activities if not in their ideologies, are significant. Right- and left-wing women both subscribed to the perspective that "the well-being of the home depends on the well-being of the union" (or the party, in the case of the Socreds). They implied that, for them, the home was the centre of society. The party/union had a key role to play in the maintenance of the home and family. The Cold War period only increased this emphasis on the home and family as the fundamental units of society. Many in positions of power felt that women living outside the home and the traditional nuclear family constituted a "moral weakness" within capitalist societies – a weakness that would make capitalist countries ripe for a communist takeover. As Elaine Tyler May argues, conservatives attempted to control women by "containing" their sexuality within the home and family. This doctrine of containment had its counterpart in foreign policy circles, where policy makers asserted that Soviet expansionism needed to be contained.[67]

Women-only groups provide left-wing women with the chance to support union men in their strikes and campaigns against poverty. SCP women came out of the private sphere in order to support their party's agenda. Women in all three parties used women's status as mothers and nurturers as a spur to increased their political involvement outside the home. In fact, the use of separate female organizing, and maternalist discourse, allowed for a stronger, separate, and more independent women's voice within these parties, which, in turn, strengthened them. It is significant that, in this chapter, I do not focus on the CCF as much as I do on the CPC and the SCP. This is because CCF women used maternalist discourse less frequently than did women in the other parties. Furthermore, in the long term the CCF had somewhat less tolerance than did the other parties for women-only groups. Many CCF women, notably Dorothy Gretchen Steeves and Grace MacInnis, argued against groups like the CCF Women's Council, seeing them as ineffective with regard to liberating all groups of people.[68] This position proved to be a great mistake. Having separate women's groups not only strengthened women's voices in these parties, and in society in general, but also helped the parent parties' overall standing through their tireless work in election campaigns and in promoting their parties' ideologies between elections. It is significant that MacInnis was a member of the elitist faction of the CCF. When, in the mid-later 1960s, the SCP and the CCF/NDP began to marginalize women-only groups (and maternalist views) both parties declined in popular support. Populist left- and right-wing women were a major part of the grassroots support for their parties, and, when their views were marginalized, this weakened the parties' overall message. Indeed, the marginalization of women's voices was one of the factors in the SCP's loss of political power in Alberta in the early 1970s.

It would be foolish to argue that separate women's organizing is *always* a useful strategy for advancing women's rights. Estelle Freedman suggests that, unless female emancipation is put forward as a specific goal, it often does not become an issue for political movements.[69] Nonetheless, I suggest that women in these three parties carved out space for themselves as activists, public speakers, and advocates for their ideological positions. Women-only groups played crucial roles in the organization, development, and success of these movements. Similarly, women's activism during the late 1940s and 1950s helped to lay the groundwork for the rise of second-wave feminism in the 1960s. The Second World War, and the huge movement of women into the paid workforce, started a chain reaction that could not be entirely contained, notwithstanding the hopes of many conservatives. The women's groups of the 1950s offered a kind of "training ground" for more explicitly feminist groups in the 1960s and after.[70] Indeed, women like Grace MacInnis and Betty Griffin later supported various aspects of second-wave feminism.

I suggest that this chapter holds lessons for future political movements of all ideological stripes. Today, political parties and movements tend to frown upon the use of gender-specific groups, seeing them as a form of segregation. In the 1940s and 1950s this was not the case. Women-only groups played a substantial role in moving women's activism outside the home. They also represented one area in which maternalist ideology could be directed at reforming public society. In the future, political parties would do well to understand that gender-specific groups and language do not always serve to hinder their advancement – or that of women. In fact, these women-only groups provide a "safe space" wherein a new gendered order might be formulated.

6

Healthy Activity and Worthwhile Ideas

Confronting Juvenile Delinquency

Looking at how left- and right-wing women used the discourse of juvenile delinquency offers us a final window into their worldview. The issue of youth morality and immorality was an integral concern to women in the Social Credit Party, the Communist Party of Canada, and the Co-operative Commonwealth Federation. All supported providing youth with some version of "healthy activity and worthwhile ideas."[1] As we have seen in previous chapters, often too much has been made of the divisions between "left" and "right" political movements, and so it should not be surprising that left- and right-wing women shared similar ideas regarding what constituted the "youth problem." Women in all three parties asserted that the characteristics of the post-Second World War period were conducive to the decline in youth values. All argued that something needed to be done to restore what they saw as "morality," and, ultimately, the discourse of juvenile delinquency served similar purposes for them. CPC, CCF, and SCP women all used the issue of juvenile delinquency to further the political agendas of their respective parties, notwithstanding the fact that the ultimate goals of these parties differed. Even though these women differed as to the causes of delinquency, they all saw finding a solution to juvenile delinquency as key to forging the New World Order.

Discourses surrounding juvenile delinquency flourished in Cold War and 1950s Canada, and the concerns and solutions of these three groups of women were connected to capitalist "modernity." Certain aspects of the post-Second World War period – particularly rapid urbanization, industrialization, and secularization – seemed to pose new challenges for parents. Many observers worried that young people were out of control and lacked their elders' values. I provide an antidote to studies that discuss the notion of delinquency by focusing on "experts" (i.e., members of the psychiatric, psychological, and social work professions as well as others in the medical and therapeutic fields).[2] All of these experts expressed opinions on the perceived problem of youth delinquency.[3] As a number of scholars note, Cold War ideology and juvenile delinquency had a great deal of influence on immigrants, students, and other sectors of Canadian society; indeed, many in civil society subscribed to dominant discourses surrounding the Cold War and delinquency.[4] Given this, it is not surprising that CPC, CCF, and SCP women's perspectives on delinquency usually coincided with those of experts, even if their proposed solutions to it did not.

All three groups of women saw delinquency as a moral problem. CPC and CCF women argued that working-class youth were turning away from socialist and social democratic values and towards support for capitalist modernity (in the guise of American business and culture), nihilism, and materialism. They argued that the state needed to play a larger role in young people's lives by providing them with public parks and recreational facilities in order to mitigate the effects of modernity (this was seen as part of creating a strong welfare state). As we have seen, SCP women, especially those of the traditionalist and populist wing, strongly condemned capitalist modernity, arguing that it destroyed small towns, rural areas, the nuclear family, and the church. For their part, SCP women wanted to return to the "permanent" values of the nuclear family and traditional Christianity in order to stave off the pernicious effects of modern culture.[5] Both right- and left-wing women were critical of capitalism and modernity, arguing that youth delinquency was a consequence of the onset of modern life. Yet both differed when it came to how they regarded the causes of delinquency and its proposed solutions.

Although worries about delinquency reached new heights during the Cold War, concerns over the problem of youth immorality were not new. Stretching from the Progressive Era of 1890 to 1917 (with its emphasis on reforming working-class children and making them into "respectable" citizens) through to the 1920s and 1930s (with the arrival of new symbols surrounding the disorder of modern culture), the issue of youth immorality has a long history in North America.[6] During the Second World War, youth delinquency moved even more dramatically to the centre of popular concern. Jeffrey Keshen argues that the wartime situation led to increased anxiety surrounding the threat of youth delinquency.[7] Conservatives in government and the media argued that female participation in the work force needed to end as soon as the war ended. They asserted that increasing numbers of working mothers led to a rise in juvenile crime. This contributed heavily to the hopes of conservatives that the postwar period would restore the traditional gender order.[8]

The end of the Second World War ushered in a somewhat different ideological climate. Experts and individuals in civil society alike argued that the family had broken down because of the deprivation of the 1930s and the demands of the war. Thus, commentators, including those in the media and experts in the therapeutic professions, suggested that the "traditional family," consisting of the breadwinning father and dependent mother and children, needed to be strengthened.[9] Conservative commentators, like those in the SCP, feared women's new-found influence. This period of gender anxiety lent itself well to new worries about delinquency.[10]

In the short term, a conservative gender order regained dominance in postwar Canadian society. Authority figures used their expertise to support a return to an idealized past. Psychologists and physicians endorsed an ideal of mental health and well-being that involved women and children being placed in subordinate positions within the nuclear, heterosexual family.[11] Conservatives in government and the medical profession attempted to present a vision of what was "moral." For young women workers during and after the war, for example, engaging in liaisons with men on the job site was considered "immoral." Conservatives encouraged young women to "find husbands" but frowned upon women who dated too many men or those who were perceived as promiscuous.[12] Society upheld heterosexual, monogamous marriage as the only acceptable form of sexual expression. This concern about women's postwar roles was closely connected to "jitters" about problems relating to children. Fear of delinquency became a particularly important concern within the paranoid atmosphere of the Cold War. As Mary Louise Adams notes, the media portrayed anything that deviated from mainstream norms – most notably divorce, homosexuality, marital infidelity, and juvenile delinquency – as suspect and all but traitorous.[13]

The increasing fear of delinquency was connected with the "baby boom" era of affluence, which was inaugurated after the Second World War. During the 1950s, youth gained greater freedoms than were known to previous generations; they had extra money, drove cars, and went on dates without chaperones – opportunities that had largely not been available to their parents.[14] Media commentators and experts attributed youth delinquency to teenagers' increasing sexuality. In particular, federal and provincial governments brought in laws and policies intended to ameliorate delinquency – a trend that was indicative of the increase in state intervention after the Second World War.[15] This fear of youth crime in Canada after the Second World War is an example of a "moral panic."[16]

In keeping with this, prominent SCP women expressed their perspective on the issue of youth morality, linking it to women's paid work. SCP cabinet minister Ethel Wilson, in particular, connected gender with immorality among youth. Women, according to Wilson, should support policies that promoted conservative values and enshrined women's power in the home.[17] In 1966, Wilson remarked that one-quarter of Canada's workforce consisted of women; there were also many thousands of women who elected to carry on "what we might well term our native vocation – homemaking." Wilson called this "an honourable state indeed."[18] Being a full-time wife and mother demanded that women be part-time nurses, teachers, psychologists, accountants, cooks, and general servants. Given that it was difficult to combine homemaking with citizenship and work, Wilson posed the query: How can women meet "the challenge of a changing social order?"[19] In women's homes, and on the airwaves and in printed pages, came "reports of increasing juvenile delinquency, child beating, desertion of new born babies by parents," and "family desertion by one or more parents."[20] Like conservatives in the psychiatric and psychological fields, Wilson blamed working women for the problems of delinquent youth.

Ethel Wilson's views were typical of those of SCP women. She suggested that women's changing roles took Canada away from traditional values, which led to the neglect of children and the degradation of Canada's future. Wilson's status as a cabinet member, and as an SCP woman who had a foot in both the elitist and populist SCP camps, did not blunt her ardour on this issue. SCP women used delinquency to further their argument that Canada needed to return to an earlier time, when women did not engage in paid labour outside the home and children listened to the advice of their parents. Right-wing women highlighted youth delinquency because doing so served Social Credit's ideological program. And here we again see how SCP women made use of maternalist arguments: Wilson argued that society was better when women ruled the home. She did not see the domestic sphere as inferior to the public sphere of politics and economics; rather, she called upon women to defend the home against the onslaught of modernity. She asserted that the demands of modern times led to the destruction of the home as women's domain.

As mentioned, SCP women's views on female advancement were complex. They argued that conservative women should step outside the home, but with the specific goal of reforming a society that had abandoned traditional values. By the late 1960s, the SCP was in decline in Alberta, and Wilson's views on women's advancement may have contributed to the party's seeming "out of step" with urban Albertans, perhaps contributing to its eventual marginalization in Alberta politics.[21]

The SCP's approach to the problems of youth was apparent in many areas. For example, a critique of new forms of mass media, notably comic books, was common among women's groups in all three parties. This reflected their concern with the degeneracy of "modern times." Offering an explicit connection between the undermining of the family and delinquency and "mass media," a Social Credit supporter remarked: "The sly propaganda of mass publications of comic books and 'popular' magazines of book clubs and motion pictures, radio and 'uplift' organizations – all is designed to lower the moral standards of the individuals comprising our families, and thus assist in breaking down the great family tradition."[22] For SCP members, this concern with new forms of expression went along with the party's argument that mass media attacked Socred values relating to the family and traditional Christianity. They identified the nuclear, heterosexual family as the building block of society. Moreover, SCP supporters saw the Canadian nation as being a family in macrocosm. Therefore, television, radio, and crime comic books threatened its vision of Canada as white, heterosexual, and Protestant. In earlier chapters we see that women in all three parties reified the idea of "family." For the SCP, in particular, the nuclear family was an essential aspect of Canada, and modernity and capitalism were conniving to destroy it. Purveyors of mass media, then, along with communists, socialists, and other leftists, were seen as traitors to the Socred worldview. SCP supporters asserted that individual responsibility, conservative Christianity, and (at least rhetorically) anti-statism constituted solutions to the problems of modernity.[23]

In connection with this, Social Crediters stated that society was witnessing the decline of morality and the growth of "sadistic" pleasure seeking, which culminated in murders and other violent crimes. Along with the left parties, the SCP wanted to end the incentive "to peddle evil for profit."[24] One of the manifestos of the SCP states: "We must attack … [the] filth" in postwar Canadian society – that is, the perceived rise in youth crime, sex, drug use, and immorality in the mass media.[25] Commentators in the media and in the medical profession expressed similar concerns about the effect of comic books on young people.[26] After crime comics, the party argued, "let us tackle anew the abolition of those other crimes against decency, integrity and Christianity which afflict humanity today."[27] Social Crediters explicitly argued for a return to an imaginary time when delinquency did not exist. In particular, SCP women suggested that a return to biblical values might solve modern society's problems. Opposition to a materialism that had "run riot" became a key part of the SCP's platform. The SCP's notion of morality held that the material in comic books was "filth" and, therefore, needed to be eliminated lest it afflict the minds of impressionable Christian youth.[28]

An unsigned article in the *Canadian Social Crediter* offers further evidence of the Socred view of the family. Entitled "The Family and Democracy," it asserts that the "home is the cradle of society and the foundation of democracy."[29] It continues: "[The home is] the haven of the family, and the family is the basic unit of society. If then, the home goes into the discard, so does the family and so does the kind of society which we ostensibly maintain. Our very democracy is threatened."[30] Modern society, according to the Socreds, needed to adhere to "the moral law," which they believed was embodied in the Bible and Christianity. This idea had a gendered aspect to it: "The biological fact is that without a society of man and women, humanity would fail to exist."[31] According to the Socreds: "The community, and in turn the nation, is no more than a family of families."[32] This being the case, the article concludes: "It is no problem to ascertain why the family is despised in the totalitarian states[, where] it is sabotaged, hampered, and diverted from its God-ordained purpose."[33] The reactionary view of some members of the SCP, who believed that a return to an older, imagined value system was necessary, is evident here. Although it is not clear that a woman wrote the above piece, it is certainly indicative of the gendered mindset of SCP members.

Indeed, SCP women supported a kind of "Christian manhood," which not only upheld the male-breadwinner ideology but also emphasized that men should follow strict biblical teachings surrounding gender.[34] The Socred understanding of gender was often anti-modern. Those who endorsed modern manhood emphasized rationality, efficiency, belief in progress, risk management through regulation, and expert advice and knowledge.[35] Those Social Crediters who endorsed evangelicalism and traditionalism rejected this version of manhood and instead advocated a traditional form of Christian masculinity. The SCP version of manhood held that it was men's responsibility to be Christian gentlemen and to protect the home and family from external threats, notably communism and other left-wing movements. We have seen that many SCP women portrayed men as foolish, incompetent, and in need of women's help to clean up society's ills. This view, taken from first-wave feminism, held that, in an ideal world, men should be leaders in the fight against communism and modernity. Thus, SCP women's view of manhood, expressed primarily, although not exclusively, by members of the populist faction of the party, was contradictory and complex. Traditionalist SCP women argued that men had started pointless wars and needed women's help to reform society. Yet SCP women, both traditionalist and elitist, also endorsed a vision of Christian manhood and upheld men as leaders in the fight to bring about a society centred on SCP principles.

In their commentary on delinquency, SCP women offered support for women's advancement, and their use of anti-delinquent discourse supported other aspects of their ideological program. Ethel Wilson commented on a supposed increase in incidents of suicides, both attempted and successful, among young people. She asked: "Could it be that we, as adults, have failed to live what we say we believe? Or have we failed to equip them to withstand the stress and strain of the space age?"[36] Wilson remarked that adults had a responsibility to provide youths with security: "We must have confidence in our ability to meet the challenge of the future." Moreover, she contended that women with "desirable" attitudes could accomplish much by arming youth against moral weakness and the temptation of alcohol, crime comics, and communism. She expressed her hope that government initiatives like the Women's Information and Cultural Bureau would fill a need "for all those who wish[ed] to become more familiar with the responsibility of good citizenship."[37] The Women's Bureau was established in 1962, in Edmonton, to help new immigrants "integrate" into Canadian society and to provide immigrant women with information and support. It also provided information and support for Aboriginal women as well as poor and working-class women, and it offered a "safe space" for all Albertan women. Organizations like the Alberta Women's Bureau helped the rise of second-wave feminism, if unwittingly, by providing a place where women could exchange ideas and begin to discuss the formation of a women's movement.

SCP women suggested that conservative women had a role to play in making Canada a better nation – something they could do by fostering values that favoured traditionalist gender roles based on a maternalist ideology. Women like Wilson emphasized SCP women's defence of the home and the private sphere. Conservative women could help children and youth avoid delinquent pursuits. SCP women argued that, in the post-Second World War era, modernity was taking women out of the home. This, in turn, was helping to pave the way for increased youth delinquency since young people, when they lacked maternal help, turned to negative activities. This is why SCP women believed it was so important to organize to defend the home against the onslaught of modernity.[38]

SCP women's views on delinquency offer more evidence of the differences between populist and elitist members of the party. As has been mentioned, SCP women were disproportionately members of the populist wing, while SCP men were often members of the elitist wing. This being the case, it is interesting that women were concerned with the problem of youth delinquency to a far greater degree than were men. This reflects SCP women's endorsement of the "separate spheres" ideology. Due to their belief in women's maternal nature, both SCP women and SCP men saw children and youth as falling within the "women's sphere." Juvenile delinquency, and the discourse surrounding it, reflected the concerns of traditionalist, evangelical SCP supporters. Evangelical SCP populists deplored sexualized language and pictures, comic books, rock and roll, and illicit drugs, all of which they saw as elements arising from capitalist modernity and consumerism. It was the traditionalist wing of the SCP that expressed concern about youth problems. Elitist, technocratic conservatives like Ernest Manning would sometimes make comments about youth lacking the values of their elders, but, more often, their focus was on economic development and on using the state to effect economic change.[39] Thus, SCP elites introduced few laws or policies to combat delinquency. Populist conservatives, though a minority in the party, were highly critical of capitalism, if in a very different way than were members of left-wing parties. SCP women, then, organized to defend a vision of maternalism that, they asserted, was under threat from the forces of modernity and capitalism. For SCP women, maternalism was not only a strategy but also part of a deeply held conservative ideology.

On the subject of juvenile delinquency, CCF women expressed views similar to those of SCP women, although the former's vision of society differed from that of the latter. CCF member Kay McKenzie told the story of seventeen-year-old John, who had been convicted on a break-and-enter charge and who was one of many young offenders imprisoned in Oakalla Prison Farm in Burnaby, British Columbia. John's father and mother had married when his mother was only eighteen, and neither of them had been ready for the responsibilities of parenthood, especially on their small income. John's father abandoned the family when the boy was four.[40] "John never knew the relationship of father and son," McKenzie remarked, "nor did he learn from it what a man's strengths and responsibilities can be."[41] When John's mother was twenty-four, she became a waitress. This meant that the family had more money, but her shifts "came at unsuitable hours and the children were in the main left to fend for themselves."[42]

Kay McKenzie blamed the capitalist system for the problems of John's family; however, her remarks reveal the anxiety that many felt at the prospect of women entering the workforce: "When John wanted his mother, she was not there. He felt that he was not important to her and their relationship was broken."[43] Instead of blaming the absent mother for her son's turn to delinquency, McKenzie asserted that this situation could have been avoided. Reflecting the position of many CCF members, McKenzie argued that, in the form of adequate housing, supplementary economic assistance, adequate nursery schools/kindergarten programs, and family counselling, the state should provide more support for working families. She believed that the growth of the welfare state would lead to the decline of youth delinquency, concluding: "We must build a society better suited to the growth of a stable family life."[44]

McKenzie's remarks tell us much about CCF women's ideology. Many CCF members supported increasing state power in order to provide services for people, especially the poor and the working class. The election of social democratic governments at all levels, they argued, would result in a better society. This marked a clear difference from SCP women, who, at least rhetorically, disdained the state and advocated "smaller government." Like SCP women, however, CCF women suggested that working mothers needed to be at home to counsel their children, thus ensuring that they not turn towards delinquent pursuits. CCF members argued that it was fine for women to work outside the home – but only temporarily and only to supplement the family income. In an ideal, social democratic society, the state would provide higher wages, social insurance programs, and a more equitable taxation system, all of which would allow women to stay at home. In this, CCF women's views on working women reinforced male-breadwinner and maternalist ideologies. Those on the left of the political spectrum asserted that men needed to receive higher wages so that they could "keep" a family without having to force their wives and daughters to work outside the home.[45]

The CCF position on women's paid labour was broadly similar to that found in movements often seen as conservative. Kay McKenzie's remarks suggest both a condescending attitude towards working people and an unwarranted faith in the state to solve the problems of capitalism. In the invocation of the need for a father figure for John, her remarks also represent an implied endorsement of the nuclear family. The CCF endorsed the idea that the male breadwinner should be the sole source of economic support for families.[46]

Prominent CCF members like Laura Jamieson expressed concern about the impact of "modern times" on youth. Like both the CPC and the SCP, the CCF argued that young people needed to be transformed into useful members of society. Jamieson critiqued those who were in power and who had failed to solve the problem of delinquency. The public and voluntary sectors attempted to ameliorate the situation: school boards gave night school lectures on marriage and youth problems, while the YMCA and the YWCA held discussion groups on the topic of delinquency. Jamieson, however, argued that these "expert" remedies were inadequate "compared to what could be done by society if [the] men in authority were determined to prevent delinquency instead of always talking about it and dealing with it after it has happened."[47] She praised parents who established groups to talk about issues related to child rearing (some parents also set up cooperative playgrounds); however, the government offered no financial help to establish or maintain such groups: "No department of government, provincial or local, gives them any help; yet I believe they are doing by far the most important work that is being done anywhere to prevent delinquency and [to develop] citizens with well-adjusted emotional capacities so that they can give leadership instead of being a drag on society."[48] As we see, Jamieson was concerned with making "good citizens."

Jamieson and other CCF members had faith that expert knowledge, dispersed by medical professionals and social workers, could be used to solve youth problems – a faith that was perhaps misplaced. Mona Gleason suggests that social workers often supported the conservative idea that postwar youth turned to delinquency because of a lack of morals.[49] Further, as Christopher Dummitt convincingly argues, this expert knowledge was explicitly gendered as male.[50] Expert knowledge, reflecting Progressive Era values, was associated with efficiency, rationality, and containing risks. Society portrayed these values – efficiency, rationality, and risk management – as being exclusively "male."[51] Although they did not say so explicitly, Jamieson and others who advocated for expert advice regarding the problem of delinquency supported a male-centred approach to this issue. In this, CCF women's advocacy of expert knowledge differed from the position held by SCP women. Although SCP women would occasionally use expert advice if it happened to dovetail with their views, it was more common for them to be suspicious of experts, portraying them as elitists who had little knowledge of the real needs of the common people. CCF women, however, tended to valorize experts.

Laura Jamieson went on to speculate on the root causes of delinquency: "Society is responsible for delinquency in allowing itself to deteriorate and become corrupt."[52] Here she expresses the same critique of postwar modernity as did other women's groups. For example, Jamieson, like the Socreds, argued that social control broke down because young people no longer respected authority. Offering an argument typical of many CCF women, she continued: "We are at the end of an era, of a society based upon profit and greed for profit."[53] In a strong critique of the dominant system, Jamieson stated that it was capitalism that created delinquency: "The pity is that [youth] rebellion takes the destructive form of delinquency, instead of the constructive form of working for a new social order."[54] This statement suggests that delinquency would disappear when capitalism did, a common left-wing argument. When capitalism fell, so the argument went, all of the problems that went with a capitalist society – misogyny, racism, and delinquency among them – would cease to exist. This moral critique of modern capitalism was a crucial element of CCF ideology. Unlike the SCP, which also critiqued modernity and the lack of authority in postwar society, the CCF did not want to return to older values but, rather, to move towards more state governance and state-run programs in order to combat delinquency and poverty. In this sense, the CCF's approach to delinquency was typically modern, with all of the positive and negative connotations that this entails. For those on the left, the growth of the state meant welfare programs to help the disadvantaged; for those on the right, the growth of the state meant coercive government measures to control the marginalized.

The CCF, with its optimistic belief in evolutionary change, saw youth delinquency as a problem that could be solved through gradualist means. Laura Jamieson's ideas on delinquency provide a capsule version of the social democratic viewpoint. Jamieson had a particular interest in juvenile crime because of her background in law. At a public meeting in 1952, she presented her ideas on the problems of youth. "Parents and the family provide the foundation of character in children," she noted.[55] "Unless children have parents with both the desire and knowledge to train them properly, modern conditions, imposed by society, make it very difficult for children to escape delinquency."[56] To that end, teachers, social workers, and probation officers were important to a child's development.

However, Jamieson argued that parents bore the ultimate responsibility for raising children. She said that any two people could become parents, yet that many parents were "ignorant of the first principles of child-guidance, and [that] many of their children [became] delinquents."[57] After setting the stage, Jamieson turned to the heart of her talk: What was to be done about the problem of juvenile delinquency? Involving a psychiatrist was often too little, too late since the child's character had been formed before she/he went to school. Therefore, CCF women supported expert intervention as part of the solution to youth problems. Professionals like social workers and teachers could make their therapeutic skills available to young people, and this would assist in getting youth on the correct path. Many CCF women had backgrounds in social work, and, as James Struthers shows, women constituted a majority of social workers in Canada from the 1920s onward.[58] Women played a role, then, in the shaping of expert knowledge, even as many (though not all) female social workers endorsed a male-centred perspective on delinquency.[59] Most CCF women certainly did so.

The social democratic concern with gradually improving humanity through state action and expert intervention extended to helping delinquent girls. In a BC CCF Women's Council column, Laura Jamieson and other CCF women critiqued Socred MLA Buda Brown, a cabinet minister who had spoken out against the "glamourous surroundings" in the new Girls' Industrial School.[60] Dorothy Shepherd, secretary of the provincial CCF Women's Council, wrote Brown to say that "pleasant" surroundings were necessary to the rehabilitation of delinquent girls. In a newspaper interview, Jamieson, then president of the council, argued that beautiful surroundings were "quite necessary." She indicated that this beauty had to be coupled with "enlightened treatment" if the girls were to be returned to society as "useful citizens."[61] No doubt Jamieson and other social democrats genuinely wanted to help young women who came into conflict with the law. Unfortunately, reformers' attempts to help others were not always either useful or successful. As Joan Sangster argues, many industrial schools, or "training schools" as they were sometimes called, were abusive, racist, and misogynistic institutions that denied girls' sexuality, mistreated young (often First Nations) women, and rendered girls worse off than they had been before they were admitted. The reformers' view that these young women had to be changed into "useful citizens" spoke to the condescending attitude that white, middle-class people displayed towards girls from poorer, often non-white backgrounds.[62]

Thus, it was almost exclusively members of the elitist faction of the CCF, like Laura Jamieson, who spoke out against delinquency. In their support for "top-down," state-centred solutions, and in their dismissal of young women's agency, CCF women approached youth problems from an elitist standpoint. The use of male-centred social work perspectives also contributed to the elitist focus of CCF women's writings on delinquency. Given their suspicions of top-down approaches, and their strong support for working people's agency, more populist CCF members (like Evelyn Smith and Dorothy Gretchen Steeves) did not speak out on the issue of delinquency.

The discourse of delinquency meant something different to SCP women than it did to CCF women. It was primarily populist, traditionalist SCP women who argued for solutions to delinquency. Women like Ethel Wilson held that turning away from modern capitalism and state-centred approaches to improving society was the best way to get rid of delinquency. A return to older values – values that pre-existed the modern state – would offer an antidote to the problems of modernity. While CCF women also saw delinquency as a problem stemming from capitalist modernity, their solution was typically "progressive" and modern. They insisted that, in order to stamp out delinquent pursuits, the state needed to take an even stronger role in society. In effect, the CCF called for an increase in modernity in order to deal with the problems engendered by capitalist society, while the SCP argued for a retreat from modernity. Therefore, while left- and right-wing women both expressed extreme concern about the problem of juvenile delinquency, they saw different causes of, and solutions to, the problem.

CPC women also criticized capitalism and modernity in their comments on delinquency. Like CCF women, CPC women linked youth problems with poor housing conditions and urban poverty; they argued that housing in some Canadian cities was "not fit for animals."[63] In particular, members of the communist-led "5000 Homes Now" committee had a special interest in juvenile delinquency and housing. Prominent CPC supporters John Stanton and Harold Pritchett were members of this committee,[64] as were a number of party women. In a pamphlet written shortly after the end of Second World War, when housing for returning veterans was becoming a concern, the committee discussed the gendered aspects of housing and its link to delinquency. "A mother and her four small sons are living in a two-room attic," notes the pamphlet.[65] "Not long ago there was a murder in the house. The mother has collapsed as a result of worry and anxiety about her boys whom she is trying to bring up as good citizens of Vancouver."[66] Appended to this statement was an item written by the Vancouver Council of Social Agencies: "Juvenile delinquency is a rather loosely-used phrase which suggests crimes, misdemeanors and immoral conduct by boys and girls under the age of eighteen."[67] According to the council, poor housing conditions, which made normal life impossible for thousands of families, numbered among the key causes of delinquency. The CPC concluded: "Bad housing also undermines the family's sense of pride and decency leading to a general lowering of standards."[68]

Implicit in the "5000 Homes Now" statement is a moral critique of absent fathers. This was a class issue for the CPC, which connected youth delinquency with working-class men's inability to make a living. As with the CCF, the CPC used these ideas in order to critique capitalism on moral and material grounds. Left movements had done this before. Socialists from earlier decades of the twentieth century argued that women would become like prostitutes if they were "forced" to work outside the home. Powerful capitalists would exploit these women for their labour power and pay them substantially lower wages than they would male workers, thus undermining union claims for higher wages. The existence of working women was the fault of an immoral, acquisitive society that did not value human needs. While they criticized capitalists, leftist men articulated a vision of working-class masculinity that subordinated women.[69] For Canadian communists, this opposition to women's paid work was paradoxical, especially given the CPC's admiration for the Soviet Union. In the Soviet Union, and in other Eastern European communist nations, many women were engaged in paid labour outside the home.[70]

Like their counterparts in the SCP, CPC women were especially concerned about the influence of new forms of media, notably comic books, on young people. CPC women's discourse on this issue brought together elements of the views of both CCF and SCP women. Like CCF women, communist women alleged that the rise of delinquency had economic roots. And, like SCP supporters, communist women held that post-Second World War life corrupted young people. CPC members often agreed with expert writings and statements concerning delinquency. Auxiliary members of CPC-led trade unions used ideas surrounding delinquency to decry the corruption of children during the 1950s. A resolution passed at the 1955 convention of the Mine-Mill auxiliaries states: "It is generally admitted that indecent literature, such as crime, horror, sex, and war comics, is very harmful to the character education of the children who read them."[71] This kind of material was within easy reach of children. The convention resolved to take a firm stand in urging "both the federal and provincial governments to enforce legislation that [was then] on the statute books, aimed at removing indecent literature from the newsstands, by making the distribution of same a severely punishable offence." Like conservatives, communist women proposed to censor material that they deemed harmful to young people. As may be seen, people at various points of the political spectrum all suggested that postwar media had a negative impact on youth.[72]

Nonetheless, the CPC proposed different causes of delinquency than did the right. The language of delinquency made its way into the CPC press, where it was used to further buttress anti-capitalist arguments. Betty Griffin, for example, presented a strong critique of American media. In many ways, communists held rather mainstream attitudes towards sex and sexuality,[73] associating capitalism with sex perversion and debauchery. CPC women suggested that lewd movies and comics preyed upon impressionable working-class youth, the future leaders of a socialist society. Griffin even suggested that comic books should be banned in Canada, quoting Dr. Frederick Wertham's work approvingly. Wertham, author of the tract *The Seduction of the Innocent* and a strong anti-communist, critiqued modern media as undermining the moral values of American youth.[74] As part of his research, Wertham interviewed a twenty-year-old man who had killed someone during a robbery. Griffin and Wertham attributed the young man's mental state to his "being conditioned to violence by a steady diet of comic books."[75] It was not unusual for left-wing women to use ideas endorsed by conservative experts like Wertham.

The CPC's use of the delinquency issue was meant to be part of a larger critique of capitalism; however, the party largely failed to challenge elite, expert views of young people. Indeed, CPC men and women alike embraced traditional gender roles, including the male-breadwinner ideal, and railed against the capitalist system for failing to set the conditions that would allow that ideal to flourish. This may be connected to the maternalist focus of CPC women: to the belief that capitalism damaged women's and children's lives. Given this, it is not surprising that the CPC argued that left-wing women should organize to protect the family and home. Like their counterparts in the SCP, CPC women argued that women should rule the home and, by extension, children and youth, ensuring that they not be led astray by crime comics and other forms of negative media.

CPC writers' attitudes towards juvenile delinquency were explicitly linked to an anti-American perspective. Hostility towards American culture, which represented the "highest stage" of modern capitalism, was a significant impetus to the CPC's support for Canadian nationalism in the postwar period. This represents a clear difference between Canadian communists and their SCP and CCF counterparts. The CCF leadership focused only lightly on the issue of Canadian nationalism during this period, whereas SCP members openly supported the United States in its battle with the Soviet Union. SCP women's anti-war perspective, as well as their opposition to delinquency, was based on a general suspicion of modernity and capitalism, but the SCP did not link modernity specifically to the United States. The same was generally true of the CCF. Many CCF women disdained capitalism, viewing it as a predatory and unjust system. Yet, at least during the late 1940s and 1950s, the CCF did not portray capitalism as being a manifestation of specifically American cultural values.[76]

For the CPC, the situation was different. CPC women and men endorsed an anti-American perspective and connected this to their campaign against salacious literature. In one particular case, CPC member Mark Frank quoted a number of Canadian church and cultural leaders who had stated that the business of producing "smut" and "filth" resulted from a "spill-over from powerful US muck-raking concerns that [made] millions by skirting the law." They continued: "This is one form of American cultural imperialism that should be stopped at the border."[77] Communists asserted that American-produced sex and crime literature corrupted Canadian youth. Later, Frank made explicit the link between American capitalism and pornography. He quoted "Mrs. George Davis," a member of the Catholic Women's League and a strong anti-communist, as expressing support for the idea that communism and pornography were linked. Frank took issue with this notion, arguing, to the contrary, that the increase in the number of films and printed materials that emphasized sex and violence was a result of the "capitalist program and the inner crisis of a system, which [was] driving to nuclear war."[78] For CPC supporters, this state of affairs was directly linked to the United States: "It finds its most advanced representative in the United States of America and its most acute expression in the mass of poisonous ideology spread by its printing plants, its movies and its TV industry."[79]

Frank quoted Paul Neimark, an editor for *The Men's Digest*, a "pornographic best-seller," as saying that sex and socialism "don't mix." "Sex is for your own pleasure," Neimark argued, while "socialism is being made to sacrifice your happiness for other people's pleasures. Capitalism-sex is the only logical duet. Both pivot on the happiness and freedom of the individual man."[80] The CPC tried to present itself as a party of sobriety and respectability that stood in opposition to a Western, especially American, form of capitalism that fostered licentiousness, violence, racism, and hostility towards unions and socialism. Like CPC women's views on crime comics, this shows the CPC's conservative attitude towards sex and sexuality.[81] Conversely, capitalists like *Playboy* publisher Hugh Hefner linked their ideology of sexual freedom and material gain to the fight against communism, which they saw as limiting human freedom and individualism.

The idea that Western capitalism and the free market led automatically to political and civil liberties played a significant role in American anti-communism during the Cold War, and it found its expression in Canada as well. Many Canadian leftists attacked the United States because of its racism, imperialist foreign policy, and supposed decadence. This was also connected to the fact that many, though not all, CPC members disliked both the "Beatnik" movement of the 1950s and the New Left of the 1960s. Some in the Old Left of the CPC saw these movements as frivolous and middle class and as unwilling to deal with the real issues resulting from capitalism. For these reasons, the CPC opposed "bohemian sex radicalism," which it associated with capitalism and "bourgeois" pleasures.[82]

Anti-Americanism was thus a key part of the left's attack on post-Second World War media. The CCF and, especially, the CPC critiqued the hedonism of the 1950s, with its rise of affluence and its influence on men who turned away from the male-breadwinner ideal and towards self-gratification and narcissism.[83] Leftists associated postwar affluence – and the rising culture of selfishness among white, middle-class men – with American culture.[84] The infiltration of American culture into Canada engendered a new conception of masculinity, one that contrasted with the older view of a man's role in society, primarily as breadwinner and as shouldering the responsibility to care for his family.[85] Both CPC and CCF women's groups opposed this new culture of masculinity, seeing it as indicative of the crassness of modern consumerist society.[86]

As has been noted, CPC women were populists in that they fought for more rights for working people and for a more humane standard of living for all. Yet there was an authoritarian side to many in the CPC – even if it was not as prevalent as anti-communist historians in the United States and elsewhere have claimed[87] – and this is reflected in its views on delinquency. Many CPC women and men focused on delinquency as a way of arguing for a return to conventional gender roles and against licentiousness and bohemian sex radicalism. This could be seen as both populist (in that many sectors of society endorsed conservative gender values) and reactionary (in that it imposed conservative gender values on women both inside and outside the CPC). Certainly, CPC stances on these issues were inconsistent: the CPC's populist stance on workers' rights did not extend to its stance on gender. Here we see the maternalist focus of CPC women: they wanted to reinstitute the traditional nuclear family, which they saw as better than acquiescing to capitalism's destruction of the family.

The discourse of juvenile delinquency was an integral part of the overall ideologies of the CPC, the CCF, and the SCP, and it was key to their attempts to inaugurate a new societal order. SCP, CCF, and CPC women all expressed concern about a lack of morality among young people. The uncertainty of the Cold War era led to a moral panic over youth delinquency. This panic had a gendered aspect as people in all sectors of society, and on various points of the political spectrum, argued that women's paid work meant an end to traditional familial roles. This said, women in the three parties proposed different remedies for the problem of youth delinquency. SCP members saw it as their mission to bring society back to the family and church and to move it away from secularism, communism, and urbanity. Left-wing women saw things differently.

Like SCP women, CCF women portrayed the postwar world as increasingly immoral due to capitalism's encouragement of individualism and its accompanying lack of respect for one's fellow citizens. CCF members saw the evolution of socio-economic change as the way to end immorality. They presented an ethical critique of capitalism and argued that the state needed to intervene much more in public life in order to provide social services that would end delinquency. The CPC used conservative rhetoric to argue that delinquency resulted from the immorality of the capitalist state. It sometimes stated that the world needed a socialist revolution, modelled on that of the Soviet Union, before youth could be rescued. By the 1950s, however, the CPC had, in practice, moved away from advocating revolution. Indeed, CPC members, much like CCF supporters, suggested that the state could be used to foster recreation programs, public parks, and peace initiatives targeting working-class and unemployed youth.[88]

In their differing ways, CPC, CCF, and SCP women used the perceived problem of delinquency to forward the political goals of their respective parties. The issue of delinquency was one about which these women were particularly concerned: the men in these parties did not focus on this issue nearly so much as did the women. This reflected a general maternalist focus: both women and men asserted that women's concern with the problems of youth and children was an extension of their roles as mothers and nurturers.

This discourse of juvenile delinquency permeated all sectors of Canadian society: it was not only an elite preoccupation. Experts in the medical and therapeutic professions expressed concern about the problems of youth but so, too, did grassroots political women on different ends of the political spectrum. Concerns about delinquency crossed ideological and class lines. The SCP portrayed modern Canadian society as corrupt and debased, as did many on the left. Some CPC members even argued that since capitalism marketed everything it also marketed popular culture, commercializing it to the point at which "real," or "high," culture was debased.[89] The CPC criticized comic books, rock-and-roll, and what it saw as the general drift towards hedonism that characterized post-Second World War society. CCF women presented similar arguments, even as they suggested that delinquency could be reduced through expert advice and gradualist welfare state intervention.

All three of these groups presented "healthy activity and worthwhile ideas" as solutions to the problem of delinquency. Above all, they suggested that changing young people into better citizens was a worthwhile enterprise. As the statement on inculcating "healthy activities and worthwhile ideas" suggests, CPC, CCF, and SCP women held that changing human character, whether in reactionary or evolutionary (state-centred) ways, was possible. Thus, right- and left-wing women alike were "social engineers" when it came to inculcating their particular visions of the New World Order.

Conclusion

In this book, I discuss women's roles in the Communist Party of Canada, the Co-operative Commonwealth Federation, and the Social Credit Party as well as the role that women's activism and ideology played in shaping these parties' respective viewpoints. Women of both the left and the right attempted to take "their proper and rightful place" as members of the CPC, the CCF, and SCP in the battle for the New World Order.[1] This idea – that women had a "proper and rightful place" – fits in nicely with the key issues discussed in this book. Maternalism was a key element of women's political ideology: it spurred women's activism outside the home, on both the left and the right. We have seen that women, whatever their ideological background, did not view the home and family as negative or constricting; rather, they wished to remake the public sphere of politics, economics, and foreign relations in the image of the home. In this way, politically active women sought to break down barriers between the public sphere and the private sphere. For these women, gender and support for maternalism crossed ideological and, to some extent, class lines.

Even if unknowingly, these women from different political parties shared some of the same views, particularly regarding women's roles in society. In both the CCF and the SCP there were divisions between "elitist" women, who favoured centralized power and state intervention, and "populist" women, who favoured decentralization, local control, and anti-war positions. I focus on populist women because, in all three parties, they fought more explicitly for a stronger women's voice than did elitist women. In different ways, populist CCF and SCP women, as well as all CPC women, were critical of modern capitalism's hold on society.

There are a number of other, secondary, themes that emerge in connection with political women's lives. As I show in Chapters 1 and 2, class, ethnicity, and family played substantial roles in shaping women's political choices. CPC women came from working-class families who had often emigrated from Britain, Scandinavia, or Eastern Europe. These families often had a history of involvement in left-wing causes. CCF women came from a wider variety of backgrounds: many were from immigrant, working-class families from Britain and Continental Europe, but others came from wealthier, educated backgrounds. This was particularly true for those women who took on leadership positions in the CCF. Many in this group, like Grace MacInnis and Laura Jamieson, advocated for bureaucratic, statist solutions to society's problems. SCP women also came from a mixture of backgrounds: many were from working-class, or what could be termed "rural poor," families, but others – again, many who took on higher positions within the SCP would fit this category – came from middle-class, rural and urban, families. SCP women were virtually all from Protestant families who had been in North America for several generations. This class, ethnic, and familial background explains why these women sought somewhat different solutions to social problems than did their left-wing counterparts, even though they shared a maternalist viewpoint. For example, all three groups of women saw war and delinquency as moral issues. Yet CPC and CCF women sought class-based, statist, and social democratic solutions to these issues – in particular, a strengthening of the welfare state – while SCP women sought a return to traditional Christian values in order to solve modern problems.

Thus, religion was also a factor, if a minor one, in shaping women's consciousness. For SCP women, in particular, evangelicalism led them to political activism outside the home. "Traditionalist" evangelical SCP women were the backbone of the populist wing of the SCP. Indeed, when discussing SCP women, I use the terms "traditionalist" and "populist" interchangeably. Populist SCP women's views came into conflict with those of pro-business, pro-statist, elitist SCP women and men, and it was the pro-business side that ultimately prevailed. In effect, populist SCP women combined libertarian and traditionalist schools of conservative thought.[2] Rhetorically, they disdained the centralizing state, even though, in practice, SCP governments simply used the state in different ways than did Liberal, Conservative, or CCF provincial governments. Still, populist SCP women did endorse a libertarian perspective as well as the traditionalist perspective in supporting a return to the church and the family. Some CCF women, like Mildred Fahrni, subscribed to the social gospel tradition within the party, which emphasized Protestant social reform as part of the answer to society's problems. By the post-Second World War period, however, this faction within the CCF had become a minority. CPC women were almost exclusively non-religious, which is not surprising, given the Soviet Union's official disdain for religion.

The idea of place is also important in explaining women's political activism. The particular locations from which these women came played significant roles in shaping their ideologies. The strength of unions and working-class solidarities in northern British Columbia, the Kootenays, and Vancouver Island, as well as the urban experiences of Vancouver and Victoria, helped to shape the views of left-wing women in the CPC and the CCF. It is significant that more elitist, technocratic women, like Laura Jamieson and Grace MacInnis, spent the majority of their adult lives in Vancouver, where reformist discourses (borrowed from the Progressive Era) flourished. Populist women in the SCP and the CCF tended to come from rural and more isolated areas of the West: CCF supporter Evelyn Smith, for example, spent much of her time in the Kamloops area of British Columbia. Populist left-wing women like Effie Jones and Mona Morgan could be found in Vancouver, but this is not surprising as CPC women's views were associated with "rough" working-class areas like the East Side, where communism, socialism, and trade unionism flourished. Place was also of key concern for SCP women. They came from rural and small-town communities like Lethbridge, Medicine Hat, Drumheller, and Stony Plain, where their farming and evangelical backgrounds took shape. Place was tied up in whichever resources and industries – mining and forestry or farming and agriculture – were most featured. Mining and forestry produced a more leftist culture, while agriculture led to a more rightist culture.

Region was also important. For example, SCP women felt a strong disdain towards Ottawa and Toronto, certainly, but many also disliked Edmonton and Calgary (albeit to a lesser extent). It is significant that the elitist, pro-business wing of the SCP, and later the Alberta Progressive Conservative Party, had its base in the cities of Edmonton and Calgary, not in the rural areas of southern and northern Alberta. Populist women in all three parties came from places that led them to support anti-capitalist and anti-war positions. Western Canadian women in the CPC, the CCF, and the SCP disdained war-mongering elitists in the Liberal and Tory parties, which were based in Toronto, Ottawa, and Montreal.

Westerners argued that these elites had little knowledge of, or concern for, issues that were important to rural, small-town, and western Canadian people. It was believed that rootless and centralist elites had little interest in the lives of ordinary people, especially those in the outlying regions. This rootlessness made elites more willing to start wars and to promote capitalist and centralist policies that took no regard of the feelings of those based on the periphery of Canadian politics. Populist women's concerns were embedded in the communities, and region, from whence they originated. They fought for "politics on a human scale." This was the case for populist women in all three parties, and this differentiated their views from those of political women and men in Ontario and Quebec, as well as from more elitist women and men in their own parties.[3]

The political ideas discussed in this book must be contextualized within the period under consideration – 1945 to 1961. Many scholars argue that the late 1940s and, especially, the 1950s was a time of conservatism with regard to gender roles; in the United States, the fear that communism would spread led key figures in government, business, and the church to support the "containment" of women in the home. Westerners needed to be morally and sexually pure or they would be easy prey for a communist takeover. This led to the repression of gay men and lesbians and an attempt to contain women's sexuality within the nuclear, heterosexual family.[4] The fear that youth were becoming delinquents was also part of the general atmosphere of fear and conformity.[5] Historians argue that Canada followed the US model in this regard: Canadians blindly accepted the dictates of the Cold War, and the 1950s was a period of conservatism and control.[6] My findings would modify this position on the Canadian situation. The presence of right- and left-wing women in the CPC, the CCF, and the SCP; on women's councils and auxiliaries; and in the campaigns against war and delinquency suggests that not all women were confined within the household.

There was considerable political activism among women between 1945 and 1960. This contradicts previous historians, who assume a dearth of women's and feminist activity during the period from 1920 to 1960.[7] In fact, women's activism during the 1940s and 1950s laid the groundwork for the rise of second-wave feminism. Recent historical research by scholars like Tarah Brookfield and Benjamin Isitt shows that there were many ties between the Old Left of the 1930s and 1940s and the New Left of the 1960s and 1970s. In certain cases, some of the same people – men and women – continued their activism throughout the decades.[8] I suggest that women activists bridged the gap between the pre-Second World

War period to the era of second-wave feminism. Left-wing and working-class women were among the leaders of the women's movement during the years between first-wave and second-wave feminism. Liberal feminist goals, most notably the right to vote and run for public office, had been largely met in the years following the First World War.[9] Causes like fighting for equal pay legislation were far less important to middle- and upper-class feminists than they were to lower-class feminists. Indeed, it was left to working-class and socialist women to push for these issues. And they did so with some success – notably British Columbia's equal pay bill, introduced by Laura Jamieson and later hijacked by the Socreds. Second-wave feminists would later pick up on issues like equal pay for equal work and anti-war activism – both of which were championed by an earlier generation of left-wing women – and make these issues their own. Women in the labour and socialist movements continued to play important roles in second-wave feminism, building on the activism of their foremothers.[10] While the overall atmosphere of 1950s Canada, although slightly less oppressive than that in the United States, was one of conformity, a small but significant group of women spoke out against the conservatism of this period.

Right-wing women's activism during earlier decades *indirectly* foreshadowed second-wave feminism, even if most SCP women disdained the latter's goals. We have seen that populist SCP women, borrowing from first-wave "maternal" feminism, argued for a larger role for women in public life. Traditionalist SCP members like Cornelia Wood suggested that women needed to come out of the private sphere in order to "clean up" a society that men had done a poor job of administering. SCP cabinet minister Ethel Wilson helped to establish a women's bureau in Alberta, which would later provide much support to Alberta's women and to the Alberta feminist movement, as well as "Hilltop House," a refuge for abused women, the first of its kind in the province. Similarly, many SCP women spoke out in favour of an increased role for women in public life. They argued for this even as they asserted that women should support conservative political ideas. In the context of the late 1940s, the 1950s, and the early 1960s – still pre-second-wave feminist days – these were fairly radical, or at least "forward-thinking," thoughts and actions, especially for women who were members of a profoundly conservative political party.

We might think of SCP women as Christian liberals who fought for women's advancement, albeit in fairly narrow ways. They were liberal in that they endorsed a vision of anti-statism and laissez-faire capitalism, much as did nineteenth-century liberals, but Christian in that their evangelical perspective led them to advocate for a return to an idealized time when the problems of the modern order did not exist. In this light, it is important to remember middle-class and conservative women like Florence Bird and Laura Sabia, who played important roles in the advent of second-wave feminism.[11] Many of the leaders of second-wave feminist groups, like the National Action Committee on the Status of Women, were middle- or upper class and fairly conservative, even if grassroots second-wave feminists tended to be working-class. We might see SCP women as precursors to more conservative feminists from the 1960s and 1970s, even if SCP women themselves would balk at this characterization.[12] If the activism of right- and left-wing women from earlier decades was not quite a "one-and-a-half wave" of feminism, it nonetheless laid the groundwork for later feminist advances.

In the end, politicians, journalists, political pundits, and scholars sometimes make too much of the divisions between the right and the left of the political spectrum. Some argue that, in the future, a left-right populist coalition of grassroots citizens' groups against big business and big government might be the way forward in the attempt to forge a new kind of participatory democracy.[13] In this book, I indicate how such a coalition might be formed and suggest the issues upon which it might focus. The focus on grassroots organizing and fighting against elitism, corporations, war, and imperialism could be the basis upon which future generations of activists form a new kind of coalition. This left-right coalition could premise its views on a political slogan such as: "true democracy, equality, and peace." A new coalition could have a separate women's group – something that I show can be useful to women's rights activists – while also including men who share a vision of greater democracy and anti-imperialism. To be sure, this kind of coalition would likely be temporary and would contain a number of different, perhaps contradictory, views; however, it is something that is worth considering as wars and corporate capitalism continue to bedevil contemporary society.[14]

It is also worth asking whether maternalism itself might play a role in a new kind of coalition, and even in a new version of feminism. The short answer is that maternalism reflects an outdated concept of women's role in society. Second-wave feminism downplayed the relationship between women and motherhood, rightly seeing this relationship as oppressive.[15] With the decline of maternalist ideology, women's activism in all three parties went into decline. The CPC was finished as an important political group by the end of the 1950s. The CCF became the New Democratic

Party in 1961, and the more mainstream focus of the NDP led it to eschew support for second-wave feminism. Women gradually came to play a larger role in the NDP, but the party itself, and particularly its male hierarchy, did little to encourage this. As for the SCP, women were playing less of a role in the party by the end of the 1960s, and this contributed to its slow decline as a political force in Alberta. After an electoral defeat in the 1972 provincial election, the SCP in British Columbia re-emerged in 1975 as the governing party, but women's roles and issues were not important factors in its new-found lease on political life, even if particular women became important BC Socreds.

Finally, it is worth asking whether or not the continued use of maternalist views would have led to a stronger women's voice in political parties and in society in general. In spite of events like the anti-nuclear Greenham Common protest in Britain during the 1980s, the answer would have to be "no."[16] The linking of women with motherhood, and the portrayal of women as being *essentially* mothers, is a relic of a bygone era. Nonetheless, in this book I show that women's separate organizing is essential to promoting women's political participation and that, with regard to particular issues, populists of the right and the left have some of the same concerns, even if they battle for different results. All three groups of political women had a vision of a new kind of social order – one that was more authentic. And all, in different ways, criticized capitalist modernity. Perhaps future political movements will bring together the left and the right in strategic, if temporary, coalitions. If this should prove to be the case, then women in the CPC, the CCF, and the SCP may well be seen as the political antecedents to these new seekers of a new world order, both in Canada and internationally.

APPENDIX

Brief Biographies

If birth names and dates of birth and death are not listed, then they could not be found in the primary sources. For women who are still living, the death date is obviously not indicated. Birth names, if available, are indicated in parentheses.

Arsens, Lydia Augusta, 1906–83. Born in Alberta but lived much of life in Victoria area. Influenced by William Aberhart to become Social Credit member. Member of Legislative Assembly for Victoria City riding from 1953 to 1956. Restaurant owner in Victoria. Supported temperance but opposed fluoridation of water. Supported "natural" foods and was opposed to war. Member of populist faction in SC.

Bianco, Viola "Vi," 1916–53. Prominent member of Communist Party of Canada. Heavily involved in trade union and anti-war activism. Ran for public office on a number of occasions

Culhane, Claire "Kayla" (Eglin), 1918–96. Born in Montreal to mixed Russian Jewish-Irish family. Prominent CPC supporter. Lived much of adult life in Vancouver. Involved in anti-war causes and (later) prison reform and particularly in activism against the Vietnam War.

Crowe, Mary "Mollie," 1903–57. Member of CPC. From family with strong tradition of trade union politics. Of Welsh background. Lived in Alberta, in Crowsnest Pass region, then in Nelson, British Columbia. Husband Jack was prominent member of Mine-Mill Union. CPC leader Tom McEwen officiated at her funeral. Typical "rank-and-file" CPC member.

Fahrni, Mildred (Osterhout), 1900–92. Member of populist wing of Co-operative Commonwealth Federation. Followed anti-war ideology. Influenced by social work ideology and views of Mahatma Gandhi. At founding convention of CCF in Regina in 1933. Teacher at Japanese internment camp in New Denver, British Columbia, during Second World War. Spoke out against Japanese internment. Disillusioned with CCF by 1945.

Fingarson, Evelyn. Prominent SCP supporter in British Columbia.

Gardner, Elspeth Campbell (Munro), 1921–2014. Daughter of left-wing parents. Mother Elsie was member of Housewives' League and Mothers' Council during 1930s. Became labour lawyer after having articled under John Stanton. Later defended Gordon Martin, a lawyer who had been disbarred because of his leftist affiliations. Supported leftist causes for entire life.

Godfrey, Lilian ("Lil"). Prominent member of CPC and especially of the Women's Auxiliary to the IWA at Lake Cowichan, British Columbia, during 1940s.

Gresty, Florence. Prominent member of SCP women's auxiliaries in British Columbia during 1945–60 period. Served as auxiliary president in early 1950s.

Griffin, Betty (Dunbar), 1923–. CPC member. Worked at Boeing in Vancouver during Second World War. This played key role in her introduction to CPC. Attended future husband Harold (Hal) Griffin's classes on Marxist theory during war. Wrote for Women's Page of CPC newspaper for many years. Strong participant in fight against juvenile delinquency, seeing it as a manifestation of the Americanization of Canadian culture. Has remained supporter of leftist causes for whole life.

Hattersley, Ethel Vera. Prominent SCP supporter and writer. Frequent contributor to *Canadian Social Crediter*. Married to SCP economist Marshall Hattersley. Vera was a strong supporter of Douglasite economics and anti-war views. Member of populist faction in SCP.

Hilland, Gladys (Shunaman), 1915–2003. Born in Saskatchewan but lived most of adult life in British Columbia. Involved with Farmers' Unity League during 1930s. Worked at Sitka Spruce during Second World War. Became IWA member during Second World War and functioned as secretary-treasurer of IWA Local 217. Involved in 1946 strike of BC woodworkers. Was blacklisted, along with many others, in 1948 ousting of CPC members from unions. Later involved in peace movement and operated private hospital for senior citizens.

Jamieson, Laura Emma (Marshall), 1882–1964. Member of elitist wing of CCF. Born in rural Ontario but lived most of adult life in

Vancouver. Worked as teacher, secretary, then social worker before moving to British Columbia. Influenced by maternal feminist ideology and fought for suffrage rights. MLA for CCF from 1939 to 1945 and again from 1952 to 1953. Later a city councillor in Vancouver. Fought for better conditions for "delinquent" girls. Advocated for stronger welfare state and bureaucracy to improve society.

Jones, Effie, 1890–1985. Born in England but raised in Wales. Parents were both school principals. Converted to leftist politics at an early age, identifying with a group of Welsh miners. Came to Canada in 1919 and spent most of adult life in Vancouver. Initially joined CCF and was member of Housewives' League. Supported tenants being evicted from homes in 1930s and supported 1938 sit-down strike at Vancouver Post Office. Ran for mayor of Vancouver in 1947 and for city council in Vancouver on a number of later occasions. Never won election. Was leading figure in anti-war campaigns and Housewives Consumers Association during 1950s. Supported CPC for entire life.

Kerr, Elizabeth. Well known CCF member. Prominent in CCF women's councils and in organizing anti-war protests.

Landeryou, Ruth (Gemmill), 1915–2001. Prominent SCP member. President of Social Credit Women's Auxiliary from 1966 to 1968. Husband was SCP MP John Landeryou. Born in Saskatchewan but spent most of adult life in Lethbridge, Alberta. Worked at Hudson's Bay Company for twenty-sic years. Member of Rebekah Lodge and many other community organizations. Supported elitist, pro-business faction in SCP.

MacInnis, Grace Winona (Woodsworth), 1905–1991. Daughter of J.S. and Lucy Woodsworth, founding members of CCF. Born in Winnipeg, moved with family to British Columbia at young age. Attended Sorbonne in Paris. Later a secretary for her father in Ottawa. Married Angus MacInnis in 1932. Voted to support Canada's entry into Second World War. This marked a divide between her and other, more populist members of CCF like Dorothy Steeves. Supported NATO and Cold War anti-communism. Federal Member of Parliament for Vancouver-Kingsway from 1965 to 1974. Member of elitist faction of CCF.

MacLeod, Mildred. Prominent CCF member. Organized anti-war speeches and activities. Husband Alistair (1904–82) was also CCF member and well known activist in West Kootenay CCF.

Manning, Muriel Aileen (Preston), 1911–2006. Born in Saskatchewan and educated at a convent. Became pianist for William Aberhart's Prophetic Bible Institute. Married to Ernest Manning, later Alberta's premier, in 1936. Supported her husband in his political career. At times, expressed populist anti-war views, but most often played a behind-the-scenes role in Alberta politics. Her husband, as a pro-big business premier, was the leading light of elitist SCP supporters.

McKenzie, Kay. Prominent CCF member. Fought against juvenile delinquency and was frequent contributor to the *CCF News* during the 1950s. Her pro-statist views are indicative of the elitist wing of the CCF.

Morgan, Mona (Bjarnason), 1913–2004. Of Icelandic origin. Born in Wynard, Saskatchewan. Family moved to Vancouver in 1934. Married to Nigel Morgan, president of International Woodworkers of America. Played key role in 1946 strike of BC lumber workers. Hosted radio program that presented working-class issues from a woman's perspective. Helped to organized and lead Trek to Victoria in 1946 to support strikers. Later played significant role in anti-war activism in 1950s. One of the most prominent CPC women.

Robinson, Elizabeth Gladys, 1899–1960. SCP MLA in Medicine Hat from 1953 to 1960. Took husband John Lyle Robinson's former seat after he died suddenly in office. Supported women having increased role in public life and politics. She won election on three separate occasions – 1953, 1955, and 1959 – with large majorities. Like her husband, died suddenly, of an undisclosed illness, while in office. Had a foot in both populist and elitist camps of SCP.

Rogers, Edith Blanche (Cox), 1894–1985. Born in Nova Scotia but lived most of her life in Alberta. She and husband became friends with William Aberhart. Worked on federal Progressive Conservative Party campaign in 1930 but joined Social Credit in 1933. Was one of earliest organizers of SCP in northern Alberta. MLA for Ponoka, Alberta, from 1935 to 1940. Had libertarian, anti-banking perspective. Left SCP after Aberhart's death and rightward swing of party. Joined CCF shortly thereafter. Was school board trustee in Edmonton from 1959 to 1974. Member of populist wing of SCP.

Rolston, Tilly Jean (Cameron), 1887–1953. Prominent SCP MLA in British Columbia. Member of Vancouver Parks Board from 1938 to 1947 for Non-Partisan Association and MLA in Point Grey from 1941 to 1952 for Liberal-Conservative coalition then SC. Joined SCP in 1952 to support W.A.C. Bennett. Supported increased wages for women workers but also valorized women's roles in the home. Supported big business but also saw herself as an outsider in politics and disliked party lines and rigid discipline. Had a foot in both populist and elitist camps of SCP.

Smith, Evelyn (Grey), 1904–88. Daughter of socialist farmer. Trained at infant's hospital during First World War. While recovering from tuberculosis at Tranquille, British Columbia, met CCF members and converted to socialist ideology. Opposed Canada's entry into Second World War. Expelled from CCF in 1950. Became member of Socialist Fellowship and later joined Socialist Party of Canada. Supported animal welfare and was member of the Voice of Women. Opposed fluoridation of Vancouver's water supply and was sympathetic to New Left ideas. Member of populist wing in CCF.

Smith, Marion. Prominent populist SCP member. President of Social Credit Women's Auxiliaries in early 1960s. Supported increased role for women in public life. Supported maternalist ideology.

Steeves, Dorothy Gretchen (Biersteker), 1891–1974. Born and educated in the Netherlands. Met husband in 1917, married in The Hague and moved to Canada in 1919. Attended founding CCF convention in Regina in 1933. MLA in North Vancouver from 1934 to 1945. Supported credit union movement in British Columbia, opposed capital punishment and cruelty to animals. Strongly anti-war and opposed those in CCF who supported Canada's entry into Second World War. Helped to establish Socialist Fellowship in 1951. Member of populist faction of CCF.

Wilkinson, Rosamond "Rose," 1885–1968. Prominent SCP member and MLA. Born in Stamford, Lincolnshire, England. One of the few Roman Catholic SCP members. MLA in Calgary, later the Calgary North riding, from 1944 to 1963. Worked as a nurse prior to this. Influenced by William Aberhart to become SCP member. Supported women's advancement in public life but also argued that motherhood was a woman's most important role. Anti-statist and a strong supporter of C.H. Douglas's economic views. Member of populist wing of SCP.

Wilson, Ethel Sylvia (Knight), 1902–83. Born in Sunnyside, Alberta. Lived most of adult life in Edmonton. Husband Dave Wilson died in 1935 after ten years of marriage. Worked as a seamstress and for a packing firm in Edmonton. Was secretary-treasurer of Edmonton Labour Council. Was city councillor in Edmonton from 1952 to 1966 and MLA for Edmonton North from 1959 to 1971. Was cabinet minister from 1962 to 1971. Established Hilltop House, first women's shelter in Alberta, in 1962 and Alberta Women's Bureau in 1966. Defeated in 1971 provincial election when old riding was redistributed. Her Pentecostal faith played a strong role in her public life. Had a foot in both populist and elitist wings of SCP.

Wood, Cornelia Lucinda (Railey), 1892–1985. Member of populist, evangelical wing of SCP. First elected as MLA in Stony Plain, Alberta, in

1940 and stayed in this position until 1967, excepting the years from 1955 to 1958. Ran as independent in 1967 provincial election. Later mayor of the town of Stony Plain. Held anti-war, anti-banking views. Supported increased role for women in public life. She also opposed the fluoridation of water.

Notes

Introduction

1 This is not to suggest that there were not elites, or capitalists and businesspeople, in western Canada, but the majority of Canada's population and, consequently, of political and economic power, was still in central Canada. Confederation in 1867 had been designed to benefit the business class of Toronto and Montreal and to disadvantage farmers and workers in the West and elsewhere. Even in 1945, western workers and farmers were disproportionately, and negatively, influenced by Confederation and the National Policy of 1878–79. See Gerald Friesen, "Critical History in Western Canada, 1900–2000," in *The West and Beyond: New Perspectives on an Imagined Region,* ed. Alvin Finkel, Sarah Carter, and Peter Fortna, 3–9 (Edmonton: Athabasca University Press, 2010); R.T. Naylor, "The Rise and Fall of the Third Commercial Empire of the St. Lawrence," in *Capitalism and the National Question in Canada,* ed. Gary Teeple, 21–22 (Toronto: University of Toronto Press, 1972).

2 Wood (1892–1985) was a key female Social Credit activist in Alberta; she was arguably the best known woman in the SCP during the period that this study engages with. She is discussed in more detail in Chapter 2. The quotation is from the Provincial Archives of Alberta, Cornelia Wood Fonds, box 4, speech by Cornelia Wood, "Some Fact Bombs," presented to an annual Social Credit convention, n.d. Given the references to the Cold War, the Soviet Union, and totalitarianism, I suggest that the document was written during the 1950s, when anti-Soviet propaganda was at its height.

3 On the Cold War, see Ellen Schrecker, *Many Are the Crimes: McCarthyism in America* (Boston: Little, Brown, and Co., 1998); Reg Whitaker and Gary Marcuse, *Cold War Canada: The Making of a National Insecurity State, 1945–1957* (Toronto: University of Toronto Press, 1994), 3–24.

4 See, most notably, Tarah Brookfield, *Cold War Comforts: Canadian Women, Child Safety, and Global Insecurity, 1945–1975* (Waterloo, ON: Wilfrid Laurier University

Press, 2012); Joan Sangster, *Transforming Labour: Women and Work in Post-War Canada* (Toronto: University of Toronto Press, 2010).

5 The two key texts on left-wing women are Linda Kealey, *Enlisting Women for the Cause: Women, Labour, and the Left in Canada, 1890–1920* (Toronto: University of Toronto Press, 1998); Joan Sangster, *Dreams of Equality: Women on the Canadian Left, 1920–1950* (Toronto: McClelland and Stewart, 1989).

6 Elaine Tyler May, *Homeward Bound: American Families in the Cold War Era*, rev. ed. (New York: Basic Books, 1999) discusses the conservative gender ideal in American popular culture. For works that discuss the complexity of the period in both Canada and the United States, see Joy Parr, ed., *A Diversity of Women: Ontario, 1945–1980* (Toronto: University of Toronto Press, 1995); Veronica Strong-Boag, "Home Dreams: Women and the Suburban Experiment in Canada, 1945–60," in *Rethinking Canada: The Promise of Women's History*, 4th ed., ed. Veronica Strong-Boag, Mona Gleason, and Adele Perry, 313–44 (Toronto: Oxford University Press, 2002); Winifred Breines, *Young, White, and Miserable: Growing Up Female in the Fifties* (Boston: Beacon Press, 1992); Susan Lynn, *Progressive Women in Conservative Times: Racial Justice, Peace, and Feminism, 1945 to the 1960s* (New Brunswick, NJ: Rutgers University Press, 1992); Joanne Meyerowitz, ed., *Not June Cleaver: Women and Gender in Postwar America, 1945–1960* (Philadelphia: Temple University Press, 1994); Leila Rupp and Verta Taylor, *Survival in the Doldrums: The American Women's Rights Movement, 1945 to the 1960s* (New York: Oxford University Press, 1987). There are also a number of texts that discuss women in the particular context of western Canada. See especially Sarah Carter, Lesley Erickson, Patricia Roome, and Char Smith, eds., *Unsettled Pasts: Reconceiving the West through Women's History* (Calgary: University of Calgary Press, 2005) and Lindsey McMaster, *Working Girls in the West: Representations of Wage-Earning Women* (Vancouver: UBC Press, 2008).

7 Many texts could be cited here. See, in particular, Peter Campbell, *Rose Henderson: A Woman for the People* (Montreal and Kingston: McGill-Queen's University Press, 2010); The Clio Collective, *Quebec Women: A History* (Toronto: The Women's Press, 1987).

8 Brookfield, *Cold War Comforts*, 166–88; Dorothy Sue Cobble, *The Other Women's Movement: Workplace Justice and Social Rights in Modern America* (Princeton: Princeton University Press, 2004); Dennis A. Deslippe, *Rights, Not Roses: Unions and the Rise of Working-Class Feminism, 1945–80* (Urbana: University of Illinois Press, 2000); Daniel Horowitz, *Betty Friedan and the Making of the Feminine Mystique: The American Left, the Cold War, and Modern Feminism* (Amhers: University of Massachusetts Press, 1998); Meg Luxton, "Feminism as a Class Act: Working-Class Feminism and the Women's Movement in Canada," *Labour/Le Travail* 48 (Fall 2001): 63–88; Sangster, *Transforming Labour*; Kate Weigand, *Red Feminism: American Communism and the Making of Women's Liberation* (Baltimore: Johns Hopkins University Press, 2001).

9 See Zillah Eisenstein, *Against Empire: Feminisms, Racism, and the West* (London: Zed Books, 2004), 148–62.

10 For a representative sample, see Kathleen M. Blee, *Inside Organized Racism: Women in the Hate Movement* (Berkeley: University of California Press, 2003); Kathleen M. Blee and Sandra McGee Deutsch, eds., *Women of the Right: Comparisons and*

Interplays across Borders (University Park.: Pennsylvania State University Press, 2012); Mary C. Brennan, *Wives, Mothers, and the Red Menace: Conservative Women and the Crusade against Communism* (Boulder: University Press of Colorado, 2008); Glen Jeansonne, *Women of the Far Right: The Mothers' Movement and World War II* (Urbana: University of Illinois Press, 1996); Michelle M. Nickerson, *Mothers of Conservatism: Women and the Postwar Right* (Princeton: Princeton University Press, 2012); Katie Pickles, *Female Imperialism and National Identity: Imperial Order Daughters of the Empire* (Manchester, UK: Manchester University Press, 2002).

11 The two key texts upon which I expand are Alvin Finkel, "Populism and Gender: The UFA and Social Credit Experiences," *Journal of Canadian Studies* 27, 4 (1992–93): 76–97; Bob Hesketh, "From Crusaders to Missionaries to Wives: Alberta Social Credit Women, 1932–1955," *Prairie Forum* 18, 1 (1993): 53–75. The history and development of conservatism in Canada is still relatively uncharted territory, and most of the texts that deal with this area do not mention women or gender. See, for example, Philip Massolin, *Canadian Intellectuals, the Tory Tradition, and the Challenge of Modernity, 1939–1970* (Toronto: University of Toronto Press, 2001).

12 In this context, "modernity" refers to a time when rationality, mastery over nature, bureaucracy, and control over all aspects of society came into being. The growth of the state, particularly the welfare state, was a key aspect of modern times. The post-Second World War years saw modernity take on these new modes. Secularism, liberalism, the growth of the welfare state, and an increase in the amount of freedom afforded to youth were indicative of postwar modernity. See Christopher Dummitt, *The Manly Modern: Masculinity in Postwar Canada* (Vancouver: UBC Press, 2007); James C. Scott, *Seeing Like a State: How Certain Schemes to Improve the Human Condition Have Failed* (New Haven: Yale University Press, 1998).

13 This definition of maternalism draws on Linda Gordon, *Pitied But Not Entitled: Single Mothers and the History of Welfare, 1890–1935* (Cambridge: Harvard University Press, 1994); Seth Koven and Sonya Michel, eds., *Mothers of a New World: Maternalist Politics and the Origins of Welfare States* (New York: Routledge, 1993); Molly Ladd-Taylor, *Mother-Work: Women, Child Welfare, and the State, 1890–1930* (Urbana: University of Illinois Press, 1994).

14 See Susan Prentice, "Workers, Mothers, Reds: Toronto's Postwar Daycare Fight," *Studies in Political Economy* 30 (Autumn 1989): 115–41.

15 A classic definition of the public/private dichotomy – the "breadwinner ideology" – can be found in Joy Parr, *The Gender of Breadwinners: Women, Men, and Change in Two Industrial Towns, 1880–1950* (Toronto: University of Toronto Press, 1998).

16 Kathleen A. Brown, "The 'Savagely Fathered and Un-Mothered World' of the Communist Party USA: Feminism, Maternalism, and Mother Bloor," *Feminist Studies* 25, 3 (999): 539, 560; Campbell, *Rose Henderson*.

17 Temma Kaplan, "Female Consciousness and Collective Action: The Case of Barcelona, 1910–1918," *Signs* 7, 3 (1982): 565–66.

18 Gerald Friesen, *The West: Regional Ambitions, National Debates, Global Age* (Toronto: Penguin/McGill Institute, 1999). See also the essays in Robert Wardaugh, ed., *Toward Defining the Prairies: Region, Culture, and History* (Winnipeg: University of Manitoba Press, 2001). A contrary view to Friesen's arguments can be found in David Bright, "The West Wants In: Regionalism, Class, and Labour/Le Travail, 1976–2002," *Labour/Le Travail* 50 (Fall 2002): 149–61.

19 On Alberta's post-Second World War economy and political culture, see Howard Palmer with Tamara Palmer, *Alberta: A New History* (Edmonton: Hurtig, 1990), 303–25; Peter J. Smith, "Alberta: A Province Just Like Any Other?," in *The Provincial State: Politics in Canada's Provinces and Territories*, ed. Keith Brownsey and Michael Howlett, 246–51 (Toronto: Copp Clark Pitman Ltd., 1992). On British Columbia, see Michael Howlett and Keith Brownsey, "British Columbia: Public Sector Politics in a Rentier Resource Economy," in *The Provincial State: Politics in Canada's Provinces and Territories*, ed. Keith Brownsey and Michael Howlett, 272–73 (Toronto: Copp Clark Pitman Ltd., 1992); See also Benjamin Isitt, *Militant Minority: British Columbia Workers and the Rise of a New Left, 1948–1972* (Toronto: University of Toronto Press, 2011), 30–43; Hugh J.M. Johnston, ed., *The Pacific Province: A History of British Columbia* (Vancouver: Douglas and McIntyre, 1996).

20 John Agnew and Luca Muscara, *Making Political Geography*, 2nd ed. (Lanham, MD: Rowman and Littlefield, 2012); Agnew, *Place and Politics: The Geographical Mediation of State and Society* (Boston: Allen and Unwin, 1987). On western Canada in particular, two recent collections offer new views of the region. See Finkel et al., *West and Beyond*; Adele Perry, Esyllt Jones, and Leah, eds., *Place and Replace: Essays on Western Canada* (Winnipeg: University of Manitoba Press, 2013).

21 The term "embeddedness" is from Maureen G. Reid, *Taking Stands: Gender and the Sustainability of Rural Communities* (Vancouver: UBC Press, 2003); Mercedes Steedman, "The Red Petticoat Brigade: Mine Mill Women's Auxiliaries and the Threat from Within, 1940s-1970s," in *Whose National Security? Canadian State Surveillance and the Creation of Enemies*, ed. Gary Kinsman, Dieter K. Buse, and Mercedes Steedman, . 55–68 (Toronto: Between the Lines, 2000).

22 Donald E. Blake, *Two Political Worlds: Parties and Voting in British Columbia* (Vancouver: UBC Press, 1985), 36–43; Alvin Finkel, *The Social Credit Phenomenon in Alberta* (Toronto: University of Toronto Press, 1989), 130–34; Gordon Hak, "The Communists and the Unemployed in the Prince George District, 1930–1935," *BC Studies* 68 (Winter 1985–86): 45–61.

23 In the May 2015 Alberta provincial election, for example, the New Democratic Party won a majority government, winning seats in the urban areas of Edmonton, Calgary, Lethbridge, Red Deer, and Medicine Hat as well as in some working-class ridings in northern Alberta. The conservative Wild Rose Party, in some ways an ideological descendent of Social Credit, dominated rural Alberta, especially in the southern part of the province. The Progressive Conservative Party was reduced to a rump, based primarily in wealthy and suburban areas of Calgary. See *Calgary Herald*, 6 May 2015; *Edmonton Journal*, 6 May 2015.

24 In the case of SCP women, there are references to the mid-later 1960s. I do not feel that this changes the overall focus of the text. SCP women possessed broadly the same ideology from 1945 to 1970, even as the party's grip on political power in Alberta and British Columbia loosened over time.

25 On the CPC's origins, see Ian Angus, *Canadian Bolsheviks: The Early Years of the Communist Party of Canada*, 2nd ed. (Victoria: Trafford Publishing, 2004); Ivan Avakumovic, *The Communist Party of Canada: A History* (Toronto: McClelland and Stewart, 1975); John Manley, "Does the International Labour Movement Need Salvaging? Communism, Labourism, and the Canadian Trade Unions, 1921–28," *Labour/Le Travail* 41 (Spring 1998): 148–52; John Manley, "Moscow Rules? 'Red

Unionism' and 'Class against Class' in Britain, Canada, and the United States, 1928–1935," *Labour/Le Travail* 56 (Fall 2005): 9–50; William Rodney, *Soldiers of the International: The Communist Party of Canada, 1919–1929* (Toronto: University of Toronto Press, 1968).

26 The Comintern introduced this change in CPC strategy. With the rise of Nazism in Germany, the Comintern advocated cooperation with socialists, social democrats, and liberal and conservative societal elements in order to present a united front against fascism. This lasted until 1939, with the union of Nazi Germany and the Soviet Union in the Nazi-Soviet Pact. See Fernando Claudin, *The Communist Movement: From Comintern to Cominform, Part Two: The Zenith of Stalinism*, trans. Francis MacDonagh (New York: Monthly Review Press, 1975), 307–15, 590–97; Duncan Hallas, *The Comintern* (London: Bookmarks, 1985), 155–67; Kevin McDermott and Jeremy Agnew, *The Comintern: A History of International Communism from Lenin to Stalin* (London: MacMillan, 1996), 204–19.

27 There were exceptions. In cities like Vancouver, CPC members were still being elected to municipal office – City Council, Park Board, and School Board – as late as the 1980s and 1990s. Many individual CPC members continued to support leftist protest in various areas (e.g., anti-war activism, pro-union marches, and anti-poverty activities). On the CPC's decline, see Norman Penner, *Canadian Communism: The Stalin Years and Beyond* (Toronto: Methuen, 1988), 237–48; Merrily Weisbord, *The Strangest Dream: Canadian Communists, the Spy Trials, and the Cold War* (Toronto: Lester and Orpen Dennys, 1983); Whitaker and Marcuse, *Cold War Canada.*

28 I say "ostensible" because many have argued that, in practice, the CCF/NDP's policies, at both the federal and provincial levels, were little different from those of the Liberal Party or the Conservative Party. For an earlier critique, see Gary Teeple, "'Liberals in a Hurry': Socialism and the CCF-NDP," in *Capitalism and the National Question in Canada*, ed. Gary Teeple, 229–50 (Toronto: University of Toronto Press, 1972).

29 On the CCF and its origins in agrarian populism and protest, see Seymour Martin Lipset, *Agrarian Socialism: The Co-operative Commonwealth Federation in Saskatchewan. A Study in Political Sociology*, rev. ed. (New York: Anchor Books, 1968); W.L. Morton, *The Progressive Party in Canada* (Toronto: University of Toronto Press, 1950); Paul F. Sharp, *The Agrarian Revolt in Western Canada: A Survey Showing American Parallels* (Omaha: University of Nebraska Press, 1997).

30 Although it must be said that the inclusion of UFA members was, at best, a mixed blessing for the CCF since many UFA members and MPs held reactionary views. See Alvin Finkel, "Obscure Origins: The Confused Early History of the Alberta CCF," in *"Building the Co-operative Commonwealth": Essays on the Democratic Socialist Tradition in Canada*, ed. J. William Brennan, 99–115 (Regina: Canadian Plains Research Center, 1984).

31 Benjamin Isitt, "Elusive Unity: The Canadian Labour Party in British Columbia, 1924–28," *BC Studies* 163 (Autumn 2009): 33–64. See also Isitt, *Militant Minority.*

32 The League for Social Reconstruction, founded in 1932, was the "braintrust" for the CCF and consisted of university professors, intellectuals, and urban, middle-class reformers. A representative example of an LSR member is Frank Underhill (1889–1971), a professor of history at the University of Toronto and – much later – Carleton University. Underhill was a prolific writer and, initially, supported

a moderate, "Fabian" approach to the implementation of socialism in Canada. Underhill's vision of socialism, or social democracy, emphasized a gradualist, electoral approach to improving society, state planning, and Keynesian economic ideas. This was a common perspective among LSR supporters and many early CCF members. Underhill joined the Liberal Party during the 1950s. See R. Douglas Francis, *Frank H. Underhill: Intellectual Provocateur* (Toronto: University of Toronto Press, 1986); Michiel Horn, *The League for Social Reconstruction: Intellectual Origins of the Democratic Left in Canada, 1930–1942* (Toronto: University of Toronto Press, 1980).

33 Even in earlier decades, many argued that the Soviet threat was exaggerated, if not illusory. See William Appleman Williams, *The Tragedy of American Diplomacy*, 50th ed. (New York: W.W. Norton, 2009 [1962]).

34 Important general works on the CCF, and its successor the NDP, include Ivan Avakumovic, *Socialism in Canada: A Study of the CCF-NDP in Federal and Provincial Politics* (Toronto: McClelland and Stewart, 1978); Dan Azoulay, *Keeping the Dream Alive: The Survival of the Ontario CCF-NDP, 1950–1963* (Montreal and Kingston: McGill-Queen's University Press, 1997); Gerald L. Caplan, *The Dilemma of Canadian Socialism: The CCF in Ontario* (Toronto: McClelland and Stewart, 1973); Desmond Morton, *NDP: Social Democracy in Canada*, 2nd ed., (Toronto: Samuel Stevens Hakkert and Company, 1977); Alan Whitehorn, *Canadian Socialism: Essays on the CCF-NDP* (Toronto: Oxford University Press, 1992); Walter D. Young, *The Anatomy of a Party: The National CCF, 1932–61* (Toronto: University of Toronto Press, 1969).

35 Fahrni (1900–92) and Jamieson (1883–1964) were both prominent CCF members. Jamieson was a CCF MLA in the Vancouver area from 1939 to 1945 and again from 1952 to 1953 as well as a city councillor. Fahrni was a pacifist and a disciple of the ideas of Mahatma Gandhi. She was one of the few political activists of any stripe to oppose the internment of Japanese Canadians during the Second World War. Both are discussed in more detail in Chapter 1.

36 A definition and explanation of technocracy can be found in Nancy Christie, *Engendering the State: Family, Work, and Welfare in Canada* (Toronto: University of Toronto Press, 2000).

37 Christina J. Nichol, "In Pursuit of the Voter: The British Columbia CCF, 1945–1950," in *"Building the Co-operative Commonwealth": Essays on the Democratic Socialist Tradition in Canada*, ed. J. William Brennan, 131–35 (Regina: Canadian Plains Research Center, 1984).

38 For general works on women in the CCF, see Dan Azoulay, "Winning Women for Socialism: The Ontario CCF and Women, 1947–1961," *Labour/Le Travail* 36 (Fall 1995): 59–90; Dean Beeby, "Women in the Ontario CCF, 1940–1950," *Ontario History* 74, 4 (1982): 258–83; Joan Sangster, "The Role of Women in the Early CCF, 1933–1940," in *Beyond the Vote: Canadian Women and Politics*, ed. Linda Kealey and Joan Sangster, 124–32 (Toronto: University of Toronto Press, 1989); Georgina M. Taylor, "'The Women … Shall Help to Lead the Way': Saskatchewan CCF-NDP Women Candidates in Provincial and Federal Elections, 1934–1965," in *"Building the Co-operative Commonwealth": Essays on the Democratic Socialist Tradition in Canada*, ed. J. William Brennan, 141–54 (Regina: Canadian Plains Research Center, 1984).

39 David R. Elliot and Iris Miller, *Bible Bill: A Biography of William Aberhart* (Edmonton: Reidmore Books, 1987).

40 On Douglas, see Bob Hesketh, *Major Douglas and Alberta Social Credit* (Toronto: University of Toronto Press, 1997); John A. Irving, *The Social Credit Movement in Alberta* (Toronto: University of Toronto Press, 1959).

41 Finkel, *Social Credit Phenomenon in Alberta*, 41–47; David Laycock, *Populism and Democratic Thought on the Canadian Prairies* (Toronto: University of Toronto Press, 1990), 35–40; J.R. Mallory, *Social Credit and the Federal Power in Canada*, rev. ed. (Toronto: University of Toronto Press, 1976), 69–76.

42 Gordon Hak, "Populism and the 1952 Social Credit Breakthrough in British Columbia," *Canadian Historical Review* 85, 2 (2004): 277–96; Leonard B. Kuffert, " 'Reckoning with the Machine': The British Columbia Social Credit Movement as Social Criticism, 1932–52," *BC Studies* 124 (Winter 1999/2000): 9–39; David Mitchell, *W.A.C. Bennett and the Rise of British Columbia* (Vancouver: Douglas and McIntyre, 1983); Martin Robin, *Pillars of Profit: The Company Province, 1934–1972* (Toronto: McClelland and Stewart, 1973), 128–97.

43 Anti-modernism was a common theme in conservative thought, especially among women. See June Melby Benowitz, *Days of Discontent: American Women and Right-Wing Politics, 1933–1945* (DeKalb: Northern Illinois University Press, 2002).

44 See, in particular, Kuffert, "Reckoning with the Machine."

45 On the early radicalism of the BC CPC and CCF, see Isitt, *Militant Minority*, chap. 1.

46 Finkel, *Social Credit Phenomenon in Alberta*, 125–30, 134, 210.

47 This is not to imply that Alberta has always lacked a left-wing tradition. Indeed, left movements like the One Big Union, the early CCF, and even the CPC had strong followings in Alberta prior to 1945, and, in the post-Second World War years, peace movements and ethnic organizations like the Association of the United Ukrainian Canadians also enjoyed significant support. Still, from 1945 onward, and especially from the 1950s onward, many in mainstream Albertan society eschewed left-wing, or even liberal, viewpoints and turned towards right-wing solutions to social and economic problems. In May 2015, the Alberta New Democratic Party won a majority government in the province, suggesting that a significant number of Albertans desired a shift towards more left-wing views. Yet, given the staunchly moderate, even centrist, orientation of the present-day NDP at both the federal and provincial levels, it remains to be seen how leftist this branch of the NDP will end up being. See David Bright, *The Limits of Labour: Class Formation and the Labour Movement in Calgary, 1883–1929* (Vancouver: UBC Press, 1998); *Edmonton Journal*, 6 May 2015. The most recent text on the labour movement, and labour and leftist activism, in Alberta contains no mention of left-wing women during the 1940s and 1950s, although it does indicate the strong presence of a left-wing tradition in the province. See Alvin Finkel, *Working People in Alberta: A History* (Edmonton: Athabasca University Press, 2012), 109–48.

48 There was also a minority tradition of left and labour women's activism in the province in earlier decades. See Andree Levesque, *Red Travellers: Jeanne Corbin and Her Comrades* (Montreal and Kingston: McGill-Queen's University Press, 2006); Patricia Roome, "Amelia Turner and Calgary Labour Women, 1919–1935," in *Beyond the Vote: Canadian Women in Politics*, ed. Linda Kealey and Joan Sangster,

89–117 (Toronto: University of Toronto Press, 1989). This, too, seems to have faded by the post-Second World War period.

49 On Evangelicalism, see Robert Burkinshaw, *Pilgrims in Lotus Land: Conservative Protestantism in British Columbia* (Vancouver: UBC Press, 1995), 9–12; Sara Diamond, *Not by Politics Alone: The Enduring Influence of the Christian Right* (New York: Guilford Press, 1998), 9–11; Darren Dochuk, *From Bible Belt to Sunbelt: Plain-Folk Religion, Grassroots Politics, and the Rise of Evangelical Conservatism* (New York: W.W. Norton and Co., 2012); Kevin Kruse, *One Nation under God: How Corporate America Invented Christian America* (New York: Basic Books, 2015); John G. Stackhouse, Jr., *Canadian Evangelicalism in the Twentieth Century: An Introduction to Its Character* (Toronto: University of Toronto Press, 1993), 6–17.

50 Burkinshaw, *Pilgrims in Lotus Land*, 196–97. Conservatives in Cold War Canada produced "red-baiting" propaganda on United Church members, portraying them as communists and socialists for their anti-war, and pro-social and economic justice, stance. On the persecution of United Church members, see Steve Hewitt, "Sunday Morning Subversion: The Canadian Security State and Organized Religion in the Cold War," in *Love, Hate, and Fear in Canada's Cold War*, ed. Richard Cavell, 57–74 (Toronto: University of Toronto Press, 2004).

51 Burkinshaw, *Pilgrims in Lotus Land*, 196–97.

52 Burkinshaw, *Pilgrims in Lotus Land*. On this point, see also Walter E. Ellis, "Some Aspects of Religion in British Columbia Politics" (MA thesis, University of British Columbia, 1956). In the 1930s, by contrast, Social Credit voters in Alberta were not primarily evangelicals but, rather, workers and farmers drawn to William Aberhart's populist, anti-poverty message. See Finkel, *Social Credit Phenomenon in Alberta*, 30; Larry Hannant, "The Calgary Working Class and the Social Credit Movement in Alberta, 1932–35," *Labour/Le Travail* 16 (Fall 1985): 97–116.

53 This had a long history in western Canada. See Laycock, *Populism and Democratic Thought*.

54 Mallory, *Social Credit*; Martin Robin, *Pillars of Profit: The Company Province, 1934–1972* (Toronto: McClelland and Stewart, 1973).

55 Gary R. Miedema, *For Canada's Sake: Public Religion, Centennial Celebrations, and the Re-Making of Canada in the 1960s* (Montreal and Kingston: McGill-Queen's University Press, 2005); Doug Owram, *Born at the Right Time: A History of the Baby Boom Generation* (Toronto: University of Toronto Press, 1996).

56 Finkel, *Social Credit Phenomenon in Alberta*, 202–03. See also Michael Kazin, *The Populist Persuasion: An American History*, rev. ed. (Ithaca, NY: Cornell University Press, 2012); Mark Leier, *Red Flags and Red Tape: The Making of a Labour Bureaucracy* (Toronto: University of Toronto Press, 1995).

57 In particular, Paul Weyrich and George Wallace stand out as examples of right-wing populists who were critical of big business. See Christopher Lasch, *The True and Only Heaven: Progress and Its Critics* (New York: W.W. Norton and Company, 1991), 504–08.

58 On this topic, see especially Trevor Harrison, *Of Passionate Intensity: Right-Wing Populism and the Reform Party of Canada* (Toronto: University of Toronto Press, 1995); E.F. Schumacher, *Small Is Beautiful: Economics as if People Mattered* (New York: Harper and Row, 1973); Jeff Taylor, *Politics on a Human Scale: The American Tradition of Decentralism* (Lanham, MD: Lexington Books, 2013).

59 On the CPC and its work in local communities, see, in particular, Robin D.G. Kelley, *Hammer and Hoe: Alabama Communists during the Great Depression* (Chapel Hill: University of North Carolina Press, 1990); Ian McKay, *Rebels, Reds, Radicals: Rethinking Canada's Left History* (Toronto: Between the Lines, 2005); James Mochoruk, *The People's Co-op: The Life and Times of a North End Institution* (Halifax: Fernwood, 2000); Andrew Parnaby, *Citizen Docker: Making a New Deal on the Vancouver Waterfront, 1919–1939* (Toronto: University of Toronto Press, 2008). Bryan Palmer contends that US communists were increasingly controlled by Moscow during the Stalin period, although he, too, emphasizes the need to discuss top-down control *and* local conditions. See Bryan D. Palmer, "Rethinking the History of United States Communism," *American Communist History* 2, 2 (December 2003): 139–73.

60 The definition of "historical materialism" is from Pat Armstrong and Hugh Armstrong, *Theorizing Women's Work* (Toronto: Garamond Press, 1990); Rosemary Hennessy and Chrys Ingraham, "Introduction: Reclaiming Anticapitalist Feminism," in *Materialist Feminism: A Reader in Class, Difference, and Women's Lives*, ed. Rosemary Hennessy and Chrys Ingraham, 8–9 (New York and London: Routledge, 1997). "Radical Feminism" refers to a particular vision of feminism, advanced in the late-1960s and 1970s, stating that women constituted a "sex class" and that women's oppression resulted exclusively from the domination of men in a patriarchal society. This contrasted with liberal feminists, who argued for improvements to an unjust legal system to remedy women's problems; and socialist feminists, who stated that it was capitalist social relations, coupled with patriarchy, that accounted for women's oppression. Radical feminists often advanced a separatist agenda and advocated for the need to establish women-only organizations, notably "consciousness-raising" groups, transition houses for women leaving abusive relationships, and rape crisis centres. See Alice Echols, *Daring to Be Bad: Radical Feminism in America, 1967–1975* (Minneapolis: University of Minnesota Press, 1989), 3–5 and passim. "Poststructuralism" refers to an intellectual movement that emphasizes the importance of language and words rather than economics or ideology, focuses on micronarratives in history that explore languages and symbols of oppression, and upholds discontinuity, rupture, and chance in discussing history. This definition is from Joan Sangster, *Earning Respect: The Lives of Working Women in Small-Town Ontario, 1920–1950* (Toronto: University of Toronto Press, 1995), 8–9.

61 Representative examples of new research in women's and gender history are Brookfield, *Cold War Comforts*; Lara Campbell, *Respectable Citizens: Gender, Family, and Unemployment in Ontario's Great Depression* (Toronto: University of Toronto Press, 2009); Katrina Srigley, *Breadwinning Daughters: Young Working Women in a Depression-Era City, 1929–1939* (Toronto: University of Toronto Press, 2010); Jennifer A. Stephen, *Pick One Intelligent Girl: Employability, Domesticity, and the Canadian Welfare State, 1939–1947* (Toronto: University of Toronto Press, 2007).

Chapter 1: Women No Longer Need Fear Want or Illness

1 "Social democracy" refers to a belief system – stemming from the German Social Democratic Party of the nineteenth century and other similar parties – that advocates working within the dominant political system in order to effect reforms that

benefit working people and other oppressed groups. Thus, the CCF – advocates of social democracy – and its precursor parties like the Socialist Party of Canada supported running candidates for public office as the best way of ameliorating the problems of capitalist society. If enough CCF members could be elected to municipal, provincial, and federal office, then the party could advocate for welfare state measures like higher wages, day care centres, and a fairer taxation policy. This vision of political action often led to compromise with more conservative political parties and movements. "Social democracy" is distinct from "democratic socialism," a more general term that refers to the possibility of workers and socialists taking over the capitalist state and running it in accordance with working-class interests. Some early CCF members advocated for democratic socialism but most were reformist, "welfare statist," social democrats, which is why I refer to CCF members as "social democrats." On social democracy, see Mark Leier, *Where the Fraser River Flows: The Industrial Workers of the World in British Columbia* (Vancouver: New Star Books, 1990), 90–94.

2 Laura E. Jamieson, *Women Dry Those Tears* (Vancouver: CCF Women's Council of BC with the assistance of Ontario CCF Women, 1945), 14. On the optimism of the immediate post-Second World War years, see Joy Parr, *Domestic Goods: The Material, the Moral, and the Economic in the Postwar Years* (Toronto: University of Toronto Press, 1998), 34–37.

3 See, in particular, Christopher Dummitt, *The Manly Modern: Masculinities in Postwar Canada* (Vancouver: UBC Press, 2007); Bill Osgerby, *Playboys in Paradise: Masculinity, Youth, and Leisure Style in Modern America* (London: Berg, 2001).

4 Indeed, the Canadian and American governments – both federal and provincial/state governments – worked with "private" industry to regulate the economy, create jobs, control workers' collective action, and to build "mega-projects" like canals, railways, roads, and, more recently, dams. Ultimately, most businesses wanted state regulation in order to prevent competition and to ensure that laws and policies favoured big business against workers, unions, and smaller competitors. See Gabriel Kolko, *The Triumph of Conservatism: A Reinterpretation of American History, 1900–1916* (New York: The Free Press, 1977); Martin J. Sklar, *The Corporate Reconstruction of American Capitalism, 1890–1916: The Market, the Law, and Politics* (New York: Cambridge University Press, 1988); Tom Traves, *The State and Enterprise: Canadian Manufacturers and the Federal Government, 1917–1931* (Toronto: University of Toronto Press, 1979).

5 On left-wing women's ideological background, see especially Joan Sangster, *Dreams of Equality: Women on the Canadian Left, 1920–1950* (Toronto: McClelland and Stewart, 1989), 14, 19–24.

6 See, for example, Irene Howard, *The Struggle for Social Justice in British Columbia: Helena Gutteridge, the Unknown Reformer* (Vancouver: UBC Press, 1992); Mick Lowe, *One Woman Army: The Life of Claire Culhane* (Toronto: Macmillan, 1992). There were many other women, of the left and the right, whom I might have included in Chapters 1 and 2; however, space dictated that I include the most significant women and those whom I felt I offered new information. This was not the case for Gutteridge and Culhane; thus, I did not include them here.

7 A useful feminist explanation of the uses of biography for historians can be found in Katrina Srigley, *Breadwinning Daughters: Young Working Women in a Depression-Era City, 1929–1939* (Toronto: University of Toronto Press, 2010), 9–11.

8 In addition to the texts on "place" mentioned in Chapter 1, see a recent popular study of women in BC politics, Anne Edwards, *Seeking Balance: Conversations with BC Women in Politics* (Halfmoon Bay, BC: Caitlin Press, 2008).

9 Here, the term "ideology" refers to a set of ideas, symbols, and signifiers that, collectively, make up the worldview or belief system of a particular group of people. An ideology consists of a core of ideas, different strands of this core, and outlying ideas that still make up part of the general ideology. Ideologies are used to justify and uphold the actions, views, and statements of different social and political groups on all points of the political and social spectrum. Therefore, an ideology could be used either to uphold the dominant system of power or to challenge it. See Terry Eagleton, *Ideology: An Introduction* (London: Verso, 1991), 1–10 and passim; Michael Freeden, *Liberalism Divided: A Study in British Political Thought, 1914–1939* (Oxford: Clarendon Press, 1986), 2–5.

10 Although it should be said that I did not find many pronouncements by either CCF or CPC women (or SCP women, for that matter) on issues related to abortion and birth control. These issues, arguably, did not become mainstream for the left until the advent of second-wave feminism; earlier feminists who supported eugenics and birth control, like Violet McNaughton and Irene Parlby, could not be defined as "leftist" in any real sense of that term. Until the 1960s redefined these issues as feminist and libertarian (libertarian in the sense that women had the right to control their bodies and what was done to them) abortion and birth control were connected with the eugenics and population control movements, and were not seen as leftist issues. Abortion, birth control, and gay and lesbian rights are relatively recent additions to the left's ideological repertoire. This certainly does not imply that these are not important issues – indeed, they are very important – but simply that leftists from the pre-1960s era would not have focused on them nearly as much as the generations of the 1960s and after. See Erika Dyck, *Facing Eugenics: Reproduction, Sterilization, and the Politics of Choice* (Toronto: University of Toronto Press, 2013), 85–95, 193–95; Angus McLaren and Arlene Tigar McLaren, *The Bedroom and the State: The Changing Practices and Politics of Contraception and Abortion in Canada, 1880–1997*, 2nd ed. (Toronto: Oxford University Press, 1997), 160 and passim.

11 The fifteen hundred number comes from my own observations on left- and right-wing women and from the estimates given by historians of these parties. See, on the CPC, Ivan Avakumovic, *The Communist Party in Canada: A History* (Toronto: McClelland and Stewart, 1975). On the CCF, see Walter D. Young, *The Anatomy of a Party: The National CCF, 1932–61* (Toronto: University of Toronto Press, 1969).

12 *Pacific Tribune*, 29 November 1957.

13 Ibid.

14 On the mining communities of the Crowsnest Pass, see Tom Langford and Chris Frazier, "The Cold War and Working-Class Politics in the Coal Mining Communities of the Crowsnest Pass, 1945–1958," *Labour/Le Travail* 49 (Spring 2002): 43–81.

15 *Pacific Tribune*, 29 November 1957.

16 Ibid.

17 Ibid.

18 John Douglas Belshaw, *Colonization and Community: The Vancouver Island Coalfield and the Making of the British Columbian Working Class* (Montreal and Kingston: McGill-Queen's University Press, 2002).

19 Here see Betty Griffin and Susan Lockhart, *Their Own History: Women's Contribution to the Labour Movement of British Columbia* (New Westminster: United Fishermen and Allied Workers' Union/CAW Seniors Club, 2002), 106–08.

20 On Griffin, see *Pacific Tribune*, 9 February 1951, 5 October 1951, 8 February 1952, 24 October 1952, 28 November 1952; Harold Griffin, *Radical Roots: The Shaping of British Columbia* (Vancouver: Broadway Printers, 1999); Griffin and Lockhart, *Their Own History*, 108; Maurice Rush, "*We Have a Glowing Dream": Recollections of Working-Class and People's Struggles in BC, 1935–1995* (Vancouver: Centre for Socialist Education, 1996), appendix F-1.

21 On Morgan, see *Pacific Tribune*, 28 February 1947, 21 March 1947, 13 October 1950, 9 February 1951. University of Toronto, Thomas Fisher Rare Book Library, Robert Kenny Collection, box 23, file 14, pamphlet, *Vote Mona Morgan for Alderman*, n.d. See also Griffin and Lockhart, *Their Own History*, 85–89; Jerry Lembcke and William M. Tattam, *One Union in Wood: A Political History of the International Woodworkers of America* (Madeira Park, BC: Harbour Publishing, 1984); Andrew Neufeld and Andrew Parnaby, *The IWA in Canada: The Life and Times of an Industrial Union* (Vancouver: IWA Canada/New Star Books, 2000); Sangster, *Dreams of Equality*, 188.

22 On Kathleen Morgan, see *Pacific Tribune*, 13 October 1961.

23 Lembcke and Tattam, *One Union in Wood;* Neufeld and Parnaby, *IWA in Canada.*

24 On the different "CP families" in the Vancouver area, see Rush, *We Have a Glowing Dream.*

25 Levesque, *Red Travellers.*

26 Benjamin Isitt, *Militant Minority: British Columbia Workers and the Rise of a New Left, 1948–1972* (Toronto: University of Toronto Press, 2011). On consumer protest, see Brian Thorn, "'Women Are Truly Wonderful in Their Ingenuity': Radical Housewives and Consumer Protest during the Cold War Era," *left history* 18, 1 (2014): 9–36.

27 On Elsie Munro and the Houswives' League, see Irene Howard, "The Mothers' Council of Vancouver: Holding the Fort for the Unemployed, 1935–1938," in *Vancouver Past: Essays in Social History. Vancouver Centennial Issue of BC Studies*, ed. Robert A.J. McDonald and Jean Barman, 249–87 (Vancouver: UBC Press, 1986); Sangster, *Dreams of Equality*, 138–42. Although many CPC women supported the HWL, it was not a communist-run organization. Anti-communist "red-baiters" tried to portray the HWL as a communist front; however, it also included women from the CCF and the Liberal Party as well as women with no formal political ties.

28 Rush, *We Have a Glowing Dream*, 4–5.

29 Simon Fraser University, Women's Labour History Collection, Sara Diamond Oral History Collection (hereafter SFU, WLHC), Sara Diamond's interview with Effie Jones, summer 1979.

30 Belshaw, *Colonization and Community.*

31 One might argue that Saskatchewan was also agricultural, but it produced a much more left-wing political culture than did neighbouring Alberta. The economic context of Saskatchewan after 1947, with Alberta's discovery of oil in that year, was very different. While Alberta became a wealthier province, Saskatchewan remained poor. As we have seen, prior to 1943, Alberta's Social Credit government was left-leaning on many issues. Saskatchewan experienced different waves of immigration

as well: many British Labour Party supporters made their way to Saskatchewan, and this was not the case with Alberta. Similarly, Douglas's CCF received much of its support from the small cities of Saskatoon and Regina rather than from the rural areas of the province. See A.W. Johnston, *Dream No Little Dreams: A Biography of the Douglas Government of Saskatchewan, 1944–1961* (Toronto: University of Toronto Press, 2015).

32 SFU, WLHC, Sara Diamond's interview with Effie Jones, summer 1979.

33 The Vancouver Housewives' League, initially founded in the mid-1930s, consisted of different groups of women in Vancouver who protested against the high prices of such foods as bread, milk, and eggs. It also presented a challenge to employers and landlords: the former paid workers low wages while the latter charged exorbitant rent. As Effie Jones noted, Liberal Party women first established the Vancouver branch of the HWL. Thus, it possessed a fairly conservative political tenor. In 1937, the Housewives Consumers Association (HCA), a national organization with a broader membership across Canada, was founded, and it fought for similar issues. The HCA, although initially not affiliated with any organization, attracted many CPC and CCF women to its cause. Some estimates place the numbers of women in the HCA as high as fifty thousand. In 1948, the same year that more conservative unionists were pushing communists out of trade unions in British Columbia, the Provincial Women's Committee of the Ontario CCF became convinced that the HCA was a communist front organization and ordered CCF women to leave the association. Those CCF women who refused to disassociate from the HCA, notably former Ontario MPP Rae Luckock, were forced out of the party. See Dan Azoulay, "'Ruthless in a Ladylike Way': CCF Women Confront the Postwar 'Communist Menace,'" *Ontario History* 89, 1 (1997): 36–43; Dean Beeby, "Women in the Ontario CCF, 1940–1950," *Ontario History* 74 (December 1982): 273, 275; Julie Guard, "Women Worth Watching: Radical Housewives in Cold War Canada," in *Whose National Security? Canadian State Surveillance and the Creation of Enemies*, ed. Gary Kinsman, Dieter K. Buse, and Mercedes Steedman (Toronto: Between the Lines, 2000), 84n; Sangster, *Dreams of Equality*, 138–39.

34 SFU, WLHC, Sara Diamond's interview with Effie Jones, Summer 1979.

35 The quotation is from University of Toronto, Kenny Collection, box 22, file 36, pamphlet, *The Buzzard*, May 1958. This pamphlet was "published by the Civic Reform Association (CRA) in the interests of protecting the public from profiteering utility companies." On Jones, see also University of Toronto, Kenny Collection, box 22, file 36, letter, 3 August 1955, Jones to R.H. Tupper, QC. On Jones's electoral campaigns, see *Pacific Tribune*, 21 November 1947, 5 December 1947, 12 December 1947, 18 November 1949, 9 December 1949; Sangster, *Dreams of Equality*, 179.

36 See Sangster, *Dreams of Equality*, 58–64, 125–27. The "First Period" refers to the period of revolutionary enthusiasm and expansionism (roughly 1917–25) after the Russian Revolution and the founding of communist parties all over the world. The "Second Period" refers to 1925–29, years when communist parties all over the world pursued a "boring from within" strategy by which communists would join trade unions, and other socialist and left-wing groups, in the hope of converting these unions and groups into supporters of communism. The "Third Period" occurred from roughly 1929 to 1935, the "Popular Front" from 1935 to 1939. All of

these changes in the CPC "line" occurred in response to changes in the policies of the Communist Party of the Soviet Union.

37 SFU, WLHC, Sara Diamond's interview with Gladys Hilland, summer 1979.

38 Griffin and Lockhart, *Their Own History*, 100–1.

39 Ibid.

40 Ibid., 101.

41 My perspective here has been influenced by the argument in Irving Martin Abella, *Nationalism, Communism, and Canadian Labour: The CIO, the Communist Party, and the Canadian Congress of Labour, 1935–1956* (Toronto: University of Toronto Press, 1973), 220–22 and passim.

42 Aileen S. Kraditor, *"Jimmy Higgins": The Mental World of the American Rank and File Communist, 1930–1958* (New York: Greenwood Press, 1988), conclusion. Kraditor's ideological views migrated from endorsing the New Left and feminism in the 1960s to supporting conservatism in the form of Ronald Reagan and the Republican Party. As of 1984, she was a prominent member of the Conservative Historians' Forum in the United States. See Aileen S. Kraditor, *The Ideas of the Woman Suffrage Movement, 1890–1920* (New York: W.W. Norton and Company, 1981), v-viii; Aileen S. Kraditor, *The Radical Persuasion, 1890–1917: Aspects of the Intellectual History and the Historiography of Three American Radical Organizations* (Baton Rouge: Louisiana State University Press, 1981), intro. and passim; Robert Westbrook, "Good-bye to All That: Aileen Kraditor and Radical History," *Radical History Review* 28–30 (1984): 69–89.

43 Sangster, *Dreams of Equality*, 58–64, 124–27.

44 More specifically, the "social gospel" refers to the idea that Protestant social reformers could bring God's kingdom to people on earth in the here and now by combatting poverty, war, violence, alcohol, and oppression. It implied that members of the Protestant churches – notably the Baptist, Methodist, and Presbyterian (later the United) Churches – must identify with the poor, the working class, and pacifism. This was positive in that it led many in the church towards a critique of capitalist social relations, but it was negative in that it usually emphasized statist, ultimately bureaucratic, solutions to social problems and a moralistic, elitist view of working people and immigrants. See especially Allen Mills, *Fool for Christ: The Intellectual Politics of J.S. Woodsworth* (Toronto: University of Toronto Press, 1991); Mariana Valverde, *The Age of Light, Soap, and Water: Moral Reform in English Canada, 1885–1925*, rev. ed. (Toronto: University of Toronto Press, 2008). For a critique of socialist and social democratic intellectuals and moral reform, see Mark Leier, "Workers and Intellectuals: The Theory of the New Class and Early Canadian Socialism," in *Making Western Canada: Essays on European Colonization and Settlement*, ed. Catherine Cavanagh and Jeremy Mouat, 133–53 (Toronto: Garamond Press, 1996).

45 On Fahrni, see University of British Columbia, Special Collections Division (hereafter UBCSC), Angus MacInnis Memorial Collection, box 69, file 2, bulletin, biographies of CCF candidates, 1946 Provincial Election; SFU Archives, Susan Walsh Oral History Collection, Susan Walsh's interview with Mildred Fahrni, 31 March 1982, Vancouver; UBCSC, UBC Oral History Collection, interview no. 90, tape 1, Chrystall Dick's interview with Mildred Fahrni, 26 July 1972, Vancouver.

46 UBCSC, Women's International League for Peace and Freedom Papers, box 5, file 7, Sheila Young, unpublished MSS, "My Memories of the First Mixed Peace Committee in Vancouver," 1947. Young notes that she and Fahrni were the only women at most pro-peace meetings in Vancouver prior to 1947.

47 SFU Archives, Susan Walsh Oral History Collection, Susan Walsh's interview with Mildred Fahrni, 31 March 1982, Vancouver; UBCSC, UBC Oral History Collection, interview no. 90, tape 1, Chrystall Dick's interview with Mildred Fahrni, 26 July 1972, Vancouver.

48 On this point see Werner Cohn, "The Persecution of the Japanese Canadians and the Political Left in British Columbia, December 1941-March 1942," *BC Studies* 68 (Winter 1985–86): 3–22.

49 The CCF Women's Council was a member organization of the Vancouver Council of Women, usually seen as a conservative organization, although, by the 1950s, it had become more moderate. See UBCSC, Vancouver Council of Women Papers, box 3, file 9, Norah M. Hill, Secretary of BC Provincial CCF Women's Council, to Mrs. Theresa Galloway, Treasurer of the VCW, 19 February 1948. Hill noted that the Vancouver CCF Women's Council had paid its five-dollar annual membership fees to the VCW. See also UBCSC, Vancouver Council of Women Papers, box 2, file 14, VCW minutes of the 65th annual meeting, 1–2 March 1960. The CCF Women's Council, as a member organization of the VCW, put forward two resolutions at this meeting. BC Social Credit leader W.A.C. Bennett's wife was also a member of the VCW. See UBCSC, Vancouver Council of Women Papers, box 3, file 10. Mrs. A.D. Beirnes, VCW Corresponding Secretary, to Mrs. Lorena Green, 4659 Clarendon Street, Vancouver, 15 September 1959. The letter notes that May Bennett of the Vancouver East Social Credit Women's Auxiliary had been accepted as a member of the VCW.

50 Nancy Knickerbocker, *No Plaster Saint: The Life of Mildred Osterhout Fahrni, 1900–1992* (Vancouver: Talonbooks, 2001).

51 Ibid.

52 British Columbia Archives (hereafter BCA), Laura Jamieson Papers, box 2, file 13, Laura Jamieson, unpublished MSS, "My First Year as a School Teacher," n.d.

53 UBCSC, Angus MacInnis Memorial Collection, box 69, file 3, election pamphlet supporting Jamieson's candidacy in the 1953 provincial election.

54 SFU Archives, Susan Walsh Oral History Collection, Susan Walsh's interview with Mildred Fahrni, 31 March 1982, Vancouver; SFU Archives, Susan Walsh Oral History Collection, Susan Walsh's interview with Harold Winch and Jessie (Mendels) Winch, 18 May 1982, Vancouver (hereafter Walsh's interview with Winch and Winch).

55 Here see Carol Lee Bacchi, *Liberation Deferred? The Ideas of the English-Canadian Suffragists, 1877–1918* (Toronto: University of Toronto Press, 1983). Where middle- and upper-class suffragettes fought for political rights and acceptance within the dominant system, socialist and communist women supported economic equality for poor and working-class women and men. Not all first-wave feminists held racialist or elitist views. Liberal, pacifist, ethnic, and even socialist women endorsed the suffrage campaign. First-wave feminism was a complex and multifaceted phenomenon. For examples of more radical suffrage supporters, see Howard, *Struggle for Social Justice*; Barbara Ann Roberts, *A Reconstructed World: A Feminist Biography of Gertrude Richardson* (Montreal and Kingston: McGill-Queen's University Press, 1996). For a

case study of how some non-Anglo-Saxon women understood suffrage rights, see Varpu Lindstrom, *Defiant Sisters: A Social History of Finnish Immigrant Women in Canada*, 3rd ed. (Beaverton, ON: Aspasia Books, 2003).

56 Here, see Brian T. Thorn, "Visions of the New World Order: Women and Gender in Radical and Reactionary Movements in Post-World War II Western Canada," (PhD diss, Trent University, 2006), chap. 3. I do not have the space to go into detail about Jamieson's support for colonialism and orientalism. On the colonialist tendency in Western culture, the classic text is Edward W. Said, *Orientalism*, rev. ed. (New York: Vintage Books, 1994).

57 UBCSC, Angus MacInnis Memorial Collection, box 69, file 3, election pamphlet supporting Jamieson's candidacy in the 1953 provincial election; SFU Archives, Susan Walsh Oral History Collection, Susan Walsh's interview with Hilda Kristiansen, 26 February 1982, Vancouver.

58 BCA, Laura Jamieson Papers, box 2, file 16, New Vista Society, minutes of director's meeting, 14 May 1956, held at 1873 Adanac Street, Vancouver (Jamieson's residence). See also Linda Louise Hale, "Appendix: Votes for Women: Profiles of Prominent British Columbia Suffragists and Social Reformers," in *In Her Own Right: Selected Essays on Women's History in BC*, ed. Barbara Latham and Cathy Kess (Victoria: Camosun College, 1980), 294.

59 UBCSC, Dorothy Gretchen Steeves Papers, box 1, file 1, autobiographical notes by Steeves, n.d.; *Vancouver Sun*, 14 February 1945.

60 SFU Archives, Susan Walsh Oral History Collection, Susan Walsh's interview with Daisy Webster, 2 March 1982, Vancouver.

61 Ibid., Walsh's interview with Winch and Winch.

62 UBCSC, Dorothy Gretchen Steeves Papers, box 1, file 1, autobiographical notes by Steeves, n.d.

63 For examples of women's political and reform work that predates the suffrage era, see Sharon Anne Cook, *"Through Sunshine and Shadow": The Woman's Christian Temperance Union, Evangelicalism, and Reform in Ontario, 1874–1930* (Montreal and Kingston: McGill-Queen's University Press, 1995); Lynne Marks, *Revivals and Roller Rinks: Religion, Leisure, and Identity in Late-Nineteenth-Century Small Town Ontario* (Toronto: University of Toronto Press, 1996).

64 UBCSC, Dorothy Gretchen Steeves Papers, box 1, file 1. autobiographical notes by Steeves, n.d.

65 SFU Archives, Susan Walsh Oral History Collection, Walsh's interview with Winch and Winch.

66 On Steeves's views on international relations, see Chapter 3. On the rise of the Socialist Fellowship, see Christina J. Nichol, "In Pursuit of the Voter: The British Columbia CCF, 1945–1950," in *"Building the Co-operative Commonwealth": Essays on the Democratic Socialist Tradition in Canada*, ed. J. William Brennan, 131–35 (Regina: Canadian Plains Research Center, 1984).

67 SFU Archives, Susan Walsh Oral History Collection, Walsh's interview with Winch and Winch.

68 Ibid., Susan Walsh's interview with Daisy Webster, 2 March 1982, Vancouver.

69 The two quotations regarding Steeves's personality are from SFU Archives, Susan Walsh Oral History Collection, Walsh's interview with Winch and Winch.

70 SFU Archives, Susan Walsh Oral History Collection, Susan Walsh's interview with Hilda Kristiansen, 26 February 1982, Vancouver.

71 Ibid., Walsh's interview with Winch and Winch.

72 On Steeves see also Susan Walsh, "Equality, Emancipation, and a More Just World: Leading Women in the British Columbia Co-operative Commonwealth Federation" (MA thesis, Simon Fraser University, 1984); Susan Walsh, "The Peacock and the Guinea Hen: Political Profiles of Dorothy Gretchen Steeves and Grace MacInnis," in *The Neglected Majority: Essays in Canadian Women's History*, ed. Alison Prentice and Susan Mann Trofimenkoff, 2:144–59 (Toronto: McClelland and Stewart, 1985).

73 SFU Archives, Susan Walsh Oral History Collection, Susan Walsh's interviews with Grace MacInnis, 12 November 1981, 22 March 1982, Vancouver (hereafter Walsh's interviews with MacInnis).

74 As we have seen, many early socialists and communists favoured the breadwinner ideology. See Linda Kealey, *Enlisting Women for the Cause: Women, Labour, and the Left in Canada, 1890–1920* (Toronto: University of Toronto Press, 1998); Janice Newton, *The Feminist Challenge to the Canadian Left, 1900–1918* (Toronto: University of Toronto Press, 1995).

75 SFU Archives, Susan Walsh Oral History Collection, Walsh's interviews with MacInnis.

76 Young, *Anatomy of a Party*, 167–68.

77 SFU Archives, Susan Walsh Oral History Collection, Walsh's interviews with MacInnis; SFU Archives, Susan Walsh Oral History Collection, Susan Walsh's interview with Daisy Webster, 2 March 1982, Vancouver; *Vancouver Sun*, 6 October 1972; Ann Farrell, *Grace MacInnis: A Story of Love and Integrity* (Markham, ON: Fitzhenry and Whiteside, 1994); Walsh, "Peacock and the Guinea Hen," 153–59.

78 Isitt, *Militant Minority*; Nichol, "In Pursuit of the Voter," 132–35.

79 On Smith's early life, see UBCSC, Evelyn Grey Smith Papers, box 11, files 1–4, Rachel Epstein's interview with Evelyn Grey Smith, 1991 (hereafter Epstein's interview with Smith).

80 On Evelyn's family life and, particularly, her sister Constance, see Karen Duder, "Public Acts and Private Languages: Bisexuality and the Multiple Discourses of Constance Grey Swartz," *BC Studies* 136 (Winter 2002–03): 7–9. Duder argues, convincingly in my view, that Eve's sister Constance had many close, possibly sexual, relationships with women, although her parents continually pushed Constance towards heterosexuality and family.

81 UBCSC, Evelyn Grey Smith Papers, box 11, files 1–4, Epstein's interview with Smith, 1991. The 1991 date for these interviews must mean that the interviews were placed in the archives during that year since Eve Smith died in 1988. On Smith's background and family life, see the popular biography by Arthur Cathers, *Beloved Dissident: Eve Smith (1904–1988)* (Blyth, ON: Drumadravy Books, 1997), 5, 13–15, 21, 29, 31, 39, 45, 59, 61, 76, 98, 110, 116–21, 131.

82 The Regina Manifesto was the founding document of the CCF, so called because it originated during the CCF's founding conference in Regina in 1933. The manifesto, written primarily by Frank Scott and Frank Underhill, was a fairly moderate document. It expressed support for the creation of a welfare statist society (although the term "welfare statist" was not specifically used) by electoral means: CCF members should strive to vote for CCF candidates for public office at all levels of government in Canada. The final sentence of the document did state that the

CCF would not rest until capitalism had been eradicated and replaced by a society based on the co-operative commonwealth. Despite this statement, the Regina Manifesto was a blueprint for Canadian social democracy and not a statement in support of radical socialism or communism. See Desmond Morton, *NDP: Social Democracy in Canada*, 2nd ed. (Toronto: Samuel Stevens Hakkert and Company, 1977), 12–13; Young, *Anatomy of a Party*.

83 UBCSC, Evelyn Grey Smith Papers, box 11, files 1–4, Epstein's interview with Smith, 1991.

84 Cathers, *Beloved Dissident*, 116.

85 UBCSC, Evelyn Grey Smith Papers, box 7, file 16, Smith to the BC CCF Provincial Executive, 21 September 1950; UBCSC, Evelyn Grey Smith Papers, box 7, file 16, Smith to the CCF Provincial Executive, 25 August 1950.

86 The "Old Left" refers to the communist and social democratic left from the period encompassing roughly 1930 to 1959. In its Canadian manifestation, the Old Left was made up of the CPC, the CCF, and a few other (smaller) parties who argued that the working class was the primary social force that could mitigate the effects of capitalism and bring in a more humane system. The "New Left" refers to the many groups of left radicals who emerged during the 1960s and in subsequent years. In contrast to their counterparts from earlier decades, the New Left emphasized the "new social movements" – feminists, gay and lesbian activists, environmentalists, and students to name but a few – as the forces who would effect change in society. See John Henry Harter, *New Social Movements, Class, and the Environment: A Case Study of Greenpeace, Canada* (Newcastle-Upon-Tyne: Cambridge Scholars Press, 2011); Isitt, *Militant Minority*, 109–37; Bryan D. Palmer, *Canada's 1960s: The Ironies of Identity in a Rebellious Era* (Toronto: University of Toronto Press, 2009).

87 Cathers, *Beloved Dissident*, 6.

88 UBCSC, Evelyn Grey Smith Papers, box 11, files 1–4, Epstein's interview with Smith, 1991.

89 Thomas P. Socknat, "The Pacifist Background of the Early CCF," in *"Building the Co-operative Commonwealth": Essays on the Democratic Socialist Tradition in Canada*, ed. J. William Brennan, 23–35 (Regina: Canadian Plains Research Center, 1984).

90 On the views of earlier CCF women, see Sangster, *Dreams of Equality*, 91–98.

91 For a study of dominant concepts of homo- and heterosexuality during this period, see Daniel J. Robinson and David Kimmel, "The Queer Career of Homosexual Security Vetting in Cold War Canada," in *Gender and History in Canada*, ed. Joy Parr and Mark Rosenfeld, 317–88 (Toronto: Copp Clark, 1996).

92 On history, politics, and "place," see John Agnew and Luca Muscara, *Making Political Geography*, 2nd ed. (Lanham, MD: Rowman and Littlefield, 2012); Robert A.J. MacDonald, *Making Vancouver: Class, Status, and Social Boundaries, 1863–1913* (Vancouver: UBC Press, 1996).

Chapter 2: Ladies, Let Us Hold High the Banner!

1 Glenbow Archives, Vera Gillespie Fonds, file 1, report of the 31st Annual Convention of the Social Credit Women's Auxiliary (SCWA), 3 December 1968, Edmonton.

2 On the decline of Social Credit during the late 1960s, see Alvin Finkel, *The Social Credit Phenomenon in Alberta* (Toronto: University of Toronto Press, 1989),

167–201; Howard Palmer with Tamara Palmer, *Alberta: A New History* (Edmonton: Hurtig, 1990), 321–25.

3 This "lament for a patriarchy lost" is a standard theme in right-wing discourse surrounding the family. In more recent times, reactionaries, both female and male, have argued that the nuclear, heterosexual family has "broken down" as a result of the supposed permissiveness of the modern era, particularly the 1960s. The women studied here felt similarly, seeing the post-Second World War period as one of moral decay and societal breakdown. The increased freedom that youth gained after the Second World War played a key role in formulating this viewpoint. See Karen Dubinsky, *Lament for a "Patriarchy Lost"? Anti-Feminism, Anti-Abortion, and R.E.A.L. Women in Canada* (Ottawa: Canadian Research Institute for the Advancement of Women, 1985), 27–40 and passim; Andrea Dworkin, *Right-Wing Women* (New York: Perigee Books, 1983); Barbara Ehrenreich, *Fear of Falling: The Inner Life of the Middle Class* (New York: Pantheon Books, 1989), 168–95; Rebecca E. Klatch, *Women of the New Right* (Philadelphia: Temple University Press, 1987).

4 C.B. Macpherson described the social basis of the SCP as being "petit-bourgeois," and this was true, to some degree, of the party's leadership: many were wealthy farmers and small business owners. See C.B. Macpherson, *Democracy in Alberta: Social Credit and the Party System*, new ed. (Toronto: University of Toronto Press, 2013). Yet many of the party's rank and file were poor farmers who owned little land. Some were even urban workers in cities like Edmonton, Calgary, Lethbridge, and Medicine Hat. See Edward Bell, *Social Classes and Social Credit in Alberta* (Montreal and Kingston: McGill-Queen's University Press, 1994).

5 This statement should *not* imply that rank-and-file SCP women and men were any less valuable to the movement. Indeed, I would argue that elites in political parties owe much more to the grassroots members then they often admit. This statement simply acknowledges that leaders in political parties often leave behind more detailed records. Like in the CPC and the CCF, more educated and wealthier Socreds became leaders in the party.

6 Finkel, *Social Credit Phenomenon in Alberta*, 89, 196.

7 Glenbow Archives, Vera Gillespie Fonds, file 1, report of the 31st Annual Convention of the SCWA, Edmonton, 3 December 1968.

8 Information on the auxiliaries' structure can be found in Vancouver City Archives (VCA), Henrietta M. Thompson Papers, box 1, file 3, Alberta Social Credit League, Constitution and Bylaws, approved by the Annual Convention, Calgary, Alberta, 27–28 November 1947. For British Columbia, see VCA, Henrietta M. Thompson Papers, box 1, file 3, British Columbia Social Credit League, Constitution and Bylaws, effective 1 December 1950.

9 *Edmonton Journal*, 12 February 1960.

10 Glenbow Archives, Eva Reid Fonds, file 152, pamphlet, A.J. Hooke, *Social Credit Women Members of the Legislature*, n.d. See also Cynthia Loch-Drake, "'A Non-Drinker, a Non-Smoker, She was a Good-Living Woman'": Pentacostalism and the Class Politics of Alberta Meat-Packing Unionist Ethel Wilson," paper presented at the International Conference on the Study of Canada, Trent University, 23 May 2015.

11 On the strength of evangelical religion in Lethbridge, and in Alberta in general, see W.E. Mann, *Sect, Cult, and Church in Alberta* (Toronto: University of Toronto Press, 1955), 19.

12 Glenbow Archives, Vera Gillespie Fonds, file 1, pamphlet, *Social Credit 70: Women's Auxiliaries of the ASCL*, pamphlet published by the Women's Auxiliaries of the Alberta Social Credit League, 1970.

13 Ibid. This identification with Native people did not suggest any anti-racist or pro-Native viewpoint on Landeryou's part. Indeed, the general Socred viewpoint on First Nations people reflected that of the dominant political class in Canada: First Nations cultures were something to be admired in museums, but Native land claims or calls for the end of the residential school system were not to be taken seriously. Indeed, Social Credit discourse surrounding race and racism was implicitly ethnocentric since the new world that the SCP supported was white, although this aspect of SCP ideology was rarely stated publicly. See Ward Churchill, *Indians Are Us? Culture and Genocide in Native North America* (Toronto: Between the Lines, 1994); Howard Palmer, *Patterns of Prejudice: Nativism in Alberta* (Toronto: McClelland and Stewart, 1982).

14 Glenbow Archives, Vera Gillespie Fonds, file 1, pamphlet, *Social Credit 70: Women's Auxiliaries of the ASCL.*

15 Glenbow Archives, Vera Gillespie Fonds, file 1, report of the 31st Annual Convention of the SCWA, 3 December 1968, Edmonton.

16 Ibid.

17 In addition to the works already cited on right-wing women's ideology, see Paola Bacchetta and Margaret Power, eds., *Right-Wing Women: From Conservatives to Extremists around the World* (New York: Routledge, 2002); Kathleen Blee, *Women of the Klan: Racism and Gender in the 1920s* (Berkeley: University of California Press, 1991); Julie V. Gottlieb, *Feminine Fascism: Women in Britain's Fascist Movement, 1923–1945* (London: I.B. Tauris, 2000).

18 Provincial Archives of Alberta (hereafter PAA), Cornelia Wood Fonds, box 24, item 479, Wood's passport, expired 1 August 1955.

19 *Calgary Herald*, 11 October 1966.

20 PAA, Cornelia Wood Fonds, box 24, item 463, marriage certificate for Russell Edgerton Wood and Cornelia Lucinda Railey, 24 December 1912.

21 Women in rural areas of Canada formed branches of the Women's Institutes all across the country in order to provide advice and support for other women in isolated areas. See Monda Halpern, *And on That Farm He Had a Wife: Ontario Farm Women and Feminism, 1900–1970* (Montreal and Kingston: McGill-Queen's University Press, 2001).

22 *Calgary Herald*, 11 October 1966; PAA, SCWA Papers, box 1, file 18, program for *Stars in Time*, a pantomime commemorating the fiftieth anniversary of the vote for women in Alberta.

23 Ibid.

24 On Blackmore and the anti-Semites within the SCP, see Glenbow Archives, John Horn Blackmore Fonds, files 261, 300, 442. Though Wood did not express anti-Semitic views, she, like Blackmore, owned copies of *American Nationalist*, a right-wing, nativist publication from the United States that opposed civil rights for African Americans, the State of Israel, and Jewish organizations of all stripes.

25 On anti-Semitism in the SCP, see Janine Stingel, *Social Discredit: Anti-Semitism, Social Credit, and the Jewish Response* (Montreal and Kingston: McGill-Queen's University Press, 2000). Ernest Manning expelled the anti-Semites from the party

in 1948, while William Aberhart never expressed anti-Semitic views. See Bob Hesketh, *Major Douglas and Alberta Social Credit* (Toronto: University of Toronto Press, 1997); Finkel, *Social Credit Phenomenon in Alberta*, 104–06.

26 The quotations are from PAA, Cornelia Wood Fonds, box 1, items 129–49, minutes of the 29th Annual Convention of the SCWA, Palliser Hotel, Calgary, 21 November 1966.

27 Nadja Durbach, *Bodily Matters: The Anti-Vaccination Movement in England, 1853–1907* (Durham, NC: Duke University Press, 2005), esp. chap. 3; Norman Gevitz, ed., *Other Healers: Unorthodox Medicine in America* (Baltimore: Johns Hopkins University Press, 1988).

28 On this issue, see Christopher Dummitt, *The Manly Modern: Masculinity in Postwar Canada* (Vancouver: UBC Press, 2007).

29 A critique of expert knowledge can be found in Michel Foucault, *Discipline and Punish: The Birth of the Prison*, trans. Alan Sheridan (New York: Pantheon Books, 1977). For a study of psychiatry, see Mona Gleason, *Normalizing the Ideal: Psychology, Schooling, and the Family in Postwar Canada* (Toronto: University of Toronto Press, 1999).

30 *Edmonton Journal*, 21 February 1952.

31 PAA, Cornelia Wood Fonds, box 14, item 296, address on the Speech from the Throne in the Alberta Legislature by Wood, 23 February 1952.

32 Catherine Carstairs and Rachel Elder, "Expertise, Health, and Popular Opinion: Debating Water Fluoridation, 1945–80," *Canadian Historical Review* 89, 3 (2008): 345–71.

33 Leonard B. Kuffert, "'Reckoning with the Machine': The British Columbia Social Credit Movement as Social Criticism, 1932–52," *BC Studies* 124 (Winter 1999–2000): 9–39. The term "island communities" is from Robert H. Wiebe, *The Search for Order, 1877–1920* (New York: Hill and Wang, 1967), xiii. The term is also used, more recently, in T.J. Jackson Lears, *Rebirth of a Nation: The Making of Modern America, 1877–1920* (New York: HarperCollins, 2009).

34 Lisa McGirr, *Suburban Warriors: The Origins of the New American Right* (Princeton: Princeton University Press, 2001), chap. 4.

35 On evangelical Christianity's attack on modernity, see David Bebbington, "Evangelicalism in Its Settings: The British and American Movements Since 1940," in *Evangelicalism: Comparative Studies of Popular Protestantism in North America, the British Isles, and Beyond, 1700–1990*, ed. Mark A. Noll, David W. Bebbington, and George A. Rawlyk, 366–69 (New York: Oxford University Press, 1994); George A. Rawlyk, *Wrapped Up in God: A Study of Several Canadian Revivals and Revivalists* (Burlington, ON: Welch Publishing Co., 1988), 128–29, 135–40.

36 On first-wave feminism, see Carol Lee Bacchi, *Liberation Deferred? The Ideas of the English-Canadian Suffragists, 1877–1918* (Toronto: University of Toronto Press, 1983); Franca Iacovetta, "'A Respectable Feminist': The Political Career of Senator Cairine Wilson, 1921–1962," in *Beyond the Vote: Canadian Women in Politics* ed. Linda Kealey and Joan Sangster (Toronto: University of Toronto Press, 1989), 65–66. Wilson endorsed state assistance to single mothers and poor working women. She was an exemplar of the "New Liberalism" of the late nineteenth and early twentieth centuries.

37 On the WCTU and the IODE, see Sharon Anne Cook, *"Through Sunshine and Shadow": The Woman's Christian Temperance Union, Evangelicalism, and Reform in Ontario, 1874–1930* (Montreal and Kingston: McGill-Queen's University Press, 1995); Katie Pickles, *Female Imperialism and National Identity: Imperial Order Daughters of the Empire* (Manchester, UK: Manchester University Press, 2009); Mariana Valverde, *The Age of Light, Soap, and Water: Moral Reform in English Canada, 1885–1925*, rev. ed. (Toronto: University of Toronto Press, 2008).

38 Jennifer Burns, *Goddess of the Market: Ayn Rand and the American Right* (New York: Oxford University Press, 2009); Justin Raimondo, *Reclaiming the American Right: Lost Legacy of the Conservative Movement*, rev. ed. (Wilmington, DE: ISI Books, 2008), 183–200. Paterson and Lane, the latter the heir to the *Little House on the Prairie* fortune, were both libertarian, anti-communist opponents of the New Deal; both argued that the United States needed to return to small government and small-town values.

39 Philip Massolin, *Canadian Intellectuals, the Tory Tradition, and the Challenge of Modernity, 1939–1970* (Toronto: University of Toronto Press, 2001).

40 I say "continentalist" because we might argue that SCP women were part of a tradition of women's conservatism that included US right-wing women as well. An in-depth study of the comparisons and contrasts among Canadian and American conservative women is beyond the scope of this book. For an international perspective on rightist women, see Kathleen M. Blee and Sandra McGee Deutsch, eds., *Women of the Right: Comparisons and Interplays across Borders* (University Park: Pennsylvania State University Press, 2012).

41 *Victoria Times-Colonist*, 28 February 1983; *Vancouver News-Herald*, 14 October 1953; Library and Archives Canada (LAC), Canadian Security and Intelligence Fonds, vols. 778–82, part 39, *Ukrainske-Slovo* [Ukrainian word], 15 February 1956.

42 PAA, Cornelia Wood Fonds, box 14, item 304, pamphlet, *Fluoridation of Water*, taken from speech made by Lydia Arsens in the BC Legislature, 22 February 1955.

43 Frank Zelko, *Make It a Green Peace! The Rise of Countercultural Environmentalism* (New York: Oxford University Press, 2013).

44 *Vancouver News-Herald*, 14 October 1953.

45 Massachusetts candy manufacturer Robert Welch founded the John Birch Society in 1958 to combat communism and to support "limited government" and traditional values: this was very similar to SCP populist ideology. See Gary Allen with Larry Abraham, *None Dare Call It Conspiracy* (San Diego, CA: Dauphin Publications, 2013); David Brion Davis, ed., *The Fear of Conspiracy: Images of Un-American Subversion from the Revolution to the Present* (Ithaca: Cornell University Press, 1971); Jeff Taylor, *Politics on a Human Scale: The American Tradition of Decentralism* (Lanham, MD: Lexington Books, 2013).

46 PAA, SCWA Papers, box 1, file 9, report of the 8th Annual Provincial Convention of the SCWA, Palliser Hotel, Calgary, 4 December 1945.

47 Gladys A. Willison, *Stars in Time: A History of the Alberta Social Credit Women's Auxiliaries* (Edmonton: The Women's Auxiliaries of the Alberta Social Credit League, 1973), 53–54. This is an "official" history of the SCWA.

48 On Rose Wilkinson, see also Tom Langford, "Why Alberta Vacillated over Wartime Day Nurseries," *Prairie Forum* 28, 2 (2003): 184; Gilbert Levine, ed., *Patrick*

Lenihan: From Irish Rebel to Founder of Canadian Public Sector Unionism (St. John's: Canadian Committee on Labour History, 1998), 128.

49 Willison, *Stars in Time*, 54.

50 For example, Arkansas's Hattie Caraway became the first female US senator in 1931 after inheriting her late husband's seat in the US Senate. She won a special election in January 1932 to serve out the remaining months of her husband's term in office and then won a full term in the US Senate in November 1932. See Alan Brinkley, *Voices of Protest: Huey Long, Father Coughlin, and the Great Depression* (New York: Vintage Books, 1983), 47–53.

51 Willison, *Stars in Time*, 54.

52 This was a strange statement to make, considering that the population of Alberta numbered more than a million in 1955. Howard and Tamara Palmer note that the 1951 census put the province's population at 939,000, while the 1961 census states that Alberta's population was 1.3 million. See Howard Palmer with Tamara Palmer, *Alberta, A New History* (Edmonton: Hurtig, 1990), 303.

53 PAA, SCWA Papers, box 1, file 10. Mrs. J.L. Robinson, speech at the 18th Annual SCWA Convention, Palliser Hotel, Calgary, 29 November 1955.

54 Although the British influence over Canada was changing and slowly fading during the 1950s and 1960s. See C.P. Champion, *The Strange Demise of British Canada, 1964–68* (Montreal and Kingston: McGill-Queen's University Press, 2010); Jose Igartua, *The Other Quiet Revolution: National Identities in English Canada, 1945–71* (Vancouver: UBC Press, 2006).

55 The quotations are from a speech cited in the Socred newspaper the *Busy Bee*, vol. 2, no. 3, December 1957.

56 The quotations are from the *Canadian Social Crediter*, vol. 8, no. 2, February 1956.

57 Ibid.

58 *Maclean's*, 1 September 1952; *Vancouver Sun*, 5 February 1953; *Vancouver Province*, 13 October 1953; *Christian Science Monitor*, 17 March 1942; University of British Columbia, Special Collections Division (hereafter UBCSC), Dorothy Gretchen Steeves Papers, box 7, file 2, unpublished article, Dave Driver, "Log of the House," n.d.

59 *Vancouver Sun*, 5 February 1953; *Vancouver Province*, 13 October 1953.

60 On these points, see Andrea B. Smith, "The CCF, the NPA, and Civic Change: Provincial Forces behind Vancouver Politics, 1930–1940," *BC Studies* 53 (Spring 1982): 45–65.

61 *Vancouver Sun*, 13 October 1953; *Vancouver Province*, 13 October 1953.

62 On the "back to the land" program, see James Struthers, *No Fault of Their Own: Unemployment and the Canadian Welfare State, 1914–1941* (Toronto: University of Toronto Press, 1983), 8–9, 156–57.

63 Rolston's views on Second World War-era wartime day nurseries – established by the federal government in Ottawa to provide childcare for women with children who were working in war industries in Ontario and Quebec – demonstrate her conservative perspective on working women. In 1943, Laura Jamieson and Rolston debated this issue in the *Vancouver Sun*. Some CCF and CPC women supported providing women with day care so that they could better support their families, while most SCP women opposed nurseries and argued for the return of the women to the family home. See *Vancouver Sun*, 4 March 1943; Ruth Roach Pierson, *"They're Still Women after All": The Second World War and Canadian*

Womanhood (Toronto: McClelland and Stewart, 1986), 49–61. A full discussion of wartime day nurseries is beyond the scope of this book.

64 *Christian Science Monitor*, 17 March 1942; UBCSC, Dorothy Gretchen Steeves Papers, box 7, file 2, unpublished article, Dave Driver, "Log of the House," n.d. On Rolston, see also Juliette Proom, "Tilly Jean Rolston: She Knew How to Throw a Party," in *Not Just Pin Money: Selected Essays on the History of Women's Work in British Columbia*, ed. Barbara K. Latham and Roberta J. Pazdro, 381–88 (Victoria: Camosun College, 1984).

65 On Rogers, see Glenbow Archives, Eva Reid Fonds, file 152, notes by Reid on women MLAs in Alberta, n.d. These notes seem to have been written during the 1950s.

66 For Rogers' CCF connections, see Glenbow Archives, Alberta CCF/NDP Fonds, file 232, notebook, minutes of meetings of the Edmonton CCF women's clubs. The minutes of the 10 February 1947 meeting note that Rogers was "in the chair."

67 Glenbow Archives, Eva Reid Fonds, file 152, Pamphlet, A.J. Hooke, *Social Credit Women Members of the Legislature*, n.d. Given the reference to Socred cabinet member Ethel Wilson, this pamphlet was written during the 1950s.

68 Glenbow Archives, Eva Reid Fonds, file 152, Notes by Reid on women MLAs in Alberta, n.d. On Rogers' background, see also John A. Irving, *The Social Credit Movement in Alberta* (Toronto: University of Toronto Press, 1959), 186–96.

69 Glenbow Archives, Edith Rogers Fonds, file 1, address delivered by "Mrs. Edith Rogers" to Legislative Assembly of Alberta in support of the taxation of banks (second reading), 30 September 1937.

70 Ibid.

71 Ibid.

72 Ibid.

73 For a description of the Old Right, and its particular relevance to women, see Burns, *Goddess of the Market*.

74 Alvin Finkel, "Populism and Gender: The UFA and Social Credit Experiences," *Journal of Canadian Studies* 27, 4 (1992–93): 76–97. Baker and Barritt returned to the United Farm Women of Alberta after leaving SC.

75 John G. Stackhouse Jr., *Canadian Evangelicalism in the Twentieth Century: An Introduction to Its Character* (Toronto: University of Toronto Press, 1993), 22, 35–45.

76 Ibid., 35–45.

77 Finkel, *Social Credit Phenomenon in Alberta*, intro. and passim.

78 Kathleen Blee, *Inside Organized Racism: Women in the Hate Movement* (Berkeley: University of California Press, 2002).

79 Bacchetta and Power, *Right-Wing Women*; Ruth Frankenberg, *White Women, Race Matters: The Social Construction of Whiteness* (Minneapolis: University of Minnesota Press, 1993).

80 Bob Hesketh, "From Crusaders to Missionaries to Wives: Alberta Social Credit Women, 1932–1955" *Prairie Forum* 18, 1 (1993): 54.

81 It is interesting to compare SCP women with former British prime minister Margaret Thatcher. Thatcher famously argued for a return to Victorian values in Britain. In an interview with London's *Evening Standard*, shortly before the 1983 British election, Thatcher talked of how her grandmother had taught her about

"Victorian values" such as cleanliness, patriotism, self-reliance, and hard work. See Kevin A. Morrison, "There's No Place Like Home: Margaret Thatcher at No. 10 Downing Street," in *Thatcher and After: Margaret Thatcher and Her Afterlife in Contemporary Culture*, ed. Louisa Hadley and Elizabeth Ho (New York: Routledge, 2010), 131n. Yet, where populist SCP women honestly hoped for a return to traditional, older values as an antidote to the problems of modernity, Lady Thatcher used the state to engineer more modern forms of state governance in Britain. We might think of Thatcher as similar to the "elitist, pro-business" wing of the SCP, even as she paid tribute to socially conservative values.

82 Trinity Western University Archives, Robert N. Thompson Fonds, box 1, file 23, statement by "Mrs. I. Smith," chairman of the SCP Women's Auxiliary Committee, souvenir program, National Social Credit Party Convention, founding convention of the federal Social Credit Ladies' Auxiliary of Canada, Ottawa, 4 July 1961.

Chapter 3: Peace Is the Concern of Every Mother

1 *Pacific Tribune*, 25 May 1951. A version of this chapter appeared in *Peace and Change* under the title "Peace Is the Concern of Every Mother: Communist and Social Democratic Women's Anti-War Activism in British Columbia, 1948–1960," *Peace and Change: A Journal of Peace Research* 35, 4 (2010): 626–57.

2 For the CPC, see Stephen Lyon Endicott, *James G. Endicott: Rebel out of China* (Toronto: University of Toronto Press, 1980); for the CCF, see the work of Thomas Socknat cited in the introduction and below in note 5.

3 The sources I was able to find for Chapters 3 to 6 are better than those I was able to find for earlier chapters. If some of the women mentioned in the latter do not reappear, this is due to issues with primary sources. There were other primary sources that I could have used, but I have chosen to use those that I feel are the best and that are most representative of these different topics.

4 For an overview of earlier reform movements in Canada, see Mariana Valverde, *The Age of Light, Soap, and Water: Moral Reform in English Canada, 1885–1925*, rev. ed. (Toronto: University of Toronto Press, 2008).

5 For background on these arguments, see Kathleen A. Brown, "The 'Savagely Fathered and Un-Mothered World of the Communist Party USA: Feminism, Maternalism, and Mother Bloor," *Feminist Studies* 25, 3 (1999): 539, 560; Peter Campbell, *Rose Henderson: A Woman for the People* (Montreal and Kingston: McGill-Queen's University Press, 2010); Temma Kaplan, "Female Consciousness and Collective Action: The Case of Barcelona, 1910–1918," *Signs* 7, 3 (1982): 565–66.

6 The literature here is vast. See, in the Canadian context, Tarah Brookfield, *Cold War Comforts: Canadian Women, Child Safety, and Global Insecurity, 1945–1975* (Waterloo, ON: Wilfrid Laurier University Press, 2012); Lara Campbell, " 'Women United against the War': Gender Politics, Feminism, and Vietnam Draft Resistance in Canada," in *New World Coming: The Sixties and the Shaping of Global Consciousness*, ed. Karen Dubinsky, Catherine Krull, Susan Lord, Sean Mills, and Scott Rutherford, 339–46 (Toronto: Between The Lines, 2009); Kay Macpherson, "The Voice of Women," in *Up and Doing: Canadian Women and Peace*, ed. Janice Williamson and Deborah Gorham, 204–10 (Toronto: The Women's Press, 1989);

James Naylor, "Pacifism or Anti-Imperialism? The CCF Response to the Outbreak of World War II," *Journal of the Canadian Historical Association* 8 (1997): 213–37; Barbara Roberts, *A Reconstructed World: A Feminist Biography of Gertrude Richardson* (Montreal and Kingston: McGill-Queen's University Press, 1996); Barbara Roberts, *"Why Do Women Do Nothing to End the War?" Canadian Feminist-Pacifists and the Great War* (Ottawa, ON: Canadian Research Institute for the Advancement of Women, 1985); Barbara Roberts, "Women's Peace Activism in Canada," in *Beyond the Vote: Canadian Women and Politics*, ed. Linda Kealey and Joan Sangster, 276–308, (Toronto: University of Toronto Press, 1989); Joan Sangster, *Dreams of Equality: Women on the Canadian Left, 1920–1950* (Toronto: McClelland and Stewart, 1989), 165–66; Thomas P. Socknat, "The Pacifist Background of the Early CCF," in *"Building the Co-Operative Commonwealth": Essays on the Democratic Socialist Tradition in Canada*, ed. J. William Brennan, 57–64 (Regina: Canadian Plains Research Center, 1984); Thomas P. Socknat, *Witness against War: Pacifism in Canada, 1900–1945* (Toronto: University of Toronto Press, 1987); Veronica Strong-Boag, "Peace-Making Women: Canada, 1919–1939," in *Women and Peace: Theoretical, Historical and Practical Perspectives*, ed. Ruth Roach Pierson, 170–91 (London: Croom Helm, 1987). In the American context, see Jacqueline B. Castledine, *Cold War Progressives: Women's Interracial Organizing for Peace and Freedom* (Urbana: University of Illinois Press, 2012); Harriet Hyman Alonso, *Peace as a Women's Issue: A History of the US Movement for World Peace and Women's Rights* (Syracuse, NY: Syracuse University Press, 1993); Frances H. Early, *A World without War: How US Feminists and Pacifists Resisted World War I* (Syracuse, NY: Syracuse University Press, 1997); Dee Garrison, "'Our Skirts Gave Them Courage': The Civil Defense Protest Movement in New York City, 1955–1961," in *Not June Cleaver: Women and Gender in Postwar America, 1945–1960*, ed. Joanne Meyerowitz, 201–21 (Philadelphia: Temple University Press, 1994); Robbie Lieberman, *The Strangest Dream: Communism, Anticommunism, and the US Peace Movement, 1945–1963* (Syracuse, NY: Syracuse University Press, 2000); Amy Swerdlow, *Women Strike for Peace: Traditional Motherhood and Radical Politics in the 1960s* (Chicago: University of Chicago Press, 1993).

7 Hence, this chapter's focus on the period from 1948 to 1960. I found very few commentaries in the communist or social democratic press, or in archival collections, dealing with the CPC or CCF on the Cold War and peace issues prior to 1948.

8 On Bianco's background. see *Pacific Tribune*, 20 May 1949, 3 June 1949, 10 June 1949, 17 April 1953.

9 The quotations are from *Pacific Tribune*, 6 May 1949, 2 June 1950.

10 *Pacific Tribune*, 11 May 1951.

11 See the works in note 6.

12 *Pacific Tribune*, 11 May 1951.

13 Here I draw on arguments made in Linda Kealey, *Enlisting Women for the Cause: Women, Labour, and the Left in Canada, 1890–1920* (Toronto: University of Toronto Press, 1998); Sangster, *Dreams of Equality*.

14 Todd McCallum, " 'Not a Sex Question?' The One Big Union and the Politics of Radical Manhood," *Labour/Le Travail* 42 (1998): 15–54.

15 University of British Columbia, Special Collections Division (hereafter UBCSC), Harold Prichett-IWA District Council No. 1 Papers, box 8, file 6, Mrs. Raymond

Lang, Secretary to Local 1–30, Ladies' Auxiliaries IWA (Lake Cowichan, BC), to George Brown, Director of Organization, CIO, Portland, Oregon, 26 July 1945.

16 *Pacific Tribune*, 22 October 1948.

17 Ibid.

18 Ibid.

19 Ibid.

20 On the resilience of the far right in post-Second World War Europe, see Annie Jacobsen, *Operation Paperclip: The Secret Intelligence Program That Brought Nazi Scientists to America* (Boston: Little, Brown and Co., 2014); Mark Mazower, *Dark Continent: Europe's Twentieth Century* (New York: Vintage Books, 2000).

21 Claire (nee Eglin) Culhane was to be called "Kayla" after a deceased aunt. According to Jewish tradition, people could not pass happily into the next world until a child had been named after them. She was therefore called "Claire," the English equivalent of Kayla. Claire's husband, Gerry Culhane, a prominent communist and descendent of a long and distinguished line of Irish patriots and nationalists, took to calling his then wife "Kayla Culhane," in part to destroy the identity that "Claire" had formed apart from him. In Vancouver's left-wing circles, she was often known as "Kayla." See Mick Lowe, *One Woman Army: The Life of Claire Culhane* (Toronto: MacMillan Canada, 1992), 5–6, 47, 51–52.

22 *Pacific Tribune*, 24 August 1951.

23 Ibid.

24 On the CPC's internationalist focus, a view that included what some might read as anti-racist statements, see Fernando Claudin, *The Communist Movement: From Comintern to Cominform*, part 2: *The Zenith of Stalinism*, trans. Francis MacDonagh (New York: Monthly Review Press, 1975); Duncan Hallas, *The Comintern* (London: Bookmarks, 1985); Kevin McDermott and Jeremy Agnew, eds., *The Comintern: A History of International Communism from Lenin to Stalin* (London: Macmillan, 1996).

25 *Pacific Tribune*, 24 August 1951.

26 Swerdlow, *Women Strike for Peace*.

27 Joan Sangster and Margaret Hobbs, eds., *The Woman Worker, 1926–1929* (St. John's: Canadian Committee on Labour History, 1999), 131–34.

28 Lieberman, *Strangest Dream*, 115.

29 *Pacific Tribune*, 12 November 1948.

30 Ibid.

31 *Pacific Tribune*, 4 February 1949.

32 Ibid.

33 Ibid.

34 *Pacific Tribune*, 23 May 1952.

35 *Pacific Tribune*, 30 May 1952.

36 Ibid.

37 *Pacific Tribune*, 6 June 1952.

38 Deborah Gerson, "'Is Family Devotion Now Subversive?' Familialism against McCarthyism," *Not June Cleaver: Women and Gender in Postwar America, 1945–1960*, ed. Joanne Meyerowitz, 151–72 (Philadelphia: Temple University Press, 1994). The Smith Act, passed in 1940 in the United States and officially known as the Alien Registration Act, allowed the federal government to prosecute groups or

persons who conspired to "teach or advocate the overthrow of the established government by force or violence." This act was used to arrest many male CPC members, thus taking fathers away from their wives and children.

39 Ibid., 152–54.

40 *Pacific Tribune*, 4 July 1958.

41 Ibid.

42 The Waffle Movement of 1969–72 in the New Democratic Party was only the most prominent example of Canadian left nationalism. See Stephen Azzi, *Walter Gordon and the Rise of Canadian Nationalism* (Montreal and Kingston: McGill-Queen's University Press, 1999).

43 A standard history of Canadian-American relations is J.L. Granatstein, *Yankee Go Home? Canadians and Anti-Americanism* (Toronto: Harper Collins, 1996).

44 *Pacific Tribune*, 11 November 1949.

45 See Naylor, "Pacifism or Anti-Imperialism?," 213–37.

46 On this point, see Andree Levesque, *Red Travellers: Jeanne Corbin and Her Comrades*, Yvonne M. Klein, Trans. (Montreal and Kingston: McGill-Queen's University Press, 2006).

47 The view that women's oppression would disappear with the advent of a socialist society was fairly common among leftists. In an earlier context, see Janice Newton, *The Feminist Challenge to the Canadian Left, 1900–1918* (Toronto: University of Toronto Press, 1995).

48 For more on the CCF's ideology, in addition to the points mentioned in the introduction, see Richard Allen, *The Social Passion: Religion and Social Reform in Canada, 1914–1928* (Toronto: University of Toronto Press, 1973); Michiel Horn, *The League for Social Reconstruction: Intellectual Origins of the Democratic Left in Canada, 1930–1942* (Toronto: University of Toronto Press, 1980); Norman Penner, *The Canadian Left: A Critical Analysis* (Scarborough, ON: Prentice-Hall, 1977), 195–217; Socknat, "Pacifist Background," 57–67; Walter D. Young, *The Anatomy of a Party: The National CCF, 1932–61* (Toronto: University of Toronto Press, 1969).

49 *CCF News*, 11 May 1955.

50 Ibid. The Communist Party of Canada changed its official name to the Labour Progressive Party in 1942. The Canadian government proclaimed that the CPC was an illegal organization in 1939. In 1941, with the Nazi invasion of the Soviet Union, the federal government stated that the CPC could emerge from illegality but only if the party changed its name to the Labour Progressive Party. Presumably, the new moniker sounded less threatening to the capitalist status quo than did the old one, which included word "Communist." On this point, see Sangster, *Dreams of Equality*, 166–70.

51 Ibid.

52 Lieberman, *Strangest Dream*, 7–8, Chapter 5.

53 *CCF News*, 31 October 1951.

54 The CPC, of course, also ran candidates for all levels of government, but the party was far less successful at electing members to public office, and, in general, the CPC's image was always perceived as being on the "far left" of Canadian politics, even if this was not the reality.

55 I do not consider the New Left movements of the 1960s and 1970s to be part of mainstream Canadian politics or society. While second-wave feminists, Red Power

activists, and anti-war activists from later decades certainly influenced mainstream Canadian society, they saw themselves as creating movements that were separate from conventional society, even as they sought to transform it. See Bryan D. Palmer, *Canada's 1960s: The Ironies of Identity in a Rebellious Era* (Toronto: University of Toronto Press, 2009).

56 For a view on the downfall of the Canadian peace movement, notably the communist-influenced Canadian Peace Congress, in the 1950s, see Reg Whitaker and Gary Marcuse, *Cold War Canada: The Making of a National Insecurity State, 1945–1957* (Toronto: University of Toronto Press, 1994), 364–83. This CPC was centred in Ontario and, thus, I do not discuss it here.

57 I assume from the letter's content that "W. Dahlberg" was a woman; however, I have no evidence to confirm this assumption.

58 *CCF News*, 27 January 1960.

59 *CCF News*, 20 August 1952

60 Ibid.

61 Ibid.

62 *CCF News*, 22 October 1958.

63 Ibid.

64 Scholars who focus on the more conservative aspects of the CCF's ideology include Desmond Morton, *NDP: Social Democracy in Canada*, 2nd ed. (Toronto: Samuel Stevens Hakkert and Company, 1977); Alan Whitehorn, *Canadian Socialism: Essays on the CCF-NDP* (Toronto: Oxford University Press, 1992).

65 Christina J. Nichol, "In Pursuit of the Voter: The British Columbia CCF, 1945–51," in *Building the Co-operative Commonwealth: Essays on the Democratic Socialist Tradition in Canada*, ed. J. William Brennan, 123–35 (Regina: Canadian Plains Research Center, 1984). See also Peter Campbell, *Canadian Marxists and the Search for a Third Way* (Montreal and Kingston: McGill-Queen's University Press, 1999) for information on this under-studied left-wing tradition in Canada.

66 *CCF News*, 25 January 1961.

67 Ibid.

68 Ibid.

69 Carol Bacchi, *Liberation Deferred? The Ideas of the English-Canadian Suffragists, 1877–1918* (Toronto: University of Toronto Press, 1983), 86–103 and passim.

70 UBCSC, Angus MacInnis Memorial Collection, box 25, file 10, Motion by the "Women of the CCF," n.d. I assume that this item was written in 1948 since another item with very similar wording can be found in UBCSC, Vancouver Council of Women Papers, box 2, file 5, letter and resolution, Norah Hill, Secretary of the CCF Women's Council to the Congress of Canadian Women, 22 March 1948.

71 See Naylor, "Pacifism or Anti-Imperialism?"

72 Brookfield, *Cold War Comforts*, 166–88 and passim.

73 Kealey, *Enlisting Women to the Cause*; Sangster, *Dreams of Equality*.

74 Kate Weigand, *Red Feminism: American Communism and the Making of Women's Liberation* (Baltimore: Johns Hopkins University Press, 2001). See also Swerdlow, *Women Strike for Peace*, esp. chap. 3.

75 Dorothy Sue Cobble, *The Other Women's Movement: Workplace Justice and Social Rights in Modern America* (Princeton: Princeton University Press, 2004); Meg

Luxton, "Feminism as a Class Act: Working-Class Feminism and the Women's Movement in Canada," *Labour/Le Travail* 48 (Fall 2001): 63–88.

76 Naomi Black, *Social Feminism* (Ithaca, NY: Cornell University Press, 1989), 12–89 and passim.

77 Birth control, too, would fit into this category, although, as previously seen, this issue did not become a "front-and-centre" concern for left-wing women until the 1960s. See Erika Dyck, *Facing Eugenics: Reproduction, Sterilization, and the Politics of Choice* (Toronto: University of Toronto Press, 2013).

78 See Louise I. Carbert, *Agrarian Feminism: The Politics of Ontario Farm Women* (Toronto: University of Toronto, 1995); Monda Halpern, *And on That Farm He Had a Wife: Ontario Farm Women and Feminism, 1900–1970* (Montreal and Kingston: McGill-Queen's University Press, 2001), 3–17.

79 Whitaker and Marcuse, *Cold War Canada*, chap. 16.

80 Luxton, "Feminism as a Class Act."

81 Other texts that challenge the image of the post-Second World War period as a completely restricting one for Canadian women are Magda Fahrni, *Household Politics: Montreal Families and Postwar Reconstruction* (Toronto: University of Toronto Press, 2005); Jennifer A. Stephen, *Pick One Intelligent Girl: Employability, Domesticity, and the Gendering of the Canadian Welfare State, 1939–1947* (Toronto: University of Toronto Press, 2007). A good general overview of the conservatism and conformity of the Cold War years in the United States, and the resistance to it, can be found in Ellen Schrecker, *Many Are the Crimes: McCarthyism in America* (Boston: Little, Brown and Co., 1998).

Chapter 4: Traveling Bags for Their Trip to Russia

1 *Busy Bee*, vol. 1, no. 5, October 1956.

2 Trinity Western University Archives, Robert N. Thompson Fonds, box 1, file 23, working draft of Social Credit policy for national leadership convention, Ottawa, 4–7 July 1961.

3 Ibid.

4 For the remarks on Rhee and Nasser, see *Canadian Social Crediter* (hereafter *CSC*), vol. 9, no. 1, January 1957. There are a number of different views on Canadian foreign policy during the late 1940s and 1950s. Some argue that Canada was forced into an economic and military alliance with the United States. Here, see Stephen Clarkson, *An Independent Foreign Policy for Canada?* (Toronto: McClelland and Stewart, 1968); George Parkin Grant, *Lament for a Nation: The Defeat of Canadian Nationalism* (Toronto: McClelland and Stewart, 1965). Others argue for the "middle power" approach – that is, the notion that Canada fulfilled a mediating role between the United States and the Soviet Union, and eschewed extreme political and foreign policy positions. For examples of this argument, see Adam Chapnick, *The Middle Power Project: Canada and the Founding of the United Nations* (Vancouver: UBC Press, 2006); Douglas A. Ross, *In the Interests of Peace: Canada and Vietnam, 1954–1973* (Toronto: University of Toronto Press, 1984). Still others argue that Canada actively chose to support the American military alliance and, consequently, Cold War anticommunism. Here, see Yves Engler, *Lester Pearson's Peacekeeping: The Truth May*

Hurt (Black Point, NS: Fernwood, 2012); Engler, *The Black Book of Canadian Foreign Policy* (Black Point, NS: Fernwood, 2009); Victor Levant, *Quiet Complicity: Canadian Involvement in the Vietnam War* (Toronto: Between the Lines, 1986); Reg Whitaker and Steve Hewitt, *Canada and the Cold War* (Toronto: Lorimer, 2003).

5 *CSC*, vol. 1, no. 25, 13 December 1950.

6 British Columbia Archives (hereafter BCA), Peer Vernon Paynter Papers, box 4, file 10, unpublished MS, "Defense – to help with your speech making," n.d. I assume from the context of the arguments that the item was written during the 1950s.

7 Franca Iacovetta, *Gatekeepers: Reshaping Immigrant Lives in Cold War Canada* (Toronto: Between the Lines, 2006).

8 BCA, Peer Vernon Paynter Papers, box 4, file 10, unpublished MSS, "Defense – to help with your speech making," n.d.

9 We have seen in more recent decades that this is still a staple of Western, particularly American, foreign policy. See especially Jean Bricmont, *Humanitarian Imperialism: Using Human Rights to Sell War*, trans. Diana Johnstone (New York: Monthly Review Press, 2007); Diana Johnstone, *Fools' Crusade: Yugoslavia, NATO, and Western Delusions* (New York: Monthly Review Press, 2002).

10 BCA, Peer Vernon Paynter Papers, box 4, file 10, unpublished MS, "Defense – to help with your speech making," n.d.

11 Provincial Archives of Alberta (hereafter PAA), Social Credit Women's Auxiliary Papers (hereafter SCWA Papers), box 1, file 11, resolution passed at the 24th Annual SCWA Convention, Calgary, 20 November 1961.

12 PAA, Cornelia Wood Fonds, box 1, item 227, pamphlet, *Canadians Must Awaken*, speech by "Mrs. C.R. Wood, MLA for Stony Plain, Alberta," 8 June 1945, published by the *CSC*.

13 Wayne S. Cole, *Roosevelt and the Isolationists, 1932–1945* (Lincoln: University of Nebraska Press, 1983); Andrew L. Johns, "Doves among Hawks: Republican Opposition to the Vietnam War, 1964–1968," *Peace and Change: A Journal of Peace Research* 31, 4 (2006): 585–628; Ronald Radosh, *Prophets on the Right: Profiles of Conservative Critics of American Globalism* (New York: Simon and Schuster, 1975); Jeff Taylor, *Politics on a Human Scale: The American Tradition of Decentralism* (Lanham, MD: Lexington Books, 2013), 89–155 and passim.

14 On the decline of the Old Right in the Cold War era, see Justus D. Doenecke, *Not to the Swift: The Old Isolationists in the Cold War Era* (London: Associated University Presses, 1979); Justin Raimondo, *Reclaiming the American Right: Lost Legacy of the Conservative Movement*, 2nd ed. (Wilmington, DE: ISI Books, 2008), 173–220. On conservative women in the United States and the decline of an isolationist tradition after the Second World War, see Mary C. Brennan, *Wives, Mothers, and the Red Menace: Conservative Women and the Crusade against Communism* (Boulder: University Press of Colorado, 2008), 59–84; Michelle M. Nickerson, *Mothers of Conservatism: Women and the Postwar Right* (Princeton: Princeton University Press, 2012), 21–31; Ronnee Schreiber, *Righting Feminism: Conservative Women and American Politics*, rev. ed. (New York: Oxford University Press, 2012). For Europe, see especially Karina Urbach, ed., *European Aristocracies and the Radical Right, 1918–1939* (New York: Oxford University Press, 2007).

15 PAA, Cornelia Wood Fonds, box 1, item 227, pamphlet, *Canadians Must Awaken*, speech by "Mrs. C.R. Wood, MLA for Stony Plain, Alberta," 8 June 1945, published by the *CSC*.
16 The Hattersley quotations are all from *CSC*, vol. 7, no. 1, April 1955.
17 See Peter Brock, *Against the Draft: Essays on Conscientious Objection from the Radical Reformation to the Second World War* (Toronto: University of Toronto Press, 2006).
18 PAA, Cornelia Wood Fonds, box 1, items 41 and 42, National SCWA Bulletin, 9 March 1964.
19 *Busy Bee*, vol. 3, no. 1. January 1959.
20 Ibid.
21 On Hiss, see Athan G. Theoharis, ed., *Beyond the Hiss Case: The FBI, Congress, and the Cold War* (Philadelphia: Temple University Press, 1982). On White, see R. Bruce Craig, *Treasonable Doubt: The Harry Dexter White Spy Case* (Lawrence: University Press of Kansas, 2004). On Taft, see Radosh, *Prophets on the Right*, 178–95.
22 PAA, Cornelia Wood Fonds, box 4, item 95, address by Wood, n.d., subject "What Are We Being Offered?" On 6 January 1941, as part of his State of the Union Address, US president Franklin Delano Roosevelt spoke of "Four Freedoms" to which people "everywhere in the world" were entitled: freedom of speech and expression, freedom of worship, freedom from want, and freedom from fear. Roosevelt used the idea of the Four Freedoms as a justification for fighting Nazi fascism and Japanese authoritarianism during the Second World War. The freedoms became part of the basis for postwar optimism that a new order of freedom from poverty and oppression might be commencing in the wake of the defeat of fascism. See David M. Kennedy, *Freedom from Fear: The American People in Depression and War, 1929–1945* (New York: Oxford University Press, 1999).
23 PAA, Cornelia Wood Fonds, box 4, item 95, address given by Wood with "Mr. Bourcier" in the Lac St. Anne Constituency, week of 16–22 September 1945.
24 PAA, Cornelia Wood Fonds, box 4, item 81, election speech by Wood, 1949, introducing Walter Kuhl, Socred nominee in the Jasper-Edson federal riding.
25 PAA, Cornelia Wood Fonds, box 6, item 144, election address to the Stony Plain Constituency organization, 1948.
26 Ibid. For versions of this traditionalist argument, see Gary Allen with Larry Abraham, *None Dare Call It Conspiracy* (San Diego, CA: Dauphin Publications, 2013); Kerry Bolton, *Revolution from Above* (London: Arktos, 2011).
27 PAA, Cornelia Wood Fonds, box 14, item 301, letter to the members of the Social Credit Party, signed by Lois McDearmid, Ivy Bourcier, and Verna Cole, 16 April 1966.
28 Ibid.
29 Ibid. On the continuing strength of Douglasite ideology in some sectors of Social Credit, see Alvin Finkel, *The Social Credit Phenomenon in Alberta* (Toronto: University of Toronto Press, 1989); Bob Hesketh, *Major Douglas and Alberta Social Credit* (Toronto: University of Toronto Press, 1997).
30 *CSC*, vol. 9, no. 2. February 1957.
31 Doenecke, *Not to the Swift*; Radosh, *Prophets on the Right*. Interestingly, Senator Joseph McCarthy argued against overseas interventions in communist-led nations,

even as he zealously persecuted suspected communists and leftists in the United States. See Taylor, *Politics on a Human Scale.*

32 PAA, SCWA Papers, box 1, file 22, CBC Provincial Affairs Telecast, the Hon. Ethel Wilson, 29 June 1966.

33 Ibid.

34 *CSC*, vol. 8, no. 2. February 1956.

35 See, most notably, Daniel Bell, *The End of Ideology: On the Exhaustion of Political Ideas in the Fifties*, rev. ed. (New York: The Free Press, 1962); Daniel Boorstin, *The Genius of American Politics* (Chicago: University of Chicago Press, 1953); Arthur M. Schlesinger Jr., *The Vital Center: The Politics of Freedom* (Boston: Houghton Mifflin, 1962).

36 *CSC*, vol. 8, no. 2. February 1956.

37 Ibid.

38 The most relevant studies on regionalism in Canada are David Laycock, *Populism and Democratic Thought on the Canadian Prairies, 1910–1945* (Toronto: University of Toronto Press, 1990); W.L. Morton, *The Progressive Party in Canada* (Toronto: University of Toronto Press, 1967).

39 Doenecke, *Not to the Swift*, 21–29; Johns, "Doves among Hawks"; Bill Kauffman, *Ain't My America: The Long and Noble History of Anti-War Conservatism and Middle American Anti-Imperialism* (New York: Henry Holt and Company, 2008); Radosh, *Prophets on the Right.*

40 Randolph Silliman Bourne, *War and the Intellectuals: Selected Essays, 1915–1919* (Cambridge, MA: Hackett Publishing, 1999).

41 See Trevor Harrison, *Of Passionate Intensity: Right-Wing Populism and the Reform Party of Canada* (Toronto: University of Toronto Press, 1995).

Chapter 5: The Well-Being of the Home ...

1 Estelle Freedman, "Separatism as Strategy: Female Institution Building and American Feminism, 1870–1930," *Feminist Studies* 5, 3 (1979): 512–26.

2 On this issue, I have been influenced by Linda Briskin, "Union Women and Separate Organizing," in *Women Challenging Unions: Feminism, Democracy, and Militancy*, ed. Linda Briskin and Patricia McDermott, 89–108 (Toronto: University of Toronto Press, 1993). See also Linda Briskin and Lynda Yanz., eds., *Union Sisters: Women in the Labour Movement* (Toronto: Women's Press, 1983); Dorothy Sue Cobble, *The Other Women's Movement: Workplace Justice and Social Rights in Modern America* (Princeton: Princeton University Press, 2004); Julie White, *Sisters in Solidarity: Women and Unions in Canada* (Toronto: Thomson Educational Publishing, 1993).

3 *BC Lumber Worker*, 2nd issue, March 1957.

4 This term dates from the 1960s, with the rise of second-wave feminism. Groups of women from all classes and origins would hold consciousness-raising groups to discuss issues – both personal and political – of importance to the groups' members. The goal was to raise the female and feminist consciousness of the women in the group. See Nancy Adamson, Linda Briskin, and Margaret McPhail, *Feminist Organizing for Change: The Contemporary Women's Movement in Canada* (Toronto: Oxford University Press, 1988).

5 For the CPC, of course, 1956 and the events surrounding the Hungarian Revolution of that year, along with Cold War-era anti-communism, had already dealt a fatal blow to its support base.

6 On the CCF takeover of Canadian unions, see Irving Martin Abella, *Nationalism, Communism, and Canadian Labour: The CIO, the Communist Party, and the Canadian Congress of Labour, 1935–1956* (Toronto: University of Toronto Press, 1973), 86–138; Gordon Hak, *Capital and Labour in the British Columbia Forest Industry, 1934–1974* (Vancouver: UBC Press, 2007); Al King with Kate Braid, *Red Bait! Struggles of a Mine-Mill Local* (Vancouver: Kingbird Publishing, 1998), 51–53; Jerry Lembcke and William M. Tattam, *One Union in Wood: A Political History of the International Woodworkers of America* (Madeira Park: Harbour, 1984); Andrew Neufeld and Andrew Parnaby, *The IWA in Canada: The Life and Times of an Industrial Union* (Vancouver: IWA Canada/New Star Books, 2000). For the argument that women's activism declined in the IWA after the expulsion of the communists, see Sara Diamond, "A Union Man's Wife: The Ladies' Auxiliary Movement in the IWA, the Lake Cowichan Experience," in *Not Just Pin Money: Selected Essays on the History of Women's Work in British Columbia*, ed. Barbara K. Latham and Roberta J. Pazdro, 287–96 (Victoria: Camosun College, 1984); Lembcke and Tattam, *One Union in Wood*, 177–178.

7 Benjamin Isitt, *Militant Minority: British Columbia Workers and the Rise of a New Left, 1948–1972* (Toronto: University of Toronto Press, 2011), 88–92; Joan Sangster, *Transforming Labour: Women and Work in Post-War Canada* (Toronto: University of Toronto Press, 2010), 92–104.

8 *Busy Bee*, vol. 4, no 6A, November-December 1961.

9 Ibid.

10 Most notably in Provincial Archives of Alberta (hereafter PAA), Social Credit Women's Auxiliary Papers (hereafter SCWA Papers), box 1, file 9, minutes of the Annual Convention of the Provincial SCWA, 20 November 1944, Masonic Temple, Edmonton.

11 PAA, SCWA Papers, box 1, file 10, 17th Annual SCWA Convention, 22 November 1954, MacDonald Hotel, Edmonton.

12 PAA, SCWA Papers, box 1, file 22, unpublished MSS, "SCWA Organization and Extension: One by One," n.a., n.d.

13 Ibid. Judging by the context of the manuscript, the author wrote the piece directly following the end of the Second World War.

14 PAA, Cornelia Wood Fonds, box 1, items 129–49, Social Credit Women's Auxiliary, 26th Annual Convention, 18 November 1963, Palliser Hotel, Calgary. The doctrine of "less eligibility" argues that welfare recipients, after many years of living off the avails of the system, would become lazy and lose their self-reliance and capacity for self-improvement. On "less eligibility," see Margaret Jane Hillyard Little, *"No Car, No Radio, No Liquor Permit": The Moral Regulation of Single Mothers in Ontario, 1920–1997* (Toronto: Oxford University Press, 1998); James Struthers, *No Fault of Their Own: Unemployment and the Canadian Welfare State, 1914–1941* (Toronto: University of Toronto Press, 1983), 211–12 and passim.

15 PAA, Cornelia Wood Fonds, box 1, items 129–49, Social Credit Women's Auxiliary, 26th Annual Convention, 18 November 1963, Palliser Hotel, Calgary.

16 This view was similar to that of right-wing libertarian women in the United States. See Jennifer Burns, *Goddess of the Market: Ayn Rand and the American Right*

(New York: Oxford University Press, 2009). Although Rand herself was opposed to organized religion, her libertarian views were in step with those of many SCP women.

17 PAA, Cornelia Wood Fonds, box 1, items 129–49, Social Credit Women's Auxiliary, 26th Annual Convention, 18 November 1963, Palliser Hotel, Calgary.

18 For another view of the rhetorical, anti-statist ideology of SC, see Tom Langford, "Why Alberta Vacillated over Wartime Day Nurseries," *Prairie Forum* 28, 2 (2003): 173–94.

19 PAA, SCWA Papers, box 1, file 10, report from the 19th Annual Convention, 26 November 1956, MacDonald Hotel, Edmonton. There is no record showing whether the resolution passed or not.

20 This statement is true, *if* we accept that the 1870s, with the founding of the WCTU and the introduction of women's activism in the Salvation Army, was the start of women's political work in Canada. This is not to say that women's activism did not exist prior to the 1870s but, rather, that the WCTU and the Salvation Army were two of the first organizations in Canada that facilitated women's activity. See Sharon Anne Cook, *"Through Sunshine and Shadow": The Woman's Christian Temperance Union, Evangelicalism, and Reform in Ontario, 1874–1930* (Montreal and Kingston: McGill-Queen's University Press, 1995); Lynne Marks, *Revivals and Roller Rinks: Religion, Leisure, and Identity in Late-Nineteenth-Century Small Town Ontario* (Toronto: University of Toronto Press, 1996).

21 Alvin Finkel, *The Social Credit Phenomenon in Alberta* (Toronto: University of Toronto Press, 1989). To be fair, the same statement could be made of Liberal, Conservative, and even CCF/NDP provincial administrations.

22 *Canadian Social Crediter* (hereafter *CSC*), vol. 8, no. 8, August 1956; PAA, SCWA Papers, box 1, file 10, proceedings of the 19th Annual SCWA Convention, 26 November 1956.

23 For the conventional view that the two provincial parties were dissimilar, see David J. Mitchell, *W.A.C. Bennett and the Rise of British Columbia* (Vancouver: Douglas and McIntyre, 1983); Donald V. Smiley, "Canada's Poujadists: A New Look at Social Credit," *Canadian Forum* 42, 500 (1962): 121–23.

24 University of British Columbia, Special Collections Division (hereafter UBCSC), Social Credit Association, North Vancouver Constituency Association Papers, box 1, file 1, Zena M. Wright to Mrs. A. Caponero, 7 July 1954.

25 UBCSC, Social Credit Association, North Vancouver Constituency Association Papers, box 1, file 1, Marjorie Davies to Carole Caponero, 4 June 1954.

26 UBCSC, Social Credit Association, North Vancouver Constituency Association Papers, box 1, file 4, report of the Social Credit WA Council to the North Vancouver Constituency Social Credit Association, 19 September 1957.

27 VCA, Henrietta M. Thompson papers, box 1, file 3, newspaper Item, n.a., n.d. It appears that this item was written in 1948.

28 On big business and SCP in Alberta, see Finkel, *Social Credit Phenomenon in Alberta*, 100–10, 115–17. For British Columbia, the most recent and detailed source is Isitt, *Militant Minority*, 30–43.

29 Although, it should be noted, SCP was strong in suburban and wealthy areas of Greater Vancouver as well as on parts of Vancouver Island, a fact that enabled the party to win successive elections from 1952 to 1969 and then again from 1975 to

1986. See Jean Barman, *The West beyond the West: A History of British Columbia*, 3rd ed. (Toronto: University of Toronto Press, 2007), 325–30, 376–78.

30 Of course, the "Famous Five" inspired women throughout Canada, and elsewhere, due to their pioneering role as women activists. But the fact that all five women were from Alberta likely had a particularly strong resonance for women in Alberta.

31 Bob Hesketh, "From Crusaders to Missionaries to Wives: Alberta Social Credit Women, 1932–1955," *Prairie Forum* 18, 1 (1993): 67–68.

32 The key text on this point is still Mitchell, *W.A.C. Bennett and the Rise of British Columbia*.

33 On Mine-Mill's history, see Abella, *Nationalism, Communism, and Canadian Labour*, 108–10; King with Braid, *Red Bait!*

34 See, for example, Eileen Sufrin, *The Eaton Drive: The Campaign to Organize Canada's Largest Department Store, 1948 to 1952* (Toronto: Fitzhenry and Whiteside, 1982).

35 UBCSC, Papers of the International Union of Mine, Mill, and Smelter Workers (hereafter Mine-Mill Papers), box 17, file 1, "Draft Constitution of the Ladies' Auxiliary of the National Union of Mine, Mill, and Smelter Workers of Canada," as adopted by the 7th Annual Canadian Auxiliary Convention, July 1955.

36 A work that sums up the conventional gender perceptions of the time in Canada is Joy Parr, ed., *A Diversity of Women: Ontario, 1945–80* (Toronto: University of Toronto Press, 1995).

37 UBCSC, Mine-Mill Papers, box 17, file 2, resolution submitted to the 2nd Annual Convention of the Ladies' Auxiliary of the International Union of Mine, Mill, and Smelter Workers, San Francisco, California, 13–17 September 1948.

38 UBCSC, Mine-Mill Papers, box 17, file 2, "Report to the Fourth Annual Convention of the Auxiliaries, IUMMSW by Dorothy McDonald, Chairman, Administrative Committee, Auxiliaries," n.d. The context, especially the references to union raiding, suggests that this document was produced during the 1949–50 period.

39 Ibid.

40 Other CPC women, notably Beatrice Ferneyhough, also supported organizations like the Red Cross. Indeed, Ferneyhough was appointed director of the Junior Red Cross in British Columbia; however, the Red Cross discovered her communist connections and fired her in short order. See *Vancouver Province*, 6 January 1954; *Vancouver Sun*, 7 January 1954, 21 January 1954.

41 On the particular case of the United Steelworkers of America and the Canadian Congress of Labour raiding Mine-Mill, see Isitt, *Militant Minority*, 59–60; King with Braid, *Red Bait!*

42 Wartime day nurseries are discussed in earlier chapters. These arguably established a precedent for the expansion of daycare facilities in the 1960s and in subsequent decades. See Langford, "Why Alberta Vacillated"; Ruth Roach Pierson, *"They're Still Women after All": The Second World War and Canadian Womanhood* (Toronto: McClelland and Stewart, 1986); *Vancouver Sun*, 4 March 1943.

43 Shirley Tillotson, "'When Our Membership Awakens': Welfare Work and Canadian Union Activism, 1950–1965," *Labour/Le Travail* 40 (Fall 1997): 137–69. On RCMP surveillance of left-wing women, see Julie Guard, "Women Worth Watching: Radical Housewives in Cold War Canada," in *Whose National Security?*

Canadian State Surveillance and the Creation of Enemies, ed. Gary Kinsman, Dieter K. Buse, and Mercedes Steedman, 73–88 (Toronto: Between the Lines, 2000); Mercedes Steedman, "The Red Petticoat Brigade: Mine Mill Women's Auxiliaries and the Threat from Within, 1940s-70s," in *Whose National Security? Canadian State Surveillance and the Creation of Enemies*, ed. Gary Kinsman, Dieter K. Buse, and Mercedes Steedman, 55–71 (Toronto: Between the Lines, 2000).

44 For background on the battles within the IWA, see Abella, *Nationalism, Communism, and Canadian Labour*; Isitt, *Militant Minority*, 52–55; Lembcke and Tattam, *One Union in Wood*; Neufeld and Parnaby, *The IWA in Canada.*

45 UBCSC, Trade Union Research Bureau Papers, box 14, file 7a. District Officers Report to the 10th Annual Convention District Council No. 1, IWA-CIO, Vancouver, n.d. I assume from the context that the convention took place immediately after the strike, probably in late 1946 or early 1947.

46 *Pacific Tribune*, 21 June 1946.

47 *BC Lumber Worker*, 21 May 1946.

48 SFU Archives, Sara Diamond, Women's Labour History Collection (hereafter WLHC), interview with the Lake Cowichan Women's Auxiliary, Summer 1979, with Sara Diamond.

49 Ibid. On the 1946 strike, see Sangster, *Dreams of Equality*, 186–89.

50 The term "Jimmy Higgins," meaning a rank-and-file party member who cheerfully does menial work for the organization, is from Aileen S. Kraditor, *"Jimmy Higgins": The Mental World of the American Rank and File Communist, 1930–1958* (New York: Greenwood Press, 1988). See also Heather McLeod, "Not Another God-Dam Housewife: Ruth Bullock, the 'Woman Question' and Canadian Trotskyism" (MA thesis, Simon Fraser University, 1993).

51 SFU Archives, WLHC, interview with the Lake Cowichan Women's Auxiliary, Summer 1979, with Sara Diamond.

52 *BC Lumber Worker*, 11 March 1946.

53 SFU Archives, WLHC, interview with the Lake Cowichan Women's Auxiliary, Summer 1979, with Sara Diamond.

54 There is a large literature associated with this topic. See, for example, Molly Ladd-Taylor, *Mother-Work: Women, Child Welfare, and the State, 1890–1930* (Urbana: University of Illinois Press, 1994); Kevin P. Murphy, *Political Manhood: Red Bloods, Mollycoddles, and the Politics of Progressive Era Reform* (New York: Columbia University Press, 2010).

55 The story is told in Abella, *Nationalism, Communism, and Canadian Labour*, 111–38. For a view of the American situation, see Paul Buhle, *Taking Care of Business: Samuel Gompers, George Meany, Lane Kirkland, and the Tragedy of American Labor* (New York: Monthly Review Press, 1999).

56 *BC Lumber Worker*, 27 October 1948.

57 Ibid., 6 October 1948. The Marshall Plan, officially the European Recovery Program, was instituted by the American government and was designed to prevent the rise of communist governments in Continental Europe and to provide European trading partners that would boost the American economy. As part of the plan, the US government gave financial grants, to be used for infrastructure and welfare programs, to benefit citizens in war-torn European countries. The United States argued that, if people in Europe had stronger welfare state programs, then they

would be less likely to turn to socialist or communist governments. The program operated for four years, beginning in April 1948, although policy makers in the United States had formulated the plan in 1947. See Michael L. Hogan, *The Marshall Plan: America, Britain, and the Reconstruction of Western Europe, 1947–1952* (Cambridge: Cambridge University Press, 1987).

58 *BC Lumber Worker*, 29 November 1948.

59 Ibid.

60 Ibid.

61 *BC Lumber Worker*, 6 October 1948.

62 Ibid., 20 October 1948. The Taft-Hartley Act, named after the bill's sponsors in the US Senate and House of Representatives, was passed in 1947. In the name of dampening rank-and-file union militancy and protecting individual workers, the act instituted a series of restrictions on American unions. For example, Taft-Hartley demanded that individual workers not be dismissed from their jobs for refusing to join a union, banned mass picketing and sympathy strikes, and, perhaps most significantly, insisted that union leaders sign an affidavit stating that they were not members of the Communist Party. See George Lipsitz, *Rainbow at Midnight: Labor and Culture in the 1940s* (Urbana: University of Illinois Press, 1994), 171–79. Senator Robert Taft, mentioned earlier with regard to his Old Right, anti-imperialist views, co-sponsored this act in the (mistaken) belief that American labour unions had too much power. Later, in 1949, Taft proposed amending the law to lessen its anti-union measures, but US labour unions, wishing a total repeal of the act, refused. See Ralph Nader, *Unstoppable: The Emerging Left-Right Alliance to Dismantle the Corporate State* (New York: Nation Books, 2014), 163–65.

63 *Pacific Tribune*, 7 January 1949.

64 UBCSC, International Woodworkers of America Western Canadian Regional Council No. 1 Papers, IWA Auxiliary Conference, 3–4 February 1958, microfilm reel no. 45.

65 *BC Lumber Worker*, 2 January 1953.

66 Ibid., 2nd issue, April 1954.

67 Elaine Tyler May, *Homeward Bound: American Families in the Cold War Era*, rev. ed. (New York: Basic Books, 1999).

68 On Steeves and MacInnis, see SFU Archives, Susan Walsh Oral History Collection, Susan Walsh's interview with Grace MacInnis, 12 November 1981, Vancouver; SFUA, Susan Walsh Oral History Collection, Susan Walsh's interview with Harold Winch and Jessie (Mendels) Winch, 18 May 1982, Vancouver.

69 Freedman, "Separatism as Strategy," 522–26.

70 In the American context, see Susan Lynn, "Gender and Progressive Politics: A Bridge to Social Activism of the 1960s," in *Not June Cleaver: Women and Gender in Postwar America, 1945–1960*, ed. Joanne Meyerowitz, 103–27 (Philadelphia: Temple University Press, 1994).

Chapter 6: Healthy Activity and Worthwhile Ideas

1 The quotation is from University of British Columbia, Special Collections Division (hereafter UBCSC), United Fishermen and Allied Workers Union Papers, box 87, file 9, minutes of the Ninth Annual Convention of the Women's Auxiliaries to the UFAWU, Vancouver, 22 March 1959.

2 Works like Mary Louise Adams, *The Trouble with Normal: Postwar Youth and the Making of Heterosexuality* (Toronto: University of Toronto Press, 1997); and Mona Gleason, *Normalizing the Ideal: Psychology, Schooling, and the Family in Postwar Canada* (Toronto: University of Toronto Press, 1999), in spite of their many strengths, focus largely on perceptions of delinquency among "experts."
3 I say "perceived" because demographic evidence suggests that youth crime rates during the 1950s actually *decreased* in comparison with the Second World War era and before. The concern over youth delinquency was largely an invented moral panic. See Jeffrey A. Keshen, "Wartime Jitters over Juveniles: Canada's Delinquency Scare and Its Consequences, 1939–1945," in *Age of Contention: Readings in Canadian Social History, 1900–45*, ed. Jeffrey Keshen, 364–86 (Toronto: Harcourt Brace, 1997); Jeffrey Keshen, *Saints, Sinners, and Soldiers: Canada's Second World War* (Vancouver: UBC Press, 2004).
4 On immigrants and delinquency, see Franca Iacovetta, *Gatekeepers: Reshaping Immigrant Lives in Cold War Canada* (Toronto: Between the Lines, 2006), 187–201. On students and the Cold War, see Steve Hewitt, *Spying 101: The RCMP's Secret Activities at Canadian Universities, 1917–1997* (Toronto: University of Toronto Press, 2002), 66–90.
5 The idea of "permanent things" – notably traditions, authority, religion, and family – is an important one within modern conservative discourse. See Russell Kirk, *The Conservative Mind: From Burke to Eliot*, 7th ed. (Washington, DC: Regnery Publishing, 2001).
6 The literature on this subject is vast, and I do not have the space to address all of the pertinent texts in detail. Readers are directed to the following books: Cynthia Comacchio, *The Dominion of Youth: Adolescence and the Making of Modern Canada, 1920–1950* (Waterloo, ON: Wilfrid Laurier University Press, 2006); Tamara Myers, *Caught: Montreal's Modern Girls and the Law, 1869–1945* (Toronto: University of Toronto Press, 2006); Joan Sangster, *Girl Trouble: Female Delinquency in English Canada* (Toronto: Between the Lines, 2002); Joan Sangster, *Regulating Girls and Women: Sexuality, Family, and the Law in Ontario, 1920–1960* (Toronto: Oxford University Press, 2001); Carolyn Strange and Tina Loo, *Law and Moral Regulation in Canada, 1867–1939* (Toronto: University of Toronto Press, 1997); Carolyn Strange, *Toronto's Girl Problem: The Perils and Pleasures of the City, 1880–1930* (Toronto: University of Toronto Press, 1995).
7 Keshen, "Wartime Jitters over Juveniles," 364–74.
8 On delinquency during, and directly after, the Second World War, the key texts are Magda Fahrni, *Household Politics: Montreal Families and Postwar Reconstruction* (Toronto: University of Toronto Press, 2005); Ruth Roach Pierson, *"They're Still Women after All": The Second World War and Canadian Womanhood* (Toronto: McClelland and Stewart, 1986); Jennifer A. Stephen, *Pick One Intelligent Girl: Employability, Domesticity, and the Gendering of Canada's Welfare State, 1939–1947* (Toronto: University of Toronto Press, 2007).
9 Fahrni, *Household Politics*, 9–10.
10 Ibid., 11, 13.
11 Stephen, *Pick One Intelligent Girl*, 7. See also Gleason, *Normalizing the Ideal.*
12 Stephen, *Pick One Intelligent Girl*, 42.
13 Adams, *Trouble with Normal*, 24–25.
14 Ibid, 48–49.

15 See Comacchio, *Dominion of Youth.*

16 The term "moral panic" refers to a situation in which some sort of condition, person, or group of people comes to be seen as a threat to the dominant society and traditional values. In particular, moral panics often result from anxiety over class, race, and gender issues felt by elites and the common people. In the context of the 1950s, many argued that communism threatened the traditional order and that youth delinquency, working mothers, and increased urbanization contributed to the possibility of a communist takeover. A definition of moral panic in different contexts can be found in Stanley Cohen, *Folk Devils and Moral Panics: The Creation of the Mods and Rockers* (Oxford: Martin Robertson, 1980), 9; Mariana Valverde, *The Age of Light, Soap, and Water: Moral Reform in English Canada, 1885–1925* (Toronto: University of Toronto Press, 2008).

17 Provincial Archives of Alberta (hereafter PAA), Social Credit Women's Auxiliary (hereafter SCWA) Papers, box 1, file 22, CBC Provincial Affairs Telecast, the Hon. Ethel Wilson, 29 June 1966.

18 Ibid.

19 Ibid.

20 Ibid.

21 Ibid. For descriptions of what the dominant society thought a woman's traditional role should be, see Adams, *Trouble with Normal*; Gleason, *Normalizing the Ideal*; Stephen, *Pick One Intelligent Girl.*

22 *Canadian Social Crediter* (hereafter *CSC*), vol. 2, no. 18, 5 September 1951.

23 For the information in this section on the media, I have drawn on Noam Chomsky and Edward Herman, *Manufacturing Consent: Thought Control in a Democratic Society* (Boston: Beacon Press, 1992); Trevor Harrison, *Of Passionate Intensity: Right-Wing Populism and the Reform Party of Canada* (Toronto: University of Toronto Press, 1995).

24 *CSC*, vol. 5, no. 21, 20 October 1954.

25 Ibid.

26 Adams, *Trouble with Normal*, 142–58.

27 *CSC*, vol. 5, no. 21, 20 October 1954.

28 Ibid. For a discussion of comic books and their association with immorality during the Cold War, see Tom Engelhardt, *The End of Victory Culture: Cold War America and the Disillusioning of a Generation* (Amherst: University of Massachusetts Press, 1995), 96–98, 137–39.

29 *CSC*, vol. 2, No. 18, 5 September 1951.

30 Ibid.

31 Ibid.

32 Ibid.

33 Ibid.

34 Ibid. On masculinity, see Robert Rutherdale, "Fatherhood and the Social Construction of Memory: Breadwinning and Male Parenting on a Job Frontier, 1945–1966," in *Gender and History in Canada*, ed. Joy Parr and Mark Rosenfeld, 361–65 (Toronto: Copp Clark Ltd., 1996).

35 Christopher Dummitt, *The Manly Modern: Masculinity in Postwar Canada* (Vancouver: UBC Press, 2007), 7–15 and passim.

36 PAA, SCWA Papers, box 1, file 22. CBC Provincial Affairs Telecast, the Hon. Ethel Wilson, 29 June 1966.

37 Ibid.

38 Ibid. On Wilson and the establishment of the Women's Bureau, see Alvin Finkel, *The Social Credit Phenomenon in Alberta* (Toronto: University of Toronto Press, 1989), 96–98, 166. On state efforts to assimilate immigrants during this period, see Iacovetta, *Gatekeepers*.

39 On the Social Credit tendency towards technocracy, see Bob Hesketh, *Major Douglas and Alberta Social Credit* (Toronto: University of Toronto Press, 1997); Leonard Kuffert, "' Reckoning with the Machine': The British Columbia Social Credit Movement as Social Criticism, 1932–1952," *BC Studies* 124 (Winter 1999–2000): 9–32.

40 A piece that discusses delinquent boys in an earlier context is Bryan Hogeveen, "'You Will Hardly Believe I Turned Out So Well': Parole, Surveillance, Masculinity, and the Victoria Industrial School, 1896–1935," *Histoire Sociale/Social History* 37, 74 (2004): 201–27.

41 *CCF News*, 28 April 1954.

42 Ibid.

43 Ibid.

44 Ibid.

45 See Joy Parr, *The Gender of Breadwinners: Women, Men, and Change in Two Industrial Towns, 1880–1950* (Toronto: University of Toronto Press, 1990); Joan Sangster, *Dreams of Equality: Women on the Canadian Left, 1920–1950* (Toronto: McClelland and Stewart, 1989).

46 On the breadwinner ideology, see also Robert Griswold, *Fatherhood in America: A History* (New York: Basic Books, 1993), chap. 2 and passim; E. Anthony Rotundo, *American Manhood: Transformations in Masculinity from the Revolution to the Modern Era* (New York: Basic Books, 1993).

47 British Columbia Archives (hereafter BCA), Laura Jamieson Papers, box 2, file 15, "Broadcast – Town Meeting," 27 March 1952.

48 Ibid.

49 Gleason, *Normalizing the Ideal*, chaps. 2 and 3.

50 Dummitt, *Manly Modern*, chap. 5.

51 Ibid., chaps. 4 and 5.

52 BCA, Laura Jamieson Papers, box 2, file 15. "Broadcast – Town Meeting," 27 March 1952.

53 Ibid.

54 Ibid. See also Jamieson's statements on girls' education in her unpublished manuscript, "The Girls' Co-op Houses," n.d., which is found in BCA, Laura Jamieson Papers, box 2, file 15. I assume that the latter statement was written during the 1940s since Jamieson notes that she and some friends had established the first co-op house in 1941.

55 BCA, Laura Jamieson Papers, box 2, file 15, "Broadcast – Town Meeting," 27 March 1952.

56 Ibid.

57 Ibid.

58 James Struthers, "'Lord Give Us Men': Women and Social Work in English Canada, 1918 to 1953," in *The "Benevolent State": The Growth of Welfare in Canada*, ed. Allan Moscovitch and Jim Albert (Toronto: Garamond Press, 1987), 126–27. Shirley Tillotson, like Struthers, suggests that women constituted a majority of

workers in the therapeutic and caring professions during the 1950s but that men in these professions received far higher salaries and more prestigious positions. See Shirley Tillotson, *The Public at Play: Gender and the Politics of Recreation in Post-War Ontario* (Toronto: University of Toronto Press, 2000), 60–77.

59 The social work profession was not monolithically conservative. There were a number of radical social workers, such as Bessie Touzel, director of the Toronto Welfare Council, who fought to change an unjust system and for better services for clients. On Touzel, see Struthers "Lord Give Us Men, 135; Struthers, *The Limits of Affluence: Welfare in Ontario, 1920–1970* (Toronto: University of Toronto Press, 1994), 108–11, 274. For a radical perspective on social work, see Ben Carniol, *Case Critical: Challenging Social Services in Canada*, 4th ed. (Toronto: Between the Lines, 2000). A more recent text that shows the complexity of modern social work and its connection to the welfare state is Shirley Tillotson, *Contributing Citizens: Modern Charitable Fundraising and the Making of the Welfare State, 1920–1966* (Vancouver: UBC Press, 2009).

60 *CCF News*, 25 February 1959. Buda Brown was a Social Credit MLA in British Columbia from 1956 until she resigned in 1962. Her resignation forced a December 1962 by-election in the Vancouver-Point Grey riding. Brown served in W.A.C. Bennett's cabinet as Minister without Portfolio.

61 Ibid.

62 Sangster, *Girl Trouble*, 103–43.

63 UBCSC, Mine-Mill Papers, box 17, file 5, report to the Sixth Annual Convention of the Auxiliaries to the Officers and Members of the IUMM&SW, 1954.

64 Stanton was a well known labour lawyer and leftist activist in Vancouver, while Pritchett was one of the leaders of the IWA in British Columbia. See John Stanton, *My Past Is Now: Further Memoirs of a Labour Lawyer* (St. John's: Canadian Committee on Labour History, 1994); Stanton, *Never Say Die! The Life and Times of John Stanton, a Pioneer Labour Lawyer* (Ottawa: Steel Rail Publishing, 1987).

65 UBCSC, Trade Union Research Bureau Papers, box 54, file 23a, pamphlet, *The 5000 Homes Now Committee*, n.d.

66 Ibid.

67 Ibid.

68 Ibid. The pamphlet notes that "our veterans and the people must have homes!" and makes reference to the last days of the Second World War. Because of this, I assume that it was written during the immediate aftermath of the war. It acknowledges the help of the CCF's Grace MacInnis and Social Credit's Tilly Rolston.

69 On this point, see Franca Iacovetta, "Defending Honour, Demanding Respect: Manly Discourse and Gendered Practice in Two Construction Strikes, Toronto, 1960–1961," in *Gendered Pasts: Historical Essays in Femininity and Masculinity in Canada*, ed. Kathryn McPherson, Cecilia Morgan, and Nancy M. Forestall (Don Mills, ON: Oxford University Press, 1999), 201, 211, 222.

70 Barbara Evans Clements, *Daughters of Revolution: A History of Women in the USSR* (Arlington Heights, IL.: Harlan Davidson Inc., 1994); Alena Heitlinger, *Women and State Socialism: Sex Inequality in the Soviet Union and Czechoslovakia* (London: Macmillan, 1979).

71 UBCSC, Mine-Mill Papers, box 17, file 2, Resolution 13 passed at the 7th Annual Convention of Ladies' Auxiliaries to the Union of Mine, Mill, and Smelter Workers, Canada, Rossland, BC, 18 July 1955.

72 Ibid..

73 Indeed, many CPC men had numerous sexual partners, while rhetorically opposing premarital and extramarital sex. There are a number of CPC memoirs that discuss this. See especially Ellen Stafford, *Always and After: A Memoir* (Toronto: Viking, 1999), 89–98; Catharine Vance, *Not by Gods But by People ... The Story of Bella Hall Gauld* (Toronto: Progress Books, 1968); Louise Watson, *She Never Was Afraid: The Biography of Annie Buller* (Toronto: Progress Books, 1976). In the American context, see Vivian Gornick, *The Romance of American Communism* (New York: Basic Books, 1977), 134; Dorothy Healey and Maurice Isserman, *Dorothy Healey Remembers: A Life in the American Communist Party* (New York: Oxford University Press, 1990), 87–90.

74 Wertham is mentioned in Adams, *Trouble with Normal*, 150–56.

75 *Pacific Tribune*, 28 November 1952; Frederick Wertham, *The Seduction of the Innocent* (New York: Rinehart, 1954).

76 On Canadian-American relations during the Cold War, see Whitaker and Hewitt, *Canada and the Cold War*. During the late 1960s and early 1970s, some in the NDP, notably the left-nationalist Waffle Movement, did focus on anti-American concerns, but movements like this did not exist in the CCF/NDP during earlier years. See Stephen Azzi, *Walter Gordon and the Rise of Canadian Nationalism* (Montreal and Kingston: McGill-Queen's University Press, 1999).

77 Mark Frank, *Poison for the Young: A Major Reason for Rising Juvenile Delinquency* (Toronto: Progress Books, 1962), 20–21.

78 Ibid.

79 Ibid.

80 Ibid.

81 An important statement on the CPC and its opposition to bohemianism and "sex radicalism" can be found in Rosalyn Baxandall, "The Question Seldom Asked: Women and the CPUSA," in *New Studies in the Politics and Culture of U.S. Communism*, ed. Michael E. Brown, Randy Martin, Frank Rosengarten, and George Snedeker, 141–61 (New York: Monthly Review Press, 1993). A study showing that communists, in practice, intimated that it was acceptable for radical men, but not women, to be promiscuous, is Kathleen A. Brown and Elizabeth Faue's "Social Bonds, Sexual Politics, and Political Community on the US Left, 1920s-1940s," *left history* 7, 1 (2000): 9–45.

82 This rhetoric can also be found in other CPC publications. See, for example, Andrew Lamorie, *How They Sold Our Canada to the USA* (Gravenhurst, ON: Northern Book House, 1963), 63–64 and passim; Norman Penner, *Soldiers or Citizens?* (Toronto: National Federation of Labor Youth, 1948), 4–10. See also Brown and Faue, "Social Bonds." For the argument that there were close connections between the Old Left and the New Left in Canada, an argument with which I am in broad agreement, see Benjamin Isitt, *Militant Minority: British Columbia Workers and the Rise of a New Left, 1948–1972* (Toronto: University of Toronto Press, 2011). The above passage suggests that *some* in the CPC disdained *some* of the New Left's values. This was not the case for all CPC members.

83 Frank, *Poison for the Young*, 20–21, 23–26, 28–29, 32–33. An important study of the issues that Frank discusses is Bill Osgerby, *Playboys in Paradise: Masculinity, Youth and Leisure-Style in Modern America* (New York: Berg, 2001). See also Barbara

Ehrenreich, *The Hearts of Men: American Men and the Flight from Commitment* (Garden City, NY: Doubleday, 1983).

84 Osgerby, *Playboys in Paradise*, 4–5; Ehrenreich, *Hearts of Men*, intro.

85 Osgerby, *Playboys in Paradise*, 11–14 and passim; Ehrenreich, *Hearts of Men*, 14–28 and passim.

86 Anti-Americanism was, in turn, connected to the "Tory" anti-modernism of Donald Creighton, Harold Innis, and George Parkin Grant, which disdained technology, urbanization, and the postwar conception of progress. On this point, see Dummitt, *Manly Modern*, 14; L.B. Kuffert, *A Great Duty: Canadian Responses to Modern Life and Mass Culture, 1939–1967* (Montreal and Kingston: McGill-Queen's University Press, 2003); Philip A. Massolin, *Canadian Intellectuals, the Tory Tradition, and the Challenge of Modernity, 1939–1970* (Toronto: University of Toronto Press, 2001).

87 See, most recently, John Earl Haynes, Harvey Klehr, and Alexander Vassiliev, *Spies: The Rise and Fall of the KGB in America* (New Haven: Yale University Press, 2013).

88 On the theme of recreation, see Tillotson, *Public at Play*.

89 A discussion of this idea can be found in Russell Jacoby, *The End of Utopia: Politics and Culture in an Age of Apathy* (New York: Basic Books, 1999).

Conclusion

1 University of British Columbia, Special Collections Division, Harold Pritchett – IWA District Council No. 1 Papers, box 8, file 10, minutes of annual meeting, IWA, Local 1–80, Duncan, BC, 23 February 1948.

2 This distinction is drawn in Rebecca E. Klatch, *A Generation Divided: The New Left, the New Right, and the 1960s* (Berkeley: University of California Press, 1999).

3 For variations on this regionalist argument in the American context, see Bill Kauffman, *Ain't My America: The Long, Noble History of Anti-War Conservatism and Middle American Anti-Imperialism* (New York: Metropolitan Books, 2008); Jeff Taylor, *Politics on a Human Scale: The American Tradition of Decentralism* (Lanham, MD: Lexington Books, 2013).

4 Elaine Tyler May, *Homeward Bound: American Families in the Cold War Era*, rev. ed. (New York: Basic Books, 1999).

5 Mary Louise Adams, *The Trouble with Normal: Postwar Youth and the Making of Heterosexuality* (Toronto: University of Toronto Press, 1997); Mona Gleason, *Normalizing the Ideal: Psychology, Schooling, and the Family in Postwar Canada* (Toronto: University of Toronto, 1999).

6 See, for example, Reg Whitaker and Steve Hewitt, *Canada and the Cold War* (Toronto: Lorimer, 2003).

7 In addition to the texts that have been cited in previous chapters, see also Adams, *Trouble with Normal*; Gleason, *Normalizing the Ideal*; May, *Homeward Bound*.

8 Tarah Brookfield, *Cold War Comforts: Canadian Women, Child Safety, and Global Insecurity* (Waterloo, ON: Wilfrid Laurier University Press, 2012); Benjamin Isitt, *Militant Minority: British Columbia Workers and the Rise of a New Left, 1948–1972* (Toronto: University of Toronto Press, 2011).

9 Although, with this said, liberal women continued to play significant roles in the history of US and Canadian feminism. See Dorothy Sue Cobble, "Recapturing

Working-Class Feminism: Union Women in the Postwar Era," in *Not June Cleaver: Women and Gender in Postwar America*, ed. Joanne Meyerowitz, 57–83 (Philadelphia: Temple University Press, 1994); Patricia A. Myers, "'A Noble Effort': The National Federation of Liberal Women of Canada, 1928–1973," in *Beyond the Vote: Canadian Women in Politics*, ed. Linda Kealey and Joan Sangster, 39–62 (Toronto: University of Toronto Press, 1989).

10 Meg Luxton, "Feminism as a Class Act: Working-Class Feminism and the Women's Movement in Canada," *Labour/Le Travail* 48 (Fall 2001): 63–88.

11 Jill Vickers, Pauline Rankin, and Christine Appelle, *Politics as if Women Mattered: A Political Analysis of the National Action Committee on the Status of Women* (Toronto: University of Toronto Press, 1993). Bird, of course, could be classified as a "liberal feminist," but the general point is clear: wealthier and more centrist and conservative women were leaders in the second-wave feminist movement.

12 As far as I can tell from my research into the subject, SCP women never extensively commented on NAC or second-wave feminism in either positive or negative ways.

13 See, for example, Ralph Nader, *Unstoppable: The Emerging Left-Right Alliance to Dismantle the Corporate State* (New York: Nation Books, 2014).

14 This "left-right" coalition, on issues like the power of corporations, war and imperialism, and even crime and morality, has been suggested in a number of different texts. See, in particular, Alexander Cockburn, *A Colossal Wreck: A Road Trip through Political Scandal, Corruption, and American Culture* (London: Verso, 2013), 169–71 and passim; Nader, *Unstoppable*; Taylor, *Politics on a Human Scale*. To be clear, I am *not* arguing that right- and left-wing views are the same but, rather, that people – especially those in the grassroots and who are not party leaders – who designate themselves as right or left often share *some* of the same views on *some* of the issues. It is, therefore, worth considering the possibility of a left-right coalition on particular issues.

15 This is a generalization of course. Second-wave feminism was made up of many different movements and groups, many of whom had very different views. See, in particular, Alice Echols, *Daring to Be Bad: Radical Feminism in America, 1967–1975* (Minneapolis: University of Minnesota Press, 1989).

16 Jill Liddington, *The Road to Greenham Common: Feminism and Anti-Militarism in Britain since 1820*, rev. ed. (Syracuse: Syracuse University Press, 1991).

Bibliography

Archival Collections

Archives of Ontario
Irving Abella Oral History Collection
Communist Party of Canada Collection

British Columbia Archives
Laura Jamieson Papers
David Mitchell Oral History Collection
William Neelands Chant Papers
Peer Vernon Paynter Papers

Glenbow Archives
Alberta CCF/NDP Fonds
Vera Gillespie Fonds
John Horn Blackmore Fonds
Eva Reid Fonds
Edith Rogers Fonds

Library and Archives Canada
Canadian Security and Intelligence Service Fonds
CCF-NDP Papers
Communist Party of Canada Papers
Grace MacInnis Papers
Marjorie Mann Papers
Dorise Nielsen Papers

Provincial Archives of Alberta
Floyd Baker Fonds
Cornelia Wood Fonds
Social Credit Women's Auxiliary Papers

Simon Fraser University Archives
W.A.C. Bennett Papers
Sara Diamond Oral History Collection – Women's Labour History Collection
Susan Walsh Oral History Collection

Trinity Western University Archives
Robert M. Thompson Papers
Lyle Wicks Papers

University of British Columbia, Special Collections Division
William Bennett Memorial Collection
Mildred Fahrni Papers
Angus MacInnis Memorial Collection
Grace MacInnis Papers
Tom McEwen Fonds
Papers of the International Union of Mine, Mill, and Smelter Workers
International Woodworkers of America Western Canadian Regional Council No. 1 Papers
Harold Pritchett-IWA District Council No. 1 Papers
Evelyn Grey Smith Papers
Social Credit Association, North Vancouver Constituency Association Papers
Dorothy Gretchen Steeves Papers
Trade Union Research Bureau Papers
Arthur J. Turner Papers
UBC Oral History Collection
United Fishermen and Allied Workers Union Papers
Vancouver Council of Women Papers
Women's International League for Peace and Freedom Papers
Arnold Webster Papers
Ernest Edward Winch Papers

University of Manitoba Archives
Dorothy Livesay Papers

University of Toronto – Thomas Fisher Rare Book Library
Robert Kenny Collection

Vancouver City Archives
Henrietta M. Thompson Papers

Newspapers

BC Lumber Worker
Busy Bee
Buzzard
Calgary Herald
Canadian Social Crediter
CCF News
Champion
Christian Science Monitor
Edmonton Journal
Maclean's
Nelson Daily News
Pacific Tribune
Vancouver News-Herald
Vancouver Province
Vancouver Sun
Victoria Daily Colonist
Victoria Daily Times
Victoria Times-Colonist
Western Producer.

Other Sources

Abella, Irving Martin. *Nationalism, Communism, and Canadian Labour: The CIO, the Communist Party, and the Canadian Congress of Labour, 1935–1956*. Toronto: University of Toronto Press, 1973.

Adams, Mary Louise. *The Trouble with Normal: Postwar Youth and the Making of Heterosexuality*. Toronto: University of Toronto Press, 1997.

Adams, Rebekkah. *Glass Houses: Saving Feminist Anti-Violence Agencies from Self-Destruction*. Halifax: Fernwood, 2008.

Adamson, Nancy, Linda Briskin, and Margaret McPhail. *Feminist Organizing for Change: The Contemporary Women's Movement in Canada*. Toronto: Oxford University Press, 1988.

Agnew, John, and Luca Muscara. *Making Political Geography*. 2nd ed. Lanham, MD: Rowman and Littlefield, 2012.

Agnew, John. *Place and Politics: The Geographical Mediation of State and Society*. Boston: Allen and Unwin, 1987.

Alexander, Ruth M. *The "Girl Problem": Female Sexual Delinquency in New York, 1900–1930*. Ithaca, NY: Cornell University Press, 1995.

Alexander, Sally. *Becoming a Woman and Other Essays in 19th- and 20th-Century Feminist History*. New York: New York University Press, 1995.

Allen, Gary, with Larry Abraham. *None Dare Call It Conspiracy*. San Diego, CA: Dauphin Publications, 2013.

Allen, Richard. *The Social Passion: Religion and Social Reform in Canada, 1914–1928*. Toronto: University of Toronto Press, 1973.

Alonso, Harriet Hyman. *Peace as a Women's Issue: A History of the US Movement for World Peace and Women's Rights*. Syracuse, NY: Syracuse University Press, 1993.

Anastakis, Dimitry, ed. *The Sixties: Passion, Politics, and Style*. Montreal and Kingston: McGill-Queen's University Press, 2008.

Angus, Ian. *Canadian Bolsheviks: The Early Years of the Communist Party of Canada*. Montreal: Vanguard Publications, 1981.

Armstrong, Pat, and Hugh Armstrong. *Theorizing Women's Work*. Toronto: Garamond Press, 1990.

Avakumovic, Ivan. *The Communist Party of Canada: A History*. Toronto: McClelland and Stewart, 1975.

–. *Socialism in Canada: A Study of the CCF-NDP in Federal and Provincial Politics*. Toronto: McClelland and Stewart, 1978.

Azoulay, Dan. *Keeping the Dream Alive: The Survival of the Ontario CCF/NDP, 1950–1963*. Montreal and Kingston: McGill-Queen's University Press, 1997.

–. "'Ruthless in a Ladylike Way': CCF Women Confront the Postwar 'Communist Menace.'" *Ontario History* 89, 1 (1997): 23–52.

–. "Winning Women for Socialism: The Ontario CCF and Women, 1947–1961." *Labour/Le Travail* 36 (Fall 1995): 59–90. http://dx.doi.org/10.2307/25143974.

Azzi, Stephen. *Walter Gordon and the Rise of Canadian Nationalism*. Montreal and Kingston: McGill-Queen's University Press, 1999.

Bacchetta, Paola, and Margaret Power, eds. *Right-Wing Women: From Conservatives to Extremists around the World*. New York, London: Routledge, 2002.

Bacchi, Carol Lee. *Liberation Deferred? The Ideas of the English-Canadian Suffragists, 1877–1918*. Toronto: University of Toronto Press, 1983.

Baillargeon, Denyse. *Making Do: Women, Family, and Home in Montreal during the Great Depression*. Trans. Yvonne M. Klein. Waterloo, ON: Wilfrid Laurier University Press, 1999.

Barker, Drucilla K. "Emancipatory for Whom? A Comment on Critical Realism." *Feminist Economics* 9, 1 (2003): 103–8. http://dx.doi.org/10.1080/1354570011005927O.

Barman, Jean. *The West beyond the West: A History of British Columbia*. 3rd ed. Toronto: University of Toronto Press, 2007.

Baxandall, Rosalyn. "The Question Seldom Asked: Women and the CPUSA." In *New Studies in the Politics and Culture of US Communism*, ed. Michael E. Brown, Randy Martin, Frank Rosengarten, and George Snedeker, 141–61. New York: Monthly Review Press, 1993.

Beeby, Dean. "Women in the Ontario CCF, 1940–1950." *Ontario History* 74, 4 (1982): 259–83.

Beinin, Joel, and Zachary Lockman. *Workers on the Nile: Nationalism, Communism, Islam, and the Egyptian Working Class*. Cairo: American University in Cairo Press, 1998.

Belisle, Donica. "Toward a Canadian Consumer History." *Labour/Le Travail* 52 (Fall 2003): 181–206. http://dx.doi.org/10.2307/25149387.

Bell, Daniel. *The End of Ideology: On the Exhaustion of Political Ideas in the Fifties*. Rev. ed. New York: The Free Press, 1962.

Bell, Edward. *Social Classes and Social Credit in Alberta*. Montreal and Kingston: McGill-Queen's University Press, 1993.

Belshaw, John Douglas. *Colonization and Community: The Vancouver Island Coalfield and the Making of the British Columbian Working Class.* Montreal and Kingston: McGill-Queen's University Press, 2002.

Bennett, Judith. "Feminism and History." *Gender and History* 1, 3 (1989): 251–72. http://dx.doi.org/10.1111/j.1468–0424.1989.tb00256.x.

Benowitz, June Melby. *Days of Discontent: American Women and Right-Wing Politics, 1933–1945.* DeKalb: Northern Illinois University Press, 2002.

Bercuson, David J. *Confrontation at Winnipeg: Labour, Industrial Relations, and the General Strike.* 2nd ed. Montreal and Kingston: McGill-Queen's University Press, 1990.

–. "Labour Radicalism and the Western Industrial Frontier." *Canadian Historical Review* 58, 2 (1977): 154–75. http://dx.doi.org/10.3138/CHR-058–02–03.

Black, Edwin. *IBM and the Holocaust: The Strategic Alliance between Nazi Germany and America's Most Powerful Corporation.* London: Crown Publishers, 2001.

Black, Naomi. *Social Feminism.* Ithaca, NY: Cornell University Press, 1989.

Blackwell, Joyce. *No Peace without Freedom: Race and the Women's International League for Peace and Freedom, 1915–1975.* Carbondale: Southern Illinois University Press, 2004.

Blake, Donald E., R.K. Carty, and Lynda Erickson. *Grassroots Politicians: Party Activists in British Columbia.* Vancouver: UBC Press, 1991.

–. *Two Political Worlds: Parties and Voting in British Columbia.* Vancouver: UBC Press, 1985.

Blee, Kathleen. *Inside Organized Racism: Women and Men in the Racist Movement.* Berkeley: University of California Press, 2001.

–. *Women of the Klan: Racism and Gender in the 1920s.* Berkeley: University of California Press, 1991.

Blee, Kathleen M., and Sandra McGee Deutsch, eds. *Women of the Right: Comparisons and Interplays across Borders.* University Park: Pennsylvania State University Press, 2012.

Bolton, Kerry. *Revolution from Above.* London: Arktos, 2011.

Boorstin, Daniel J. *The Genius of American Politics.* Chicago: University of Chicago Press, 1953.

Bothwell, Robert, Ian Drummond, and John English. *Canada since 1945: Power, Politics, and Provincialism.* Rev. ed. Toronto: University of Toronto Press, 1989.

Bourne, Randolph Silliman. *War and the Intellectuals: Selected Essays, 1915–1919.* Cambridge, MA: Hackett Publishing, 1999.

Bowen, Roger. *Innocence Is Not Enough: The Life and Death of Herbert Norman.* Vancouver: Douglas and McIntyre, 1986.

Brannigan, Augustine. "Mystification of the Innocents: Crime Comics and Delinquency in Canada, 1931–1949." *Criminal Justice History* 7 (1986): 111–44.

Breines, Winifred. *Young, White, and Miserable: Growing Up Female in the Fifties.* Boston: Beacon Press, 1992.

Brennan, Mary C. *Wives, Mothers, and the Red Menace: Conservative Women and the Crusade against Communism.* Boulder: University Press of Colorado, 2008.

Brennan, J. William, ed. *"Building the Co-operative Commonwealth": Essays on the Democratic Socialist Tradition in Canada.* Regina: Canadian Plains Research Centre, 1984.

Brenner, Johanna. *Women and the Politics of Class.* New York: Monthly Review Press, 2000.

Bricmont, Jean. *Humanitarian Imperialism: Using Human Rights to Sell War.* Trans. Diana Johnstone. New York: Monthly Review Press, 2007.

Bright, David. *The Limits of Labour: Class Formation and the Labour Movement in Calgary, 1883–1929*. Vancouver: UBC Press, 1998.
–. "The West Wants In: Regionalism, Class, and Labour/Le Travail, 1976–2002." *Labour/Le Travail* 50 (Fall 2002): 149–61. http://dx.doi.org/10.2307/25149273.
Brinkley, Alan. *Liberalism and Its Discontents*. Cambridge, MA: Harvard University Press, 1998.
–. *Voices of Protest: Huey Long, Father Coughlin, and the Great Depression*. New York: Vintage Books, 1982.
Briskin, Linda. "Union Women and Separate Organizing." In *Women Challenging Unions: Feminism, Democracy, and Militancy*, ed. Linda Briskin and Patricia McDermott, 89–108. Toronto: University of Toronto Press, 1993.
Briskin, Linda, and Lynda Yanz, eds. *Union Sisters: Women in the Labour Movement*. Toronto: Women's Press, 1983.
Brock, Peter. *Against the Draft: Essays on Conscientious Objection from the Radical Reformation to the Second World War*. Toronto: University of Toronto Press, 2006.
Brookfield, Tarah. *Cold War Comforts: Canadian Women, Child Safety, and Global Insecurity*. Waterloo, ON: Wilfrid Laurier University Press, 2012.
Brown, Kathleen A., and Elizabeth Faue. "Social Bonds, Sexual Politics, and Political Community on the US Left, 1920s-1940s." *left history* 7, 1 (2000): 9–45.
Brown, Kathleen A. "The 'Savagely Fathered and Un-Mothered World' of the Communist Party, USA: Feminism, Maternalism, and 'Mother Bloor.'" *Feminist Studies* 25, 3 (1999): 537–70. http://dx.doi.org/10.2307/3178656.
Brown, Michael E., Randy Martin, Frank Rosengarten, and George Snedeker, eds. *New Studie in the Politics and Culture of US Communism*. New York: Monthly Review Press, 1993.
Brownsey, Keith, and Michael Howlett, eds. *The Provincial State: Politics in Canada's Provinces and Territories*. Toronto: Copp Clark Pitman Ltd, 1992.
Brownsey, Keith. "Tory Life: The Life Cycle of the Progressive Conservative Party of Ontario, 1935–1985." PhD diss., Queen's University, 1994.
Buck, Tim. *Keep Canada Independent*. Toronto: Progress Books, 1948.
Buckner, Phillip, ed. *Canada and the British Empire*. Oxford: Oxford University Press, 2008.
Buhle, Paul. *Taking Care of Business: Samuel Gompers, George Meany, Lane Kirkland, and the Tragedy of American Labor*. New York: Monthly Review Press, 1999.
Burkinshaw, Robert K. *Pilgrims in Lotus Land: Conservative Protestantism in British Columbia, 1917–1981*. Montreal and Kingston: McGill-Queen's University Press, 1995.
Burns, Jennifer. *Goddess of the Market: Ayn Rand and the American Right*. New York: Oxford University Press, 2009.
Burstyn, Varda. *The Rites of Men: Manhood, Masculinity, and the Culture of Sports*. Toronto: University of Toronto Press, 1999.
Burt, Sandra, and Lorraine Code, eds. *Changing Methods: Feminists Transforming Practice*. Peterborough: Broadview Press, 1995.
Campbell, Lara. *Respectable Citizens: Gender, Family, and Unemployment in Ontario's Great Depression*. Toronto: University of Toronto Press, 2009.
Campbell, Peter. *Canadian Marxists and the Search for a Third Way*. Montreal and Kingston: McGill-Queen's University Press, 1999.

–. *Rose Henderson: A Woman for the People*. Montreal and Kingston: McGill-Queen's University Press, 2010.

–. "The Heroic and the Feminist in the Life and Thought of Rose Henderson." Paper presented at "Feminism and the Making of Canada: Historical Reflections," McGill University, 9 May 2004.

–. "Working-Class Hero: Rose Henderson and the Canadian Left, 1919–20." Paper presented at the annual meeting of the Canadian Historical Association, Toronto, Ontario, 29 May 2002.

Campbell, Robert A. "'A Fantastic Rigmarole': Deregulating Aboriginal Drinking in British Columbia, 1945–62." *BC Studies* 141 (Spring 2004): 81–104.

Caplan, Gerald L. *The Dilemma of Canadian Socialism: The CCF in Ontario*. Toronto: McClelland and Stewart, 1973.

Carbert, Louise I. *Agrarian Feminism: The Politics of Ontario Farm Women*. Toronto: University of Toronto Press, 1995.

Carniol, Ben. *Case Critical: Challenging Social Services in Canada*. 4th ed. Toronto: Between the Lines, 2000.

Carstairs, Catherine. *Jailed for Possession: Illegal Drug Use, Regulation, and Power in Canada, 1920–1961*. Toronto: University of Toronto Press, 2006.

Carstairs, Catherine, and Rachel Elder. "Expertise, Health, and Popular Opinion: Debating Water Fluoridation, 1945–80." *Canadian Historical Review* 89, 3 (2008): 345–71. http://dx.doi.org/10.3138/chr.89.3.345.

Carter, Sarah, Lesley Erickson, Patricia Roome, and Char Smith, eds. *Unsettled Pasts: Reconceiving the West through Women's History*. Calgary: University of Calgary Press, 2005.

Castledine, Jacqueline B. *Cold War Progressives: Women's Interracial Organizing for Peace and Freedom*. Urbana: University of Illinois Press, 2012.

Cathers, Arthur. *Beloved Dissident: Eve Smith (1904–1988)*. Blyth, ON: Drumadravy Books, 1997.

Cavanaugh, Catherine, and Jeremy Mouat, eds. *Making Western Canada: Essays on European Colonization and Settlement*. Toronto: Garamond Press, 1996.

Cavanaugh, Catherine A, and Randi R. Warne, eds. *Telling Tales: Essays in Western Women's History*. Vancouver: UBC Press, 2000.

Cavell, Richard, ed. *Love, Hate, and Fear in Canada's Cold War*. Toronto: University of Toronto Press, 2004.

Champion, C.P. *The Strange Demise of British Canada: The Liberals and Canadian Nationalism, 1964–68*. Montreal and Kingston: McGill-Queen's University Press, 2010.

Chapnick, Adam. *The Middle Power Project: Canada and the Founding of the United Nations*. Vancouver: UBC Press, 2005.

Chomsky, Noam. *The Fateful Triangle: The United States, Israel, and the Palestinians*. Rev. ed. Montreal: Black Rose Books, 1999.

Chomsky, Noam, and Edward Herman. *Manufacturing Consent: Thought Control in a Democratic Society*. Boston: Beacon Press, 1992.

Christie, Nancy. *Engendering the State: Family, Work, and Welfare in Canada*. Toronto: University of Toronto Press, 2000.

Christie, Nancy, and Michael Gauvreau. *Christian Churches and Their Peoples, 1840–1965: A Social History of Religion in Canada*. Toronto: University of Toronto Press, 2010.

–. "Modalities of Social Authority: Suggesting an Interface for Religious and Social History." *Histoire sociale/Social History* 71 (May 2003): 1–30.

Churchill, Ward. *Indians Are Us? Culture and Genocide in Native North America*. Toronto: Between the Lines, 1994.

Clapp, Elizabeth. *Mothers of All Children: Women Reformers and the Rise of Juvenile Courts in Progressive Era America*. University Park: Pennsylvania State University Press, 1996.

Clarke, Phyllis, and William Beeching, eds. *Yours in the Struggle: Reminiscences of Tim Buck*. Toronto: NC Press, 1977.

Clarkson, Stephen. *An Independent Foreign Policy for Canada?* Toronto: McClelland and Stewart, 1968.

Claudin, Fernando. *The Communist Movement: From Comintern to Cominform*. Part 1, *The Crisis of the International*. Trans. Brian Pearce. New York: Monthly Review Press, 1975.

–. *The Communist Movement: From Comintern to Cominform*. Part 2, *The Zenith of Stalinism*. Trans. Francis MacDonagh. New York: Monthly Review Press, 1975.

Clement, Dominique. *Canada's Rights Revolution: Social Movements and Social Change, 1937–82*. Vancouver: UBC Press, 2008.

–. "Generations and the Transformation of Social Movements in Postwar Canada." *Histoire sociale/Social History* 42, 84 (2009): 361–87. http://dx.doi.org/10.1353/his.0.0077.

Clements, Barbara Evans. *Daughters of Revolution: A History of Women in the USSR*. Arlington Heights, IL: Harlan Davidson, 1994.

Clio Collective. *Quebec Women: A History*. Toronto: The Women's Press, 1987.

Cobble, Dorothy Sue. *The Other Women's Movement: Workplace Justice and Social Rights in Modern America*. Princeton: Princeton University Press, 2004.

Cochran, Burt. *Labor and Communism: The Conflict that Shaped American Unions*. Princeton: Princeton University Press, 1977.

Cockburn, Alexander. *A Colossal Wreck: A Road Trip through Political Scandal, Corruption, and American Culture*. London: Verso, 2013.

Code, Lorraine. *Rhetorical Spaces: Essays on Gendered Locations*. New York: Routledge, 1995.

–. *What Can She Know? Feminist Theory and the Construction of Knowledge*. Ithaca, NY: Cornell University Press, 1991.

Cohen, Lizabeth. *A Consumers' Republic: The Politics of Mass Consumption in Postwar America*. New York: Vintage Books, 2003.

–. *Making a New Deal: Industrial Workers in Chicago, 1919–1939*. Cambridge: Cambridge University Press, 1990.

Cohen, Stanley. *Folk Devils and Moral Panics: The Creation of Mods and Rockers*. Oxford: Martin Robinson, 1980.

Cohn, Norman. *Warrant for Genocide: The Myth of the Jewish World-Conspiracy and the Protocols of the Elders of Zion*. New York: Harper Torch, 1969.

Cohn, Werner. "The Persecution of the Japanese Canadians and the Political Left in British Columbia, December 1941–March 1942." *BC Studies* 68 (Winter 1985–86): 3–22.

Cole, Wayne S. *Roosevelt and the Isolationists, 1932–1945*. Lincoln: University of Nebraska Press, 1983.

Comacchio, Cynthia. *The Dominion of Youth: Adolescence and the Making of Modern Canada, 1920–1950*. Waterloo, ON: Wilfrid Laurier University Press, 2006.

Cook, Sharon Anne. *"Through Sunshine and Shadow": The Woman's Christian Temperance Union, Evangelicalism, and Reform in Ontario, 1874–1930*. Montreal and Kingston: McGill-Queen's University Press, 1995.

Co-operative Commonwealth Federation, "Women in Peace and War." *CCF* (1945): (n.d.).

Craig, R. Bruce. *Treasonable Doubt: The Harry Dexter White Spy Case*. Lawrence: University Press of Kansas, 2004.

Cross, Gary S. *An All Consuming Century: How Commercialism Won in Modern America*. New York: Columbia University Press, 2000.

Davis, David Brion, ed. *The Fear of Conspiracy: Images of Un-American Subversion from the Revolution to the Present*. Ithica, NY: Cornell University Press, 1971.

Dawley, Alan. *Struggles for Justice: Social Responsibility and the Liberal State*. Cambridge: The Belknap Press of Harvard University Press, 1991.

D'Emilio, John. *Sexual Politics, Sexual Communities: The Making of a Homosexual Minority in the United States, 1940–1970*. Chicago: University of Chicago Press, 1983.

de Grazia, Victoria with Ellen Furlough, eds. *The Sex of Things: Gender and Consumption in Historical Perspective*. Berkeley: University of California Press, 1996.

Deslippe, Dennis A. *"Rights, Not Roses": Unions and the Rise of Working-Class Feminism, 1945–80*. Urbana: University of Illinois Press, 2000.

Destler, Chester McArthur. *American Radicalism, 1865–1901: Essays and Documents*. New York: Octagon Books, 1963.

Diamond, Sara. *Not by Politics Alone: The Enduring Influence of the Christian Right*. New York: Guildford Press, 1998.

Dochuk, Darren. *From Bible Belt to Sun Belt: Plain-Folk Religion, Grassroots Politics, and the Rise of Evangelical Conservatism*. New York: W.W. Norton and Co, 2012.

Doenecke, Justus D. *Not to the Swift: The Old Isolationists in the Cold War Era*. London: Associated University Presses, 1979.

–. *Storm on the Horizon: The Challenge to American Intervention, 1939–1941*. New York: Rowman and Littlefield, 2003.

Domke, David. *God Willing? Political Fundamentalism in the White House, the "War on Terror," and the Echoing Press*. Ann Arbor, MI: Pluto Press, 2004.

Draper, Theodore. *The Roots of American Communism*. New York: Viking, 1957.

–. *American Communism and Soviet Russia*. New York: Viking, 1960.

Dubinsky, Karen. *Lament for a "Patriarchy Lost"? Anti-Feminism, Anti-Abortion, and REAL Women in Canada*. Ottawa: Canadian Research Institute for the Advancement of Women, 1985.

Dubinsky, Karen, Catherine Krull, Susan Lord, Sean Mills, and Scott Rutherford, eds. *New World Coming: The Sixties and the Shaping of Global Consciousness*. Toronto: Between the Lines, 2009.

Duder, Karen. "Public Acts and Private Languages: Bisexuality and the Multiple Discourses of Constance Grey Swartz." *BC Studies* 136 (Winter 2002–3): 3–24.

Dummitt, Christopher. *The Manly Modern: Masculinity in Postwar Canada*. Vancouver: UBC Press, 2007.

–. "Modern Men: Taking Risks and Making Masculinity in the Postwar Years." PhD diss., Simon Fraser University, 2004.

–. "Risk on the Rocks: Modernity, Manhood, and Mountaineering in Postwar British Columbia." *BC Studies* 141 (Spring 2004): 3–29.

Durbach, Nadja. *Bodily Matters: The Anti-Vaccination Movement in England, 1853–1907.* Durham, NC: Duke University Press, 2005.

Dworkin, Andrea. *Right-Wing Women.* New York: Perigee Books, 1983.

Dyck, Erika. *Facing Eugenics: Reproduction, Sterilization, and the Politics of Choice.* Toronto: University of Toronto Press, 2013.

Dyson, Lowell K. *Red Harvest: The Communist Party and American Farmers.* Lincoln: University of Nebraska Press, 1982.

Eagleton, Terry. *Ideology: An Introduction.* London: Verso, 1991.

Early, Frances. *A World without War: How US Feminists and Pacifists Resisted World War I.* Syracuse, NY: Syracuse University Press, 1997.

Echols, Alice. *Daring to Be Bad: Radical Feminism in America, 1967–1975.* Minneapolis: University of Minnesota Press, 1989.

Edwards, Anne. *Seeking Balance: Conversations with BC Women in Politics. Halfmoon Bay, BC.* Caitlin Press, 2008.

Egerton, George. "Between War and Peace: Politics, Religion, and Human Rights in Early Cold War Canada, 1945–50." In *Religion and the Cold War*, ed. Dianne Kirby, 163–87. New York: Palgrave Macmillan, 2003.

Ehrenreich, Barbara. *Fear of Falling: The Inner Life of the Middle Class.* New York: Pantheon Books, 1989.

–. *The Hearts of Men: American Dreams and the Flight from Commitment.* New York: Doubleday, 1983.

Eisenstein, Zillah. *Against Empire: Feminisms, Racism, and the West.* London: Zed Books, 2004.

Elkins, David J. "Politics Makes Strange Bedfellows: The BC Party System in the 1952 and 1953 Provincial Elections." *BC Studies* 30 (Summer 1976): 3–26.

Elliot, David R., and Iris Miller. *Bible Bill: A Biography of William Aberhart.* Edmonton: Reidmore Books, 1987.

Ellis, Walter E. "Some Aspects of Religion in British Columbia Politics." MA thesis, University of British Columbia, 1956.

Endicott, Stephen Lyon. *James G. Endicott: Rebel Out of China.* Toronto: University of Toronto Press, 1980.

Engelhardt, Tom. *The End of Victory Culture: Cold War America and the Disillusioning of a Generation.* Amherst: University of Massachusetts Press, 1995.

Engler, Yves. *The Black Book of Canadian Foreign Policy.* Black Point, NS: Fernwood, 2009.

–. *Lester Pearson's Peacekeeping: The Truth May Hurt.* Black Point, NS: Fernwood, 2012.

Erickson, Ingrid. "'When Will We Awaken from This Fatalism?' An Essay on First-Wave Socialism, Maternal Feminism, and the Case of Margaret Haile." Cognate Essay, Queen's University, 2007.

Ewen, Stuart. *Captains of Consciousness: Advertising and the Social Roots of the Consumer Culture.* New York: McGraw-Hill, 1976.

Ewen, Stuart, and Elizabeth Ewen. *Channels of Desire: Mass Images and the Shaping of American Consciousness.* Minneapolis: University of Minnesota Press, 1985.

Fahrni, Magda. "Counting the Costs of Living: Gender, Citizenship, and a Politics of Prices in 1940s Montreal." *Canadian Historical Review* 83, 4 (2002): 483–504. http://dx.doi.org/10.3138/CHR.83.4.483.

–. *Household Politics: Montreal Families and Postwar Reconstruction.* Toronto: University of Toronto Press, 2005.

Faludi, Susan. *Backlash: The Undeclared War on American Women*. New York: Crown, 1991.

Farrell, Ann. *Grace MacInnis: A Story of Love and Integrity.* Markham, ON: Fitzhenry and Whiteside, 1994.

Fingard, Judith, and Janet Guildford, eds. *Mothers of the Municipality: Women, Work, and Social Policy in Post-1945 Halifax*. Toronto: University of Toronto Press, 2005.

Finkel, Alvin. "Populism and Gender: The UFA and Social Credit Experiences." *Journal of Canadian Studies/ Revue d'Etudes Canadiennes* 27, 4 (1992–93): 76–97.

–. "The Rise and Fall of the Labour Party in Alberta, 1917–42." *Labour/Le Travail* 16 (Fall 1985): 61–96. http://dx.doi.org/10.2307/25142509.

–. *The Social Credit Phenomenon in Alberta*. Toronto: University of Toronto Press, 1989.

–. *Working People in Alberta: A History*. Edmonton: Athabasca University Press, 2012.

Finkel, Alvin, Sarah Carter, and Peter Fortna, eds. *The West and Beyond: New Perspectives on an Imagined Region*. Edmonton: Athabasca University Press, 2010.

Finkelstein, Norman G. *Image and Reality of the Israel-Palestine Conflict*. 2nd ed. London: Verso, 2003.

Finlay, John L. *Social Credit: The English Origins*. Montreal and Kingston: McGill-Queen's University Press, 1972.

Fleischmann, Ellen L. *The Nation and Its "New" Women: The Palestinian Women's Movement, 1920–1948*. Berkeley: University of California Press, 2003. http://dx.doi.org/10.1525/california/9780520237896.001.0001.

Forsey, Eugene. *A Life on the Fringe: The Memoirs of Eugene Forsey*. Toronto: Oxford University Press, 1990.

Fortin, Gerard, and Boyce Richardson. *Life of the Party*. Montreal: Vehicule Press, 1984.

Foster, Carrie A. *The Women and the Warriors: The US Section of the Women's International League for Peace and Freedom, 1915–1946*. Syracuse: Syracuse University Press, 1995.

Foucault, Michel. *Discipline and Punish: The Birth of the Prison*. Trans. Alan Sheridan. New York: Pantheon Books, 1977.

–. An Introduction. Robert Hurley, trans. Vol. 1, *The History of Sexuality*. New York: Vintage Books, 1990.

Frager, Ruth. *Sweatshop Strife: Class, Ethnicity and Gender in the Jewish Labour Movement, 1900–1939*. Toronto: University of Toronto Press, 1992.

Francis, R. Douglas. *Frank H. Underhill: Intellectual Provocateur*. Toronto: University of Toronto Press, 1986.

Frank, David, and Donald McGillivrary, eds. *George MacEachern: An Autobiography*. Sydney: University College of Cape Breton, 1987.

Frank, Dana. *Purchasing Power: Consumer Organizing, Gender, and the Seattle Labor Movement, 1919–1929*. New York: Cambridge University Press, 1994.

Frank, Mark. *Poison for the Young: A Major Reason for Rising Juvenile Delinquency*. Toronto: Progress Books, 1962.

Frank, Thomas. *One Market under God: Extreme Capitalism, Market Populism, and the End of Economic Democracy*. Toronto: Doubleday, 2000.

Frankenberg, Ruth. *White Women, Race Matters: The Social Construction of Whiteness*. Minneapolis: University of Minnesota Press, 1993.

Freeden, Michael. *Liberalism Divided: A Study in British Political Thought, 1914–1939*. Oxford: Clarendon Press, 1986. http://dx.doi.org/10.1093/0198274327.001.0001.

Freedman, Estelle. "Separatism as Strategy: Female Institution Building and American Feminism, 1870–1930." *Feminist Studies* 5, 3 (1979): 512–26. http://dx.doi.org/10.2307/3177511.

–. *Their Sisters' Keepers: Women's Prison Reform in America*. Ann Arbor: University of Michigan Press, 1981.

Fried, Richard M. *Nightmare in Red: The McCarthy Era in Perspective*. New York: Oxford University Press, 1990.

Friesen, Gerald. "Defining the Prairies: or, Why the Prairies Don't Exist." In *Toward Defining the Prairies: Region, Culture, and History*, ed. Robert Wardaugh, 13–28. Winnipeg: University of Manitoba Press, 2001.

–. *The West: Regional Ambitions, National Debates, Global Age*. Toronto: Penguin/McGill Institute, 1999.

Frisch, Michael. "The Memory of History." *Radical History Review* 25 (1981): 9–23. http://dx.doi.org/10.1215/01636545-1981-25-9.

Fukuyama, Francis. *The End of History and the Last Man*. New York: Avon Books, 1992.

Gendron, Robin S. *Towards a Francophone Community: Canada's Relations with France and French Africa, 1945–1968*. Montreal and Kingston: McGill-Queen's University Press, 2006.

Gevitz, Norman, ed. *Other Healers: Unorthodox Medicine in America*. Baltimore: Johns Hopkins University Press, 1988.

Gidney, Catherine. *A Long Eclipse: The Liberal Protestant Establishment and the Canadian University, 1920–1970*. Montreal and Kingston: McGill-Queen's University Press, 2004.

Gleason, Mona. *Normalizing the Ideal: Psychology, Schooling, and the Family in Postwar Canada*. Toronto: University of Toronto Press, 1999.

Gleason, Mona, and Adele Perry, eds. *Rethinking Canada: The Promise of Women's History*. 5th ed. Don Mills, ON: Oxford University Press, 2006.

Gonick, Cy. *A Very Red Life: The Story of Bill Walsh*. St. John's: Canadian Committee on Labour History, 2001.

Gonzalez, Jennifer. "Autotopographies." In *Prosthetic Territories: Politics and Hypertechnologies*, ed. Gabriel Braham, Jr., and Mark Driscoll, 133–50. Boulder: Westview Press, 1995.

Goodwyn, Lawrence. *The Populist Moment: A Short History of the Agrarian Revolt in America*. New York: Oxford University Press, 1978.

Gordon, Linda. *Pitied But Not Entitled: Single Mothers and the History of Welfare, 1890–1935*. Cambridge: Harvard University Press, 1994.

Gornick, Vivian. *The Romance of American Communism*. New York: Basic Books, 1977.

Gottlieb, Julie V. *Feminine Fascism: Women in Britain's Fascist Movement, 1923–1945*. London: I.B. Tauris, 2000.

Gramsci, Antonio. *Selections from the Prison Notebooks*. Trans. and ed. Quintin Hoare and Geoffrey Nowell Smith. New York: International Publishers, 1971.

Granatstein, J.L. *Yankee Go Home? Canadians and Anti-Americanism*. Toronto: HarperCollins, 1996.

Grant, George Parkin. *Lament for a Nation: The Defeat of Canadian Nationalism*. Toronto: McClelland and Stewart, 1965.

Green, Stephen. *Taking Sides: America's Secret Relationship with a Militant Israel*. Brattleboro, VT: Amana, 1988.

Greene, Graham. *The Quiet American.* London: Penguin Classics, 2005.

Griffin, Betty, and Susan Lockhart. *Their Own History: Women's Contributions to the Labour Movement of British Columbia.* New Westminster, BC: United Fishermen and Allied Workers' Union/CAW Seniors Club, 2002.

Griffin, Harold. *Radical Roots: The Shaping of British Columbia.* Vancouver: Broadway Printers, 1999.

Griswold, Robert. *Fatherhood in America: A History.* New York: Basic Books, 1993.

Grossberg, Laurence. *We Gotta Get Out of This Place.* New York: Routledge, 1992.

Guard, Julie. "Canadian Citizens or Dangerous Foreign Women? Canada's Radical Consumer Movement, 1947–1950." In *Sisters or Strangers? Immigrant, Ethnic, and Racialized Women in Canadian History*, ed. Marlene Epp, Franca Iacovetta, and Francis Swyripa, 161–89. Toronto: University of Toronto Press, 2004.

–. "Fair Play or Fair Pay? Gender Relations, Class Consciousness, and Union Solidarity in the Canadian UE." *Labour/Le Travail* 37 (Spring 1996): 149–77. http://dx.doi.org/10.2307/25144038.

Hadley, Louisa, and Elizabeth Ho, eds. *Thatcher and After: Margaret Thatcher and Her Afterlife in Contemporary Culture.* New York: Routledge, 2010. http://dx.doi.org/10.1057/9780230283169.

Hak, Gordon. *Capital and Labour in the British Columbia Forest Industry, 1934–1974.* Vancouver: UBC Press, 2007.

–. "The Communists and the Unemployed in the Prince George District, 1930–1935." *BC Studies* 68 (Winter 1985–86): 45–61.

–. "Populism and the 1952 Social Credit Breakthrough in British Columbia." *Canadian Historical Review* 85, 2 (2004): 277–96. http://dx.doi.org/10.3138/CHR.85.2.277.

Hallas, Duncan. *The Comintern.* London: Bookmarks, 1985.

Halpern, Monda. *And on That Farm He Had a Wife: Ontario Farm Women and Feminism, 1900–1970.* Montreal and Kingston: McGill-Queen's University Press, 2001.

Hannant, Larry. "The Calgary Working Class and the Social Credit Movement in Alberta, 1932–35." *Labour/Le Travail* 16 (Fall 1985): 97–116. http://dx.doi.org/10.2307/25142510.

Harding, Sandra, ed. *The Feminist Standpoint Theory Reader: Intellectual and Political Controversies.* New York: Routledge, 2004.

–. *The Science Question in Feminism.* Ithaca, NY: Cornell University Press, 1986.

Harrison, Trevor. *Of Passionate Intensity: Right-Wing Populism and the Reform Party of Canada.* Toronto: University of Toronto Press, 1995.

Harter, John Henry. *New Social Movements, Class, and the Environment: A Case Study of Greenpeace, Canada.* Newcastle-Upon-Tyne: Cambridge Scholars Press, 2011.

Hartsock, Nancy C.M. *The Feminist Standpoint Revisited and Other Essays.* Boulder, CO: Westview Press, 1998.

Haynes, John Earl, Harvey Klehr, and Alexander Vassiliev. *Spies: The Rise and Fall of the KGB in America.* New Haven: Yale University Press, 2013.

Healey, Dorothy, and Maurice Isserman. *Dorothy Healey Remembers: A Life in the American Communist Party.* New York: Oxford University Press, 1990.

Heitlinger, Alena. *Women and State Socialism: Sex Inequality in the Soviet Union and Czechoslovakia.* London: Macmillan, 1979.

Hennessy, Rosemary, and Chrys Ingraham. "Introduction: Reclaiming Anticapitalist Feminism." In *Materialist Feminism: A Reader in Class, Difference, and Women's Lives,* ed. Rosemary Hennessy and Chrys Ingraham, 1–14. New York, London: Routledge, 1997.

Heron, Craig. "Labourism and the Canadian Working Class," *Labour/Le Travail* 13 (Spring 1984): 45–76.

–, Heron ed. *The Workers' Revolt in Canada, 1917–1925*. Toronto: University of Toronto Press, 1998.

Hesketh, Bob. "From Crusaders to Missionaries to Wives: Alberta Social Credit Women, 1932–1955." *Prairie Forum* 18, 1 (1993): 53–75.

–. *Major Douglas and Alberta Social Credit*. Toronto: University of Toronto Press, 1997.

Hewitt, Steve. *Spying 101: The RCMP's Secret Activities at Canadian Universities, 1917–1997*. Toronto: University of Toronto Press, 2002.

Hofstadter, Richard. *The Paranoid Style in American Politics and Other Essays*. Chicago: University of Chicago Press, 1979.

Hogan, Michael L. *The Marshall Plan: America, Britain, and the Reconstruction of Western Europe, 1947–1952*. Cambridge: Cambridge University Press, 1987. http://dx.doi.org/10.1017/CBO9780511583728.

Hogeveen, Bryan. "'You Will Hardly Believe I Turned Out So Well': Parole, Surveillance, Masculinity, and the Victoria Industrial School, 1890–1935." *Histoire sociale/Social History* 37 (November 2004): 201–27.

Hoggart, Richard. *The Way We Live Now*. London: Chatto and Windus, 1995.

hooks, bell. *Talking Back: Thinking Feminism, Thinking Black*. Toronto: Between the Lines, 1988.

Horn, Michiel. *The League for Social Reconstruction: Intellectual Origins of the Democratic Left in Canada, 1930–1942*. Toronto: University of Toronto Press, 1980.

Horowitz, Daniel. *Betty Friedan and the Making of the Feminine Mystique: The American Left, the Cold War, and Modern Feminism*. Amherst: University of Massachusetts Press, 1998.

Howard, Irene. "The Mothers' Council of Vancouver: Holding the Fort for the Unemployed, 1935–1938." In *Vancouver Past: Essays in Social History*, Vancouver Centennial Edition of *BC Studies*, ed. Robert A.J. McDonald and Jean Barman, 249–87. Vancouver: UBC Press, 1986.

–. *The Struggle for Social Justice in British Columbia: Helena Gutteridge, the Unknown Reformer*. Vancouver: UBC Press, 1992.

Huntington, Samuel. *The Clash of Civilizations and the Remaking of World Order*. New York: Simon and Schuster, 1996.

Iacovetta, Franca. *Gatekeepers: Reshaping Immigrant Lives in Cold War Canada*. Toronto: Between the Lines, 2007.

Iacovetta, Franca, and Mariana Valverde, eds. *Gender Conflicts: New Essays in Women's History*. Toronto: University of Toronto Press, 1992.

Igartua, Jose. *The Other Quiet Revolution: National Identities in English Canada, 1945–71*. Vancouver: UBC Press, 2006.

Inman, Mary. *In Woman's Defense*. Los Angeles: Committee to Organize the Advancement of Women, 1940.

Irigaray, Luce. *Thinking the Difference: For a Peaceful Revolution*. Trans. Karin Montin. New York: Routledge, 1994.

Irving, John A. *The Social Credit Movement in Alberta*. Toronto: University of Toronto Press, 1959.

Isitt, Benjamin. "Elusive Unity: The Canadian Labour Party in British Columbia, 1924–28." *BC Studies* 163 (Autumn 2009): 33–64.

–. *Militant Minority: British Columbia Workers and the Rise of a New Left, 1948–1972*. Toronto: University of Toronto Press, 2011.

–. "The Search for Solidarity: The Industrial and Political Roots of the Co-operative Commonwealth Federation in British Columbia, 1913–1928." MA thesis, University of Victoria, 2003.

–. "Tug of War: The Working Class and Political Change in British Columbia, 1948–1972." PhD diss., University of New Brunswick, 2008.

Isserman, Maurice. *Which Side Were You On? The American Communist Party during the Second World War*. Middletown, CT: Wesleyan University Press, 1982.

Jacobsen, Annie. *Operation Paperclip: The Secret Intelligence Program That Brought Nazi Scientists to America*. Boston: Little, Brown and Co, 2014.

Jacoby, Russell. *The End of Utopia: Politics and Culture in the Age of Apathy*. New York: Basic Books, 1999.

Jaggar, Alison. *Feminist Politics and Human Nature*. Totowa, NJ: Rowman and Allanheld, 1983.

Jaffe, Philip J. *The Rise and Fall of American Communism*. New York: Horizon, 1975.

Jamieson, Laura E. *Women, Dry Those Tears*. Vancouver: CCF Women's Council of BC (with assistance from Ontario CCF women), 1945.

Jeansonne, Glen. *Women of the Far Right: The Mothers' Movement and World War II*. Chicago: University of Chicago Press, 1996.

Johns, Andrew L. ""Doves among Hawks: Republican Opposition to the Vietnam War: 1964–1968," *Peace and Change*." *Journal of Peace Research* 31, 4 (2006): 585–628.

Johnson, Louise C. "Socialist Feminisms." In *Feminist Knowledge: Critique and Construct*, ed. Sneja Gunew, 304–31. London: Routledge, 1990.

Johnston, A.W. *Dream No Little Dreams: A Biography of the Douglas Government of Saskatchewan, 1944–1961*. Toronto: University of Toronto Press, 2015.

Johnston, Faith. *A Great Restlessness: The Life and Politics of Dorise Nielsen*. Winnipeg: University of Manitoba Press, 2006.

Johnston, Hugh J.M., ed. *The Pacific Province: A History of British Columbia*. Vancouver: Douglas and McIntyre, 1996.

Johnstone, Diana. *Fools' Crusade: Yugoslavia, NATO, and Western Delusions*. New York: Monthly Review Press, 2002.

Kaplan, Esther. *With God on Their Side: George W. Bush and the Christian Right*. New York: The New Press, 2005.

Kaplan, Temma. "Female Consciousness and Collective Action: The Case of Barcelona, 1910–1918." *Signs* 7, 3 (1982): 545–66. http://dx.doi.org/10.1086/493899.

Kashtan, William. *You and the Depression*. Toronto: Progress Books, 1949.

Kauffman, Bill. *Ain't My America: The Long, Noble History of Antiwar Conservatism and Middle American Anti-Imperialism*. New York: Henry Holt and Company, 2008.

Kazin, Michael. *The Populist Persuasion: An American History*. Rev. ed. Ithaca, NY: Cornell University Press, 2012.

Kealey, Gregory S. "1919: The Canadian Labour Revolt." *Labour/Le Travail* 13 (Spring 1984): 11–44. http://dx.doi.org/10.2307/25140399.

–. "Stanley Brehaut Ryerson: Canadian Revolutionary Intellectual." *Studies in Political Economy* 9 (Fall 1982): 103–31.

Kealey, Linda. *Enlisting Women for the Cause: Women, Labour, and the Left in Canada, 1890–1920*. Toronto: University of Toronto Press, 1998.

Kealey, Linda, and Joan Sangster, eds. *Beyond the Vote: Canadian Women and Politics*. Toronto: University of Toronto Press, 1989.

Kee, Kevin. *Revivalists: Marketing the Gospel in English Canada, 1884–1957*. Montreal and Kingston: McGill-Queen's University Press, 2006.

Keeran, Roger. *The Communist Party and the Autoworkers Union*. Bloomington: Indiana University Press, 1980.

Kelley, Robin D.G. *Hammer and Hoe: Alabama Communists during the Great Depression*. Chapel Hill: University of North Carolina Press, 1990.

Kelly, Joan. *Women, History and Theory: The Essays of Joan Kelly*. Chicago: University of Chicago Press, 1984.

Kennedy, David M. *Freedom from Fear: The American People in Depression and War, 1929–1945*. New York: Oxford University Press, 1999.

Keshen, Jeffrey. *Saints, Sinners, and Soldiers: Canada's Second World War*. Vancouver: UBC Press, 2004.

–. "Wartime Jitters over Juveniles: Canada's Delinquency Scare and Its Consequences, 1939–1945." In *Age of Contention: Readings in Canadian Social History, 1900–1945*, ed. Jeffrey Keshen, 364–86. Toronto: Harcourt Brace, 1997.

Kimmel, David, and Gregory S. Kealey. "With Our Own Hands: Margaret Fairley and the 'Real Makers' of Canada." *Labour/Le Travail* 31 (Spring 1993): 253–85. http://dx.doi.org/10.2307/25143677.

King, Al, with Kate Braid. *Red Bait! Struggles of a Mine-Mill Local*. Vancouver: Kingbird Publishing, 1998.

Kinsman, Gary, Dieter K. Buse, and Mercedes Steedman, eds. *Whose National Security? Canadian State Surveillance and the Creation of Enemies*. Toronto: Between the Lines, 2000.

Kinzer, Stephen. *All the Shah's Men: An American Coup and the Roots of Middle East Terror*. Hoboken, NJ: J. Wiley and Sons, 2003.

Kirk, Russell. *The Conservative Mind: From Burke to Eliot*. 7th ed. Washington, DC: Regnery Publishing, 2001.

Klatch, Rebecca E. *A Generation Divided: The New Left, the New Right and the 1960s*. Berkeley: University of California Press, 1999. http://dx.doi.org/10.1525/california/9780520217133.001.0001.

–. *Women of the New Right*. Philadelphia: Temple University Press, 1987.

Klehr, Harvey. *The Heyday of American Communism: The Depression Decade*. New York: Basic Books, 1984.

Klehr, Harvey, John Earl Haynes, and Kyrill M. Anderson. *The Soviet World of American Communism*. New Haven: Yale University Press, 1998.

Klehr, Harvey, John Earl Haynes, and Fridrikh Igorevich Firsov. *The Secret World of American Communism*. New Haven: Yale University Press, 1995.

Knickerbocker, Nancy. *No Plaster Saint: The Life of Mildred Osterhout Fahrni, 1900–1992*. Vancouver: Talonbooks, 2001.

Knight, Rolf, and Homer Stevens. *Homer Stevens: A Life in Fishing*. Madeira Park, BC: Harbour Publishing, 1992.

Kolko, Gabriel. *The Triumph of Conservatism: A Reinterpretation of American History, 1900–1916*. New York: The Free Press, 1977.

Koonz, Claudia. *Mothers in the Fatherland: Women, the Family, and Nazi Politics.* New York: St. Martin's Press, 1987.

Korinek, Valerie J. *Roughing It in the Suburbs: Reading Chatelaine Magazine in the Fifties and Sixties.* Toronto: University of Toronto Press, 2000.

Koven, Seth, and Sonya Michel, eds. *Mothers of a New World: Maternalist Politics and the Origins of Welfare States.* New York, London: Routledge, 1993.

Kraditor, Aileen S. *The Ideas of the Woman Suffrage Movement, 1890–1920.* New York: W.W. Norton and Company, 1981.

–. *"Jimmy Higgins": The Mental World of the American Rank and File Communist, 1930–1958.* New York: Greenwood Press, 1988.

–. *The Radical Persuasion, 1890–1917: Aspects of the Intellectual History and the Historiography of Three American Radical Organizations.* Baton Rouge: Louisiana State University Press, 1981.

Kruse, Kevin. *One Nation under God: How Corporate America Invented Christian America.* New York: Basic Books, 2015.

Kuffert, Leonard B. *A Great Duty: Canadian Responses to Modern Life and Mass Culture, 1939–1967.* Montreal and Kingston: McGill-Queen's University Press, 2003.

–. "'Reckoning with the Machine': The British Columbia Social Credit Movement as Social Criticism, 1932–52." *BC Studies* 124 (Winter 1999/2000): 9–39.

Kunzel, Regina G. *Fallen Women, Problem Girls: Unmarried Mothers and the Professionalization of Social Work, 1890–1945.* New Haven: Yale University Press, 1993.

Ladd-Taylor, Molly. *Mother-Work: Women, Child Welfare, and the State, 1890–1930.* Urbana: University of Illinois Press, 1994.

Lamorie, Andrew. *How They Sold Our Canada to the USA.* Gravenhurst, ON: Northern Book House, 1963.

Langford, Tom. "Why Alberta Vacillated over Wartime Day Nurseries," *Prairie Forum* 28, 2 (2003): 173–94.

Langford, Tom, and Chris Frazer. "The Cold War and Working-Class Politics in the Coal Mining Communities of the Crowsnest Pass, 1945–1958." *Labour/Le Travail* 49 (Spring 2002): 43–81. http://dx.doi.org/10.2307/25149213.

Lasch, Christopher. *The True and Only Heaven: Progress and Its Critics.* New York: W.W. Norton and Company, 1991.

Latham, Barbara, and Cathy Kess, eds. *In Her Own Right: Selected Essays on Women's History in BC.* Victoria: Camosun College, 1980.

Latham, Barbara K., and Roberta J. Pazdro, eds. *Not Just Pin Money: Selected Essays on the History of Women's Work in British Columbia.* Victoria: Camosun College, 1984.

Lawson, Tony. "Ontology and Feminist Theorizing." *Feminist Economics* 9, 1 (2003): 119–50. http://dx.doi.org/10.1080/1354570022000035760.

–. "Theorizing Ontology." *Feminist Economics* 9, 1 (2003): 161–69. http://dx.doi.org/10.1080/1354570032000063038.

Laycock, David. *Populism and Democratic Thought in the Canadian Prairies, 1910–1945.* Toronto: University of Toronto Press, 1990.

Lears, T.J. Jackson. *Fables of Abundance: A Cultural History of Advertising in America.* New York: Columbia University Press, 1994.

–. *No Place of Grace: Antimodernism and the Transformation of American Culture, 1880–1920.* Chicago: University of Illinois Press, 1981.

–. *Rebirth of a Nation: The Making of Modern America, 1877–1920.* New York: HarperCollins, 2009.

Leier, Mark. "Plots, Shots, and Liberal Thoughts: Conspiracy Theory and the Death of Ginger Goodwin." *Labour/Le Travail* 39 (Spring 1997): 215–24. http://dx.doi.org/10.2307/25144113.

–. *Red Flags and Red Tape: The Making of a Labour Bureaucracy*. Toronto: University of Toronto Press, 1995.

–. *Where the Fraser River Flows: The Industrial Workers of the World in British Columbia*. Vancouver: New Star Books, 1990.

–. "Workers and Intellectuals: The Theory of the New Class and Early Canadian Socialism." In *Making Western Canada: Essays on European Colonization and Settlement*, ed. Catherine Cavanagh and Jeremy Mouat, 133–53. Toronto: Garamond Press, 1996.

Lembcke, Jerry, and William M. Tattam. *One Union in Wood: A Political History of the International Woodworkers of America*. Madeira Park. Harbour Publishing, 1984.

Levant, Victor. *Quiet Complicity: Canadian Involvement in the Vietnam War*. Toronto: Between the Lines, 1986.

Levesque, Andree. *Red Travellers: Jeanne Corbin and Her Comrades*. Yvonne M. Klein, Trans. Montreal and Kingston: McGill-Queen's University Press, 2006.

Levine, Gilbert, ed. *Patrick Lenihan: From Irish Rebel to Founder of Canadian Public Sector Unionism*. St. John's: Canadian Committee on Labour History, 1998.

Levitt, Kari. *Silent Surrender: The Multinational Corporation in Canada*. Montreal and Kingston: McGill-Queen's University Press, 2002.

Liddington, Jill. *The Road to Greenham Common: Feminism and Anti-Militarism in Britain since 1820*. Rev. ed. Syracuse: Syracuse University Press, 1991.

Lieberman, Robbie. *The Strangest Dream: Communism, Anti-Communism, and the US Peace Movement, 1945–1963*. Syracuse, NY: Syracuse University Press, 2000.

Lipset, Seymour Martin. *Agrarian Socialism: The Co-operative Commonwealth Federation in Saskatchewan: A Study in Political Sociology*. Rev. ed. New York: Anchor Books, 1968.

Lipsitz, George. *Rainbow at Midnight: Labor and Culture in the 1940s*. Urbana: University of Illinois Press, 1994.

Lindstrom, Varpu. *Defiant Sisters: A Social History of Finnish Immigrant Women in Canada*. 3rd ed. Beaverton, ON: Aspasia Books, 2003.

Little, Margaret Jane Hillyard. *"No Car, No Radio, No Liquor Permit": The Moral Regulation of Single Mothers in Ontario, 1920–1997*. Toronto: Oxford University Press, 1998.

Loch-Drake, Cynthia. "'A Non-Drinker, a Non-Smoker, She Was a Good-Living Woman': Pentacostalism and the Class Politics of Alberta Meat-Packing Unionist Ethel Wilson." Paper presented at the International Conference on the Study of Canada, Trent University, 23 May 2015.

Lowe, Mick. *One-Woman Army: The Life of Claire Culhane*. Toronto: MacMillan Canada, 1992.

Luxton, Meg. "Feminism as a Class Act: Working-Class Feminism and the Women's Movement in Canada." *Labour/Le Travail* 48 (Fall 2001): 63–88.

Lynd, Robert S., and Helen Merrell Lynd. *Middletown: A Study in American Culture*. New York: Harcourt Brace Jovanovich, 1929.

Lynn, Susan. *Progressive Women in Conservative Times: Racial Justice, Peace, and Feminism, 1945 to the 1960s*. New Brunswick: Rutgers University Press, 1992.

Macpherson, C.B. *Democracy in Alberta: Social Credit and the Party System*. Rev. ed. Toronto: University of Toronto Press, 2013.

Mallory, J.R. *Social Credit and the Federal Power in Canada.* Toronto: University of Toronto Press, 1976.

Manley, John. "Communists and Autoworkers: The Struggle for Industrial Unionism in the Canadian Automobile Industry, 1925–1936." In *Canadian Labour History: Selected Readings,* ed. David J. Bercuson and David Bright, 245–72. Toronto: Copp Clark Longman, 1994.

–. "Does the International Labour Movement Need Salvaging? Communism, Labourism, and the Canadian Trade Unions, 1921–1928." *Labour/Le Travail* 41 (Spring 1998): 147. http://dx.doi.org/10.2307/25144230.

–. "Moscow Rules? 'Red Unionism' and 'Class against Class' in Britain, Canada, and the United States, 1928–1935." *Labour/Le Travail* 56 (Fall 2005): 9–50.

–. "'Starve, Be Damned!' Communists and Canada's Urban Unemployed, 1929–1939." *Canadian Historical Review* 79, 3 (1998): 466–91. http://dx.doi.org/10.3138/CHR.79.3.466.

Mann, W.E. *Sect, Cult, and Church in Alberta.* Toronto: University of Toronto Press, 1955.

Marks, Lynne. *Revivals and Roller Rinks: Religion, Leisure, and Identity in Late-Nineteenth-Century Small Town Ontario.* Toronto: University of Toronto Press, 1996.

Marsden, George M. *Understanding Fundamentalism and Evangelicalism.* Grand Rapids, MI: William B. Eerdmans Publishing Company, 1991.

Marqusee, Mike. "Patriot Acts." *Nation,* 13 December 2004: 30–34.

Marshall, Dominique. *The Social Origins of Welfare States: Quebec Families, Compulsory Education, and Family Allowances, 1940–1955.* Trans. Nicola Doone Danby. Waterloo, ON: Wilfrid Laurier University Press, 2006.

Massolin, Philip A. *Canadian Intellectuals, the Tory Tradition, and the Challenge of Modernity, 1939–1970.* Toronto: University of Toronto Press, 2001.

May, Elaine Tyler. *Homeward Bound: American Families in the Cold War Era.* Rev. ed. New York: Basic Books, 1999.

Mazower, Mark. *Dark Continent: Europe's Twentieth Century.* New York: Vintage Books, 2000.

McCallum, Todd. "Not a Sex Question? The One Big Union and the Politics of Radical Manhood." *Labour/Le Travail* 42 (1998): 15–54. http://dx.doi.org/10.2307/25148879.

McCormack, A. Ross. *Reformers, Rebels, and Revolutionaries: The Western Canadian Radical Movement, 1899–1919.* Toronto: University of Toronto Press, 1977.

McDermott, Kevin, and Jeremy Agnew. *The Comintern: A History of International Communism from Lenin to Stalin.* London: Macmillan Press, 1996.

McDonald, Robert A.J. *Making Vancouver: Class, Status, and Social Boundaries.* Vancouver: UBC Press, 1996.

–. "'Variant of Liberalism' and the Liberal Order Framework in British Columbia." In *Liberalism and Hegemony: Debating the Canadian Liberal Revolution,* ed. Jean-Francois Constant and Michel Ducharme, 335–37. Toronto: University of Toronto Press, 2009.

McEwen, Tom. *The Forge Glows Red: From Blacksmith to Revolutionary.* Toronto: Progress Books, 1974.

McGirr, Lisa. *Suburban Warriors: The Rise of the New American Right.* Princeton: Princeton University Press, 2001.

McKay, Ian. *Reasoning Otherwise: Leftists and the People's Enlightenment in Canada, 1890–1920.* Toronto: Between the Lines, 2008.

–. *Rebels, Reds, Radicals: Rethinking Canada's Left History*. Toronto: Between the Lines, 2005.

McLaren, Angus. *Our Own Master Race: Eugenics in Canada, 1910–1944*. Toronto: University of Toronto Press, 1990.

McLaren, Angus, and Arlene Tigar McLaren. *The Bedroom and the State: The Changing Practices and Politics of Contraception and Abortion in Canada, 1880–1997*. 2nd ed. Toronto: McClelland and Stewart, 1997.

McLeod, Heather. "Not Another God-Dam Housewife: Ruth Bullock, the 'Woman Question' and Canadian Trotskyism." MA thesis, Simon Fraser University, 1993.

McMaster, Lindsey. *Working Girls in the West: Representations of Wage-Earning Women*. Vancouver: UBC Press, 2008.

McPherson, Kathryn, Cecilia Morgan, and Nancy M. Forestall, eds. *Gendered Pasts: Historical Essays in Femininity and Masculinity in Canada*. Don Mills, ON: Oxford University Press, 1999.

Meerpol, Robert and Michael. *We Are Your Sons: The Legacy of Julius and Ethel Rosenberg*. 2nd ed. Urbana: University of Illinois Press, 1986.

Melnyk, Olenka. *No Bankers in Heaven: Remembering the CCF*. Toronto: McGraw-Hill Ryerson, 1989.

Meyerowitz, Joanne. "Beyond the Feminine Mystique: A Reassessment of Postwar Mass Culture, 1946–1958." *Journal of American History* 79, 4 (1993): 1455–82. http://dx.doi.org/10.2307/2080212.

–, Meyerowitz ed. *Not June Cleaver: Women and Gender in Postwar America, 1945–1960*. Philadelphia: Temple University Press, 1994.

Miedema, Gary R. *For Canada's Sake: Public Religion, Centennial Celebrations, and the Re-making of Canada in the 1960s*. Montreal and Kingston: McGill-Queen's University Press, 2005.

Mills, Allen. *Fool for Christ: The Intellectual Politics of J.S. Woodsworth*. Toronto: University of Toronto Press, 1991.

Mills, Sean. *The Empire Within: Postcolonial Thought and Political Activism in Sixties Montreal*. Montreal and Kingston: McGill-Queen's University Press, 2010.

Mitchell, David J. *W.A.C. Bennett and the Rise of British Columbia*. Vancouver: Douglas and McIntyre, 1983.

Mitchell, Tom. "From the Social Gospel to the 'Plain Bread of Leninism': A.E. Smith's Journey to the Left in the Epoch of Reaction after World War I." *Labour/Le Travail* 33 (Spring 1994): 125–51. http://dx.doi.org/10.2307/25143791.

Mochoruk, James. *The People's Co-Op: The Life and Times of a North End Institution*. Halifax: Fernwood, 2000.

Molloy, Maureen. "Science, Myth, and the Adolescent Female: The Mazengarb Report, the Parker-Hulme Trial and the Adoption Act of 1955." *Women's Studies Journal* 9, 1 (1993): 1–25.

Mort, Frank. *Cultures of Consumption: Masculinities and Social Space in Late-Twentieth-Century Britain*. London: Routledge, 1996.

Morton, Desmond. *NDP: Social Democracy in Canada*. 2nd ed. Toronto: Samuel Stevens Hakkert and Company, 1977.

Morton, W.L. *The Progressive Party in Canada*. Toronto: University of Toronto Press, 1967.

Murphy, Kevin P. *Political Manhood: Red Bloods, Mollycoddles, and the Politics of Progressive Era Reform*. New York: Columbia University Press, 2010.

Murton, James. *Creating a Modern Countryside: Liberalism and Land Resettlement in British Columbia*. Vancouver: UBC Press, 2007.

Myers, Tamara. *Caught: Montreal's Modern Girls and the Law, 1869–1945*. Toronto: University of Toronto Press, 2006.

Nader, Ralph. *Unstoppable: The Emerging Left-Right Alliance to Dismantle the Corporate State*. New York: Nation Books, 2014.

Naison, Mark. *Communists in Harlem during the Great Depression*. New York: Grove Press, 1983.

National Women's Committee of the Communist Party of Canada. *Canada's Women*. Toronto: Progress Books, 1963.

Naylor, James. *The New Democracy: Challenging the Social Order in Industrial Ontario, 1914–1925*. Toronto: University of Toronto Press, 1991.

–. "Pacifism or Anti-Imperialism? The CCF Response to the Outbreak of World War II." *Journal of the Canadian Historical Association* 8, 1 (1997): 213–41. http://dx.doi.org/10.7202/031123ar.

Nelson, Steve, James Barrett, and Rob Ruck. *Steve Nelson: American Radical*. Pittsburgh: University of Pittsburgh Press, 1981.

Nerbas, Don. "Howard Robinson and the 'British Method': A Case Study of Britishness in Canada during the 1930s and 1940s." *Journal of the Canadian Historical Association* 20, 1 (2009): 139–60. http://dx.doi.org/10.7202/039785ar.

Neufeld, Andrew, and Andrew Parnaby. *The IWA in Canada: The Life and Times of an Industrial Union*. Vancouver: IWA Canada/New Star Books, 2000.

Newton, Janice. *The Feminist Challenge to the Canadian Left, 1900–1918*. Montreal and Kingston: McGill-Queen's University Press, 1995.

Nickerson, Michelle M. *Mothers of Conservatism: Women and the Post-War Right*. Princeton: Princeton University Press, 2012.

–. "Politically Desperate Housewives: Women and Conservatism in Post-War Los Angeles," *California History* (Summer 2009). http://dx.doi.org/10.2307/40495217.

Nielsen, Dorise W. *80 Million Women Speak for Peace*. Toronto: Women's Committee for Peace Action, 1949.

–. *New Worlds For Women*. Toronto: Progress Books, 1944.

Noll, Mark A., David W. Bebbington, and George W. Rawlyk, eds. *Evangelicalism: Comparative Studies of Popular Protestantism in North America, the British Isles, and Beyond, 1700–1990*. New York: Oxford University Press, 1994.

Nora, Pierre. "Between Memory and History: Les Lieux de Memoire." *Representations* 26, 1 (1989): 7–24. http://dx.doi.org/10.1525/rep.1989.26.1.99p0274v.

Odem, Mary. *Delinquent Daughters: Protecting and Policing Adolescent Female Sexuality in the United States, 1885–1920*. Chapel Hill: University of North Carolina Press, 1995.

Olson, Nancy Louise. "Assembling a Life: The [Auto] Biography of Alexis Amelia Alvey." MA thesis, Simon Fraser University, 1998.

Osgerby, Bill. *Playboys in Paradise: Masculinity, Youth, and Leisure-Style in Modern America*. New York: Berg, 2001.

Owram, Doug. *Born at the Right Time: A History of the Baby Boom Generation*. Toronto: University of Toronto Press, 1996.

Painter, Nell Irvin. *The Narrative of Hosea Hudson*. Cambridge: Harvard University Press, 1979.

Palmer, Bryan D. *Canada's 1960s: The Ironies of Identity in a Rebellious Era*. Toronto: University of Toronto Press, 2009.

–. "Rethinking the History of United States Communism." *American Communist History* 2, 2 (2003): 139–73. http://dx.doi.org/10.1080/1474389032000165151.

Palmer, Howard. *Patterns of Prejudice: A History of Nativism in Alberta*. Toronto: University of Toronto Press, 1982.

Palmer, Howard with Tamara Palmer. *Alberta: A New History*. Edmonton: Hurtig, 1990.

Parnaby, Andrew. *Citizen Docker: Making a New Deal on the Vancouver Waterfront, 1919–1939*. Toronto: University of Toronto Press, 2008.

Parr, Joy, ed. *A Diversity of Women: Ontario, 1945–1980*. Toronto: University of Toronto Press, 1995.

–. *Domestic Goods: The Material, the Moral, and the Economic in the Postwar Years*. Toronto: University of Toronto Press, 1999.

–. *The Gender of Breadwinners: Women, Men, and Change in Two Industrial Towns, 1880–1950*. Toronto: University of Toronto Press, 1990.

Parr, Joy, and Mark Rosenfeld, eds. *Gender and History in Canada*. Toronto: Copp Clark, 1996.

Passmore, Kevin. "'Planting the Tricolor in the Citadels of Communism': Women's Social Action in the Croix de Feu and Parti Social Francais." *Journal of Modern History* 71, 4 (1999): 814–51. http://dx.doi.org/10.1086/235360.

Paulin, Marguerite. *Maurice Duplessis: Powerbroker, Politician*. Trans. Nora Alleyn. Montreal: XYZ Publishing, 2005.

Pauwels, Jacques R. Review essay "Uber Alles! American Corporations and Hitler." *Labour/Le Travail* 51 (Spring 2003): 223–49. http://dx.doi.org/10.2307/25149339.

Penner, Norman. *Canadian Communism: The Stalin Years and Beyond*. Toronto: Methuen, 1988.

–. *The Canadian Left: A Critical Analysis*. Scarborough, ON: Prentice-Hall, 1977.

–. *Soldiers or Citizens?* Toronto: National Federation of Labor Youth, 1948.

Perry, Adele, Esyllt Jones, and Leah Morton, eds. *Place and Replace: Essays on Western Canada*. Winnipeg: University of Manitoba Press, 2013.

Pessen, Edward. *Losing Our Souls: The American Experience in the Cold War*. Chicago: Ivan R. Dee, 1993.

Peter, Fabienne. "Critical Realism, Feminist Epistemology, and the Emancipatory Potential of Science: A Comment on Lawson and Harding." *Feminist Economics* 9, 1 (2003): 93–101. http://dx.doi.org/10.1080/13545700110059289.

Phillips, Anne. *Divided Loyalties: Dilemmas of Sex and Class*. London: Virago, 1987.

Pickles, Katie. *Female Imperialism and National Identity: Imperial Order Daughters of the Empire*. Manchester, UK: Manchester University Press, 2002. http://dx.doi.org/10.7228/manchester/9780719063909.001.0001.

Pierson, Ruth Roach. *"They're Still Women after All": The Second World War and Canadian Womanhood*. Toronto: McClelland and Stewart, 1986.

–, Pierson ed. *Women and Peace: Theoretical, Historical, and Practical Perspectives*. London: Croom Helm, 1987.

Pinard, Maurice. *The Rise of a Third Party: A Study in Crisis Politics*. Enlarged ed. Montreal and Kingston: McGill-Queen's University Press, 1975.

Postman, Neil. *Amusing Ourselves to Death*. New York: Penguin, 1985.

Power, Elaine. "Making the Borders Thin: Reflections on Becoming a Researcher." *Atlantis* 24, 1 (1999): 15–24.

Power, Margaret. *Right-Wing Women in Chile: Feminine Power and the Struggle against Allende, 1964–1973*. University Park: Pennsylvania State University Press, 2002.

Prentice, Susan. "Workers, Mothers, Reds: Toronto's Postwar Daycare Fight." *Studies in Political Economy* 30 (Autumn 1989): 115–41.
Purvey, Diane. "Review of Catherine A. Cavanaugh and Randi R. Warne, eds., *Telling Tales: Essays in Western Women's History*." *Labour/Le Travail* 50 (Fall 2002): 326–29. http://dx.doi.org/10.2307/25149294.
Radosh, Ronald. *Prophets on the Right: Profiles of Conservative Critics of American Globalism*. New York: Simon and Schuster, 1975.
–. *Rosenberg File: With an Introduction Containing Revelations from National Security Agency and Soviet Sources*. 2nd ed. New Haven: Yale University Press, 1997.
Radway, Janice. *Reading the Romance: Women, Patriarchy and Popular Literature*. Chapel Hill: University of North Carolina Press, 1984.
Raimondo, Justin. *Reclaiming the American Right: Lost Legacy of the Conservative Movement*. 2nd ed. Wilmington, DE: ISI Books, 2008.
Ramsay, Robin. *The Rise of New Labour*. North Pomfret, VT.: Pocket Essentials, 2002.
Rappaport, Erika Diane. *Shopping for Pleasure: Women in the Making of London's West End*. Princeton: Princeton University Press, 2000.
Rawlyk, G.A. *The Canada Fire: Radical Evangelicalism in British North America, 1775–1812*. Montreal and Kingston: McGill-Queen's University Press, 1994.
–. *Wrapped Up in God: A Study of Several Canadian Revivals and Revivalists*. Burlington, ON: Welch Publishing, 1988.
Reed, Maureen G. "Taking Stands: A Feminist Perspective on 'Other' Women's Activism in Forestry Communities of Northern Vancouver Island." *Gender, Place and Culture* 7, 4 (2000): 363–87. http://dx.doi.org/10.1080/713668882.
–. *Taking Stands: Gender and the Sustainability of Rural Communities*. Vancouver: UBC Press, 2003.
Rees, Tim, and Andrew Thorpe, eds. *International Communism and the Communist International 1919–43*. Manchester: Manchester University Press, 1998.
Rennie, Bradford James. *The Rise of Agrarian Democracy: The United Farmers and Farm Women of Alberta, 1909–1921*. Toronto: University of Toronto Press, 2000.
Ribuffo, Leo P. *The Old Christian Right: The Protestant Far Right from the Great Depression to the Cold War*. Philadelphia: Temple University Press, 1983.
Richmond, Alex. "Women in the Ontario and BC CCF, 1932–1942: Political Osmosis at Work." Paper presented at the annual meeting of the Canadian Historical Association, Toronto, 28 May 2002.
Roberts, Barbara. *A Reconstructed World: A Feminist Biography of Gertrude Richardson*. Montreal and Kingston: McGill-Queen's University Press, 1996.
–. *"Why Do Women Do Nothing to End the War?" Canadian Feminist-Pacifists and the Great War*. Ottawa: Canadian Research Institute for the Advancement of Women, 1985.
Roberts, Wayne. "Rocking the Cradle for the World: The New Woman and Maternal Feminism, Toronto, 1874–1914." In *A Not Unreasonable Claim: Women and Reform in Canada, 1880s-1920s*, ed. Linda Kealey, 15–45. Toronto: Women's Press, 1979.
Robin, Martin. "British Columbia: The Politics of Class Conflict." In *Canadian Provincial Politics: The Party Systems of the Ten Provinces*, ed. Martin Robin, 27–68. Scarborough: Prentice-Hall, 1972.
–. *Pillars of Profit: The Company Province, 1934–1972*. Toronto: McClelland and Stewart, 1973.
Rodney, William. *Soldiers of the International: A History of the Communist Party of Canada, 1919–1929*. Toronto: University of Toronto Press, 1968.

Roediger, David R. *The Wages of Whiteness: Race and the Making of the American Working Class*. New York: Verso, 1991.
Romero, Patricia W. E. *Sylvia Pankhurst: Portrait of a Radical*. New Haven, NY: Yale University Press, 1987.
Rooke, P.T., and R.L. Schnell. *No Bleeding Heart: Charlotte Whitton – A Feminist on the Right*. Vancouver: UBC Press, 1987.
Roosevelt, Kermit. *Countercoup: The Struggle for Control of Iran*. New York: McGraw-Hill, 1979.
Ross, Douglas A. *In the Interests of Peace: Canada and Vietnam, 1954–1973*. Toronto: University of Toronto Press, 1984.
Rotundo, E. Anthony. *American Manhood: Transformations in Masculinity from the Revolution to the Modern Era*. New York: Basic Books, 1993.
Rupp, Leila J., and Verta Taylor. *Survival in the Doldrums: The American Women's Rights Movement, 1945 to the 1960s*. New York: Oxford University Press, 1987.
Rush, Maurice. *"We Have a Glowing Dream": Recollections of Working-Class and People's Struggles in BC from 1935–1996*. Vancouver: Centre for Socialist Education, 1996.
Ryan, Oscar. *Tim Buck: A Conscience for Canada*. Toronto: Progress Books, 1975.
Ryerson, Stanley B. *Why Be a Doormat?* Toronto: Progress Books, 1948.
Rymph, Catherine E. *Republican Women: Feminism and Conservatism from Suffrage through to the New Right*. Chapel Hill: University of North Carolina Press, 2006.
Said, Edward. *Orientalism*. Rev. ed. New York: Vintage Books, 1994.
Sangster, Joan. *Dreams of Equality: Women on the Canadian Left, 1920–1950*. Toronto: McClelland and Stewart, 1989.
–. *Earning Respect: The Lives of Working-Women in Small-Town Ontario, 1920–1960*. Toronto: University of Toronto Press, 1995.
–. "Feminism and the Making of Canadian Working-Class History: Exploring the Past, Present and Future." *Labour/Le Travail* 46 (Fall 2000): 127–65. http://dx.doi.org/10.2307/25149098.
–. *Girl Trouble: Female Delinquency in English Canada*. Toronto: Between the Lines, 2002.
–. *Regulating Girls and Women: Sexuality, Family, and the Law in Ontario, 1920–1960*. Toronto: Oxford University Press, 1999.
–. *Transforming Labour: Women and Work in Post-War Canada*. Toronto: University of Toronto Press, 2010.
Sangster, Joan, and Margaret Hobbs, eds. *The Woman Worker, 1926–1929*. St. John's: Canadian Committee on Labour History, 1999.
Saunders, Frances Stonor. *Who Pays the Piper? The CIA and the Cultural Cold War*. London: Granta, 1999.
Schlesinger Jr., Arthur M. *The Vital Center: The Politics of Freedom*. Boston: Houghton Mifflin, 1962.
Schmitz, David F. *"Thank God They're on Our Side": The United States and Right-Wing Dictatorships*. Chapel Hill: University of North Carolina Press, 1999.
Schott, Linda. *Reconstructing Women's Thoughts: The Women's International League for Peace and Freedom before World War II*. Palo Alto: Stanford University Press, 1997.
Schrecker, Ellen, ed. *Cold War Triumphalism: The Misuse of History after the Fall of Communism*. New York: The New Press, 2004.
–. *Many Are the Crimes: McCarthyism in America*. Boston: Little, Brown, 1998.
Schreiber, Ronnee. *Righting Feminism: Conservative Women and American Politics*. Rev. ed. New York: Oxford University Press, 2012.

Schumacher, E.F. *Small Is Beautiful: Economics as if People Mattered*. New York: Harper and Row, 1973.

Scott, Jack. *A Communist Life: Jack Scott and the Canadian Workers Movement, 1927–1985*. Ed. Bryan D. Palmer. St. John's: Canadian Committee on Labour History, 1988.

Scott, James C. *Seeing Like a State: How Certain Conditions to Improve the Human Condition Have Failed*. New Haven: Yale University Press, 1998.

Scott, Joan Wallach. *Gender and the Politics of History*. New York: Columbia University Press, 1988.

Sharp, Paul. *The Agrarian Revolt in Western Canada: A Survey Showing American Parallels*. Revised ed. Regina: Canadian Plains Research Center, 1997.

Sherman, Paddy. *Bennett*. Toronto: McClelland and Stewart, 1966.

Sklar, Holly. "Brave New World Order." In *Collateral Damage: The "New World Order" at Home and Abroad*, ed. Cynthia Peters, 3–46. Boston: South End Press, 1992.

Sklar, Martin J. *The Corporate Reconstruction of American Capitalism, 1890–1916: The Market, the Law, and Politics*. New York: Cambridge University Press, 1988.

Smiley, Donald V. "Canada's Poujadists: A New Look at Social Credit." *Canadian Forum* 42, 500 (1962): 121–3.

Smith, Andrea B. "The CCF, NPA, and Civic Change: Provincial Forces behind Vancouver Politics, 1930–1940." *BC Studies* 53 (Spring 1982): 45–65.

Smith, Dorothy E. *The Everyday World as Problematic: A Feminist Sociology*. Boston: Northeastern University Press, 1987.

Smith, Sidonie. *Subjectivity, Identity, and the Body: Women's Autobiographical Writing Practices in the Twentieth Century*. Bloomington: Indiana University Press, 1993.

Socknat, Thomas P. *Witness against War: Pacifism in Canada, 1900–1945*. Toronto: University of Toronto Press, 1987.

Solinger, Rickie. *Wake Up Little Susie: Single Pregnancy and Race Before Roe V. Wade*. New York: Routledge, 1992.

Spivak, Gayatri Chakravorty. *A Critique of Postcolonial Reason: Toward a History of the Vanishing Present*. Cambridge, London: Harvard University Press, 1999.

Srigley, Katrina. *Breadwinning Daughters: Young Working Women in a Depression-Era City, 1929–1939*. Toronto: University of Toronto Press, 2010.

Stackhouse Jr., John G. *Canadian Evangelicalism in the Twentieth Century: An Introduction to Its Character*. Toronto: University of Toronto Press, 1993.

Stafford, Ellen. *Always and After: A Memoir*. Toronto: Viking, 1999.

Stanton, John. *My Past Is Now: Further Memoirs of a Labour Lawyer*. St. John's: Canadian Committee on Labour History, 1994.

–. *Never Say Die! The Life and Times of John Stanton, a Pioneer Labour Lawyer*. Ottawa: Steel Rail Publishing, 1987.

Starobin, Joseph R. *American Communism in Crisis, 1943–1957*. Cambridge: Harvard University Press, 1972.

Steeves, Dorothy. *The Compassionate Rebel: Ernest Winch and the Growth of Socialism in Western Canada*. Vancouver: J.J. Douglas, 1977.

Stephen, Jennifer A. *Pick One Intelligent Girl: Employability, Domesticity, and the Gendering of the Canadian Welfare State, 1939–1947*. Toronto: University of Toronto Press, 2007.

Stewart, Walter. *The Life and Politics of Tommy Douglas*. Toronto: McArthur, 2003.

Stingel, Janine. *Social Discredit: Anti-Semitism, Social Credit, and the Jewish Response*. Montreal and Kingston: McGill-Queen's University Press, 2000.

Strange, Carolyn. *Toronto's Girl Problem: The Perils and Pleasures of the City, 1880–1930*. Toronto: University of Toronto Press, 1995.

Strange, Carolyn, and Tina Loo. *Making Good: Law and Moral Regulation in Canada, 1867–1939*. Toronto: University of Toronto Press, 1997.

Strong-Boag, Veronica. *The New Day Recalled: Lives of Girls and Women in English Canada, 1919–1939*. Markham, ON. Penguin Books, 1988.

Strong-Boag, Veronica, and Anita Clair Fellman, eds. *Rethinking Canada: The Promise of Women's History*. 3rd ed. Toronto: Oxford University Press, 1997.

Strong-Boag, Veronica, Mona Gleason, and Adele Perry, eds. *Rethinking Canada: The Promise of Women's History*. 4th ed. Toronto: Oxford University Press, 2002.

Struthers, James. *The Limits of Affluence: Welfare in Ontario, 1920–1970*. Toronto: University of Toronto Press, 1994.

–. "'Lord Give Us Men': Women and Social Work in English Canada, 1918 to 1953." In *The "Benevolent State": The Growth of Welfare in Canada*, ed. Allan Moscovitch and Jim Albert, 126–43. Toronto: Garamond Press, 1987.

–. *No Fault of Their Own: Unemployment and the Canadian Welfare State, 1914–1941*. Toronto: University of Toronto Press, 1983.

Sufrin, Eileen. *The Eaton Drive: The Campaign to Organize Canada's Largest Department Store, 1948 to 1952*. Toronto: Fitzhenry and Whiteside, 1982.

Susman, Warren I. *Culture as History: The Transformation of American Culture in the Twentieth Century*. New York: Pantheon Books, 1984.

Swanson, Jean. *Poor-Bashing: The Politics of Exclusion*. Toronto: Between the Lines, 2001.

Swerdlow, Amy. *Women Strike for Peace: Traditional Motherhood and Radical Politics in the 1960s*. Chicago: University of Chicago Press, 1993.

Taylor, Jeff. *Politics on a Human Scale: The American Tradition of Decentralism*. Lanham, MD: Lexington Books, 2013.

Taylor, Jeffery. *Fashioning Farmers: Ideology, Agricultural Knowledge and the Manitoba Farm Movement, 1890–1925*. Regina: Canadian Plains Research Center, 1994.

Teeple, Gary, ed. *Capitalism and the National Question in Canada*. Toronto: University of Toronto Press, 1972.

Theoharis, Athan G., ed. *Beyond the Hiss Case: The FBI, Congress, and the Cold War*. Philadelphia: Temple University Press, 1982.

Thomson, Gerald E. "'A Baby Show Means Work in the Hardest Sense': The Better Baby Contests of the Vancouver and New Westminster Local Councils of Women, 1913–1929." *BC Studies* 128 (Winter 2000/01): 5–36.

Thompson, E.P. *The Making of the English Working Class*. London: Penguin Books, 1980.

Thompson, John Herd, and Stephen J. Randall. *Canada and the United States: Ambivalent Allies*. 3rd ed. Montreal and Kingston: McGill-Queen's University Press, 2002.

Thompson, Robert N. *Canadians, It's Time You Knew*. Ottawa: The Aavangen Press, 1961.

Thorn, Brian T. "'Peace Is the Concern of Every Mother': Communist and Social Democratic Women's Anti-War Activism in British Columbia, 1948–1960." *Peace and Change: Journal of Peace Research* 35, 4 (2010): 626–57. http://dx.doi.org/10.1111/j.1468-0130.2010.00658.x.

–. "Visions of the New World Order: Women and Gender in Radical and Reactionary Movements in Post-World War II Western Canada." PhD diss., Trent University, 2006.

–. " 'Women Are Truly Wonderful in Their Ingenuity': Radical Housewives and Consumer Protest during the Cold War Era." *left history* 18, 1 (2014): 9–36.

Tillotson, Shirley. *Contributing Citizens: Modern Charitable Fundraising and the Making of the Welfare State, 1920–1966*. Vancouver: UBC Press, 2009.

–. *The Public at Play: Society, Recreation, and the State in Postwar Canada*. Toronto: University of Toronto Press, 2001.

–. "'When Our Membership Awakens': Welfare Work and Canadian Union Activism, 1950–1965." *Labour/Le Travail* 40 (Fall 1997): 137–69. http://dx.doi.org/10.2307/25144166.

Toews, Anne. "For Liberty, Bread, and Love: Annie Buller, Becky Buhay, and the Forging of Communist Militant Femininity in Canada." MA thesis, Simon Fraser University, 2009.

Tomblin, Stephen G. "W.A.C. Bennett and Province-Building in British Columbia." *BC Studies* 85 (Spring 1990): 45–61.

Traves, Tom. *The State and Enterprise: Canadian Manufacturers and the Federal Government, 1917–1931*. Toronto: University of Toronto Press, 1979.

Urbach, Karina, ed. *European Aristocracies and the Radical Right, 1918–1939*. New York: Oxford University Press, 2007

Valverde, Mariana. *The Age of Light, Soap, and Water: Moral Reform in English Canada, 1885–1925*. Rev. ed. Toronto: University of Toronto Press, 2008.

–. "Racial Poison: Drink, Male Vice, and Degeneration in First-Wave Feminism." In *Women's Suffrage in the British Empire: Citizenship, Nation, and Race*, ed. Ian Christopher Fletcher, Laura E. Nym Mayhall, and Phillipa Levine, 33–50. New York: Routledge, 2000.

Vance, Catharine. *Not by Gods but by People: The Story of Bella Hall Gauld*. Toronto: Progress Books, 1968.

Vellacott, Jo. *From Liberal to Labour with Women's Suffrage: The Story of Catherine Marshall*. Montreal and Kingston: McGill-Queen's University Press, 1993.

Vickers, Jill, Pauline Rankin, and Christine Appelle. *Politics as if Women Mattered: A Political Analysis of the National Action Committee on the Status of Women*. Toronto: University of Toronto Press, 1993.

Vogel, Lise, ed. "Red Feminism: A Symposium." Special Issue, *Science and Society* 66, 4 (2002). http://dx.doi.org/10.1521/siso.66.4.498.21112.

Waiser, Bill. "Introduction: Place, Process, and the New Prairie Realities." *Canadian Historical Review* 84, 4 (2003): 509–16. http://dx.doi.org/10.3138/CHR.84.4.509.

Walsh, Susan. "Equality, Emancipation and a More Just World: Leading Women in the British Columbia Co-operative Commonwealth Federation." MA thesis, Simon Fraser University, 1984.

–. "The Peacock and the Guinea Hen: Political Profiles of Dorothy Gretchen Steeves and Grace MacInnis." In *The Neglected Majority: Essays in Canadian Women's History*, vol. 2. ed. Alison Prentice and Susan Mann Trofimenkoff, 144–59. Toronto: McClelland and Stewart, 1985.

Wardaugh, Robert, ed. *Toward Defining the Prairies: Region, Culture, and History*. Winnipeg: University of Manitoba Press, 2001.

Ware, Vron. *Beyond the Pale: White Women, Racism, and History*. London: Verso, 1992.

Watson, Louise. *She Never Was Afraid: The Biography of Annie Buller*. Toronto: Progress Books, 1976.

Weigand, Kate. *Red Feminism: American Communism and the Making of Women's Liberation*. Baltimore: Johns Hopkins University Press, 2001.

Weisbord, Merrily. *The Strangest Dream: Canadian Communists, the Spy Trials, and the Cold War*. Toronto: Lester and Orpen Dennys, 1983.

Wertham, Frederic. *The Seduction of the Innocent.* New York: Rinehart, 1954.

Westbrook, Robert. "Good-bye to All That: Aileen Kraditor and Radical History." *Radical History Review* 28–30 (1984): 69–89. http://dx.doi.org/10.1215/01636545-1984-28-30-69.

Westphall, Richard. "Newton and His Biographer." In *Introspection in Biography: The Biographer's Quest for Self-Awareness,* ed. Samuel H. Baron and Carl Pletsch, 175–90. Hillsdale: The Analytic Press, 1985.

Whitaker, Reg, and Steve Hewitt. *Canada and the Cold War.* Toronto: Lorimer, 2003.

Whitaker, Reg, and Gary Marcuse. *Cold War Canada: The Making of a National Insecurity State, 1945–1957.* Toronto: University of Toronto Press, 1994.

White, Howard, ed. *A Hard Man to Beat: The Story of Bill White, Labour Leader, Historian, Shipyard Worker, Raconteur – An Oral History.* Vancouver: Pulp Press, 1983.

White, Julie. *Sisters in Solidarity: Women and Unions in Canada.* Toronto: Thomson Educational Publishing, 1993.

Whitehorn, Alan. *Canadian Socialism: Essays on the CCF-NDP.* Toronto: Oxford University Press, 1992.

Wiebe, Robert H. *The Search for Order, 1877–1920.* New York: Hill and Wang, 1967.

Williams, William Appleman. *Empire as a Way of Life: An Essay on the Causes and Character of America's Present Predicament along with a Few Thoughts about an Alternative.* New York: Oxford University Press, 1980.

–. *The Tragedy of American Diplomacy.* 50th Edition. New York: W.W. Norton, 2009 [1962].

Williamson, Janice, and Deborah Gorham, eds. *Up and Doing: Canadian Women and Peace.* Toronto: The Women's Press, 1989.

Willison, Gladys A. *Stars in Time: A History of the Alberta Social Credit Women's Auxiliaries.* Edmonton: Women's Auxiliaries of the Alberta Social Credit League, 1973.

Wiseman, Nelson. *In Search of Canadian Political Culture.* Vancouver: UBC Press, 2007.

–. "The Pattern of Prairie Politics." In *Party Politics in Canada,* 7th ed., ed. Hugh G. Thorburn, 428–45. Toronto: Prentice-Hall Canada, 1996.

–. *Social Democracy in Manitoba: A History of the CCF-NDP.* Winnipeg: University of Manitoba Press, 1983.

Worley, Ronald. *The Wonderful World of W.A.C. Bennett.* Toronto: McClelland and Stewart, 1971.

Wrigley, Julia. "From Housewives to Activists: Women and the Division of Political Labor in the Boston Antibusing Movement." In *No Middle Ground: Women and Radical Protest,* ed. Kathleen M. Blee, 250–88. New York: New York University Press, 1998.

Ybarra, Michael J. *Washington Gone Crazy: Senator Pat McCarran and the Great American Communist Hunt.* Hanover, NH: Steerforth, 2004.

Young, Walter D. *The Anatomy of a Party: The National CCF, 1932–1961.* Toronto: University of Toronto Press, 1969.

–. "Ideology, Personality and the Origins of the CCF in British Columbia." *BC Studies* 32 (Winter 1976–77): 139–62.

Zelko, Frank. *Make It a Green Peace! The Rise of Countercultural Environmentalism.* New York: Oxford University Press, 2013.

–. "Making Greenpeace: The Development of Direct Action Environmentalism in British Columbia." *BC Studies* 142/143 (Summer/Autumn 2004): 197–239.

Index